BURNT

BURNT

A MEMOIR OF FIGHTING FIRE

CLARE FRANK

ABRAMS PRESS, NEW YORK

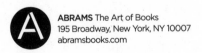

ABRAMS The Art of Books
195 Broadway, New York, NY 10007
abramsbooks.com

Dedicated to my three families:
one born of blood, one of marriage, and one of fire.

And to Brody.

CONTENTS

If you light a fire to destroy me, I will climb to heaven on its flames.

—SAINT FLORIAN, PATRON SAINT OF FIREFIGHTERS

AUTHOR'S NOTE

For privacy and clarity, I changed some names and time sequences. I also left out many people who influenced me and my career. Chances are, if we worked any amount of time together, you were in an earlier draft, and I thank you for being part of the adventure. What follows represents my story as I saw and felt it. It is based on memory, journal entries, photographs, research, and interviews. The dialogue is representative, not exact. I don't assert that this account reflects anyone's truth but my own. WARNING: this book contains triggers—pretty much all of them.

FIRE RANKS – AUTHOR'S PATH

1982 – 1984	FIREFIGHTER
1984 – 1990	ENGINEER
1990 – 1997	CAPTAIN
1997 – 2002	INJURED
2002 – 2004	CAPTAIN / BATTALION CHIEF *
2004 – 2005	ASSISTANT CHIEF
2005 – 2009	CHIEF
2009 – 2011	STATE DEPUTY CHIEF **
2011 – 2013	STATE CHIEF OF CO-OP FIRE
2013 – 2015	STATE CHIEF OF FIRE PROTECTION
PRESENT DAY	CIVILIAN

* Served only in acting capacity as Battalion Chief.

** This is a rank below Chief, but involved a jump to a much larger State Fire Department.

I.

IGNITION

I met my first fire at age four—the Weldon Fire in a Los Angeles neighborhood called Granada Hills. It took off in high-speed winds, ripping through ravines and toward our cul-de-sac on the valley floor. I have only two clear memories of Weldon. Its billowing plumes captivated me. And my parents exhibited zero panic. Earthquakes and wildfires were as much a part of Southern California's landscape as canyons and suburban tract housing. I imagine Dad gathered Mom, me, and my five older siblings in the backyard to watch the show as Weldon threw ash our way.

It came within a mile of our house, making it possible that Weldon was my inciting incident—the event in my impressionable years that sparked a curiosity with fire. But this theory conflicts with what the Indian pundit proffered two decades later while reading my birth chart.

"Fire, fire, fire. Never seen so much fire," he mused in a lyrical accent while tracing cryptic dots and numbers on the chart with his dark, bony finger. He looked up at me: a fit, freckled twenty-something with a strange mix of confidence and self-doubt. When he asked, "What is your work?" I told him I was a firefighter. His mouth broke into a massive, yellow-toothed smile. A breathy laugh escaped. "Ah. Cosmic joke." He looked at the chart, then back at me, and laughed again—making it clear that by nurture, nature, or both, I was meant to have a life of fire.

CHAPTER 1

MATCHSTICKS

State Fire Headquarters, 22 Months Left

I needed Bud to weigh in, so I called him on my cell from the bathroom stall inside the Shady Lady Saloon. A few blocks from headquarters in Sacramento, California, the modern speakeasy's velveted high-back booths and Roaring Twenties décor made for a comfortable meeting place after work.

"They want me in Andy's job," I whispered, even though I had the restroom to myself.

"Ken and Red? What'd they say?"

"Red said I got the top score. But I told her I didn't want the promotion. She gave me the look, then Ken asked if I trusted them, at which point I lied and said I had to pee."

"Are you in the bathroom? Don't answer that. Look, I don't think you have a choice."

"Of course I do. It's my life."

"Who picked Shady Lady?" Bud asked.

"Red suggested it."

"Who ordered the wine?"

"Ken."

"It's over. They've made their pick. The wine is to celebrate, not to cajole."

I held the phone to my ear, sat on the toilet with my pants up, and thought about the bizarre unfolding of this impending promotion. In my rookie firefighter years, I'd aspired to reach the rank of captain, *if* I could make it that far. Once I did, I swore I'd go no further. Captain is the last rank that rides on a fire engine. But I kept going. And now, Cal Fire's director and chief deputy were lobbying me to become State Chief of Fire Protection, a position six ranks above captain, and successor to the director if something took him out of play.

Part of me was flattered. It was an impressive job and I'd be the first female to rise to that position. But the other part wanted to steer clear. I had twenty-two months before retirement and liked my current gig as a two-star chief a floor away from the executive offices. Two stars were plenty. Why trade them for unknown headaches?

"You there?" Bud asked.

"Yeah. I'm here. It's just weird. I never wanted this. Pretty sure I still don't. But is it my duty? Who'd fill behind me? What if I can't come home to you on the weekends? What about Brody? Maybe I can get out of this."

Bud listened to my nonsequitur ramblings. He'd grown accustomed to them over the last seventeen years. "I'm proud of you, Sweetie. Enjoy the wine."

"Love you too." I hung up and out of habit reached back to flush. *Dammit. Drought year. Shouldn't have done that.*

When I slid back into the booth, Red smiled and asked, "How's Bud?"

Damn, she had a strong mom gene. She also looked the part. Red hair curved in exacting waves—the same every day—framing rosy cheeks and kind, knowing eyes. While motherhood seemed her strong suit, Red's finance wizardry had landed her in Ken's chief deputy spot, a non-uniformed position in charge of all the administrative shit everyone in uniform hates: budgets, information technology, legislative process, etc. Fortunately, Red lived for this stuff.

Ken caught the waitress's eye, swung his finger in a circle for another round, then added, "Oh, and a plate of fries for the table. Extra crispy, please."

This fucker knew what he was doing—pretending like he had nowhere to go and all night to ply me with alcohol and crunchy-fried deliciousness. He sipped his wine and looked around the room, waiting for me to cave. Most people did for him. His cropped salt-and-pepper hair and piercing blue eyes made a statement. But a boyish sincerity softened the look to melt adversaries.

I avoided eye contact and reached for a small box of matches kept on the table for those who needed an outdoor smoke break between drinks. I opened and closed the matchbox drawer, always needing something to keep my hands busy. Balancing the matchbox on a corner, I flicked, spinning it under my index finger. Flick. Spin. Flick.

My mind darted back to the matchbox I'd lifted from the kitchen drawer at eight years old. Readying myself for an escapade with my bestie, I slid a full-sized matchbox into my sweatshirt pouch pocket before sneaking out the side gate.

We met at the corner between our houses.

"Hey, Fat Pat."

"Hey, Clare Bare-Butt."

We tapped the street sign pole and pulled hoods up to conceal our identities. But anyone who looked out a window on this autumn Saturday afternoon would know it was us—a scrawny inseparable pair of third-graders up to no good but incapable of real harm.

We walked toward the orchard, swiveling our heads to make sure no car or pedestrian had eyes on us.

"Clear?"

"Clear. Let's go."

Scurrying onto a dirt driveway, we took cover behind an overgrown hedge that concealed a fabled abandoned mansion. Like Navy SEALs, we

crouched and moved inland. The thirty yards felt like a formidable trek with our short legs and adventure-level heart rates.

The mansion revealed itself to us all at once: chipped paint, cracked windows, and the absence of life or belongings. We crept into a ghosted courtyard piled with dry needles and leaves a light wind moved from time to time, making us jump.

Teachers and Smokey Bear had told us countless times, "Don't play with matches." I scoffed at the messaging. This was the 1970s, the era of Vietnam War protests and counterculture. It turned the fire prevention slogan into a dare. And Fat Pat and I loved dares.

"Did you bring 'em?" she asked.

"Yup." I pulled out the box of Diamond Strike Anywhere Matches.

Fat Pat's eyes got big. "You brought a whole box? Won't they notice?"

"Nah. We always have a bunch for home liturgy candles."

"Home what?"

"Dad holds church at home when we can't make it to Mass. He was a monk, and went to priest college before he met Mom, and taught God stuff at a university until we moved here."

"Wow," she said. Then we gathered dry needles, made a small pile, and squatted beside it like swamis.

I slid the box open. "You wanna go first?" I offered.

"Let's do it together." She picked a match from the box. I selected one too, then closed the lid and set the box down with the scratchy surface faced up.

"One, two, three!" We struck our phosphorus tips. A gust extinguished our matches before we touched flame to tinder. We struck again, match after match. Each time, the wind toyed with us, keeping sustained fire at bay.

Twenty matches later, we finally had ourselves a five-inch campfire.

"Stoke it," I said, mimicking Dad instructing my brother Mark. Dad expected Mark, the only boy, to carry the art of warming fires to future generations. But I tagged along everywhere with Mark and had been paying attention to fire since Weldon.

Fat Pat threw more needles on our miniature fire. They shrank instantly, like cotton candy melting on a tongue. I rushed to find thicker kindling, collecting small-branch litter congregated in the courtyard's corners.

"Keep it going!" I said. Panic had set in. I hated failure and sensed our fire would go out.

"Dump them in the middle!" Fat Pat yelled as I ran back.

I fell victim to the pressure and did it. Bull's-eye. All the sticks landed right in the center of our fire, smothering what little flame we had left. I'd put out a fire with fuel.

My stomach sank as I watched the fire take its last breath. Fat Pat shrugged, like it didn't matter. I glared at her. She was fun and my first best friend who wasn't a sibling, but I thought she lacked dedication.

A twig cracked, or a door closed, or something. We looked at each other, then at the ashen pile. Our Converse sneakers squashed remaining embers. We fled, leaving behind the litter of our failed enterprise.

From my bed that night, scenarios ran through my head. An adult had probably followed us to the mansion and called cops at the smell of smoke. I knew from movies that cops had everyone's fingerprints on file. Ours were all over the scene: on the abandoned matchbox, the gathered sticks, the spent matches. I waited for the doorbell to ring and rubbed my wrists, prepping them for handcuffs. When it didn't ring, I convinced myself that Fat Pat and I had misconstrued the sound, and no adult had come. By now, the wind would have resuscitated embers we missed in our hasty escape. An inferno was a certainty. I apologized to God and poked my head out from under the blankets to see if smoke had reached my bedroom yet. Eventually, I fell asleep into a nightmare that I'd burned down Ventura, California.

A week later, a 12,000-acre wildfire raged through Ventura County— the Potrero Fire. Everyone talked about it.

"How 'bout that fire?"

"We have to be so careful this time of year."

"Yeah, those Santa Anas can turn a spark into a firestorm."

At night, I watched the news on our black-and-white TV. White flames danced across the landscape. I thought they were beautiful. In hindsight, I

realize my fear during my venture with Fat Pat was task failure and getting caught. Nothing about fire—its power, heat, or unpredictable movement—inspired fright in me.

<p style="text-align:center">✳✳✳</p>

The Shady Lady waitress returned. I abandoned my matchbox for fries.

"Look, guys," I said to Ken and Red. "I'm good where I am. You bump me up, now you've got two newbies fumbling around trying to make it work during a serious drought."

Ken disregarded the point with a hand wave. "Red found a way to budget for overlap. We'll appoint you early. You shadow Andy until he retires in six months. By then, you'll be an old salt." Ken took a slow sip of wine, letting it sink in.

Red nodded. "While you're shadowing Andy, you can train someone to fill behind you."

I swilled wine in my mouth to buy myself time. They'd played an unexpected card. Spinning my glass at its stem, I countered, "Why put all that effort in when you're going to have to groom someone again in twenty-two months?"

They squinted at me. They'd forgotten I'd joined at age seventeen. Plus my ponytail and juvenile spirit made me look younger than someone who'd started thirty-one years ago.

"You don't *have* to retire," Ken said. "You could be one of those dinosaurs that puts in forty years."

"Nope. I promised Bud: the day I'm age eligible is my last day. Believe it or not, he'd like to spend more than just weekends with me."

Ken shrugged. "Fine. I'll deal with it in twenty-two months." He was unflappable.

They both stared at me. Bud was right. I wasn't getting out of this.

I picked up the matchbox again and slid its drawer open, deciding the best use of the time was to give Ken and Red fair warning. "There're two things you need to know."

They raised their chins, urging the information out of me.

"First, I don't know shit about silviculture." Until I said it, I didn't understand this was my main reason for balking. Silviculture is the art and science behind forest management, and the department grew from these roots. When I started, my patch said DEPARTMENT OF FORESTRY. Managing California's forests and rangelands led to protecting them from destructive wildland fires. Fire protection contracts all over the state followed as cities spread into rural areas. The department amassed resources everyone wanted to access, making it a behemoth all-risk fire department with over 800 fire stations, the largest firefighting air fleet in the world, 40 fire crew camps, a host of communications and command centers, 10,000 people at peak season, a management structure that resembled a small military, and a patch that said CAL FIRE.

The department's scale didn't bother me one bit. But I had no experience on the forestry side, unlike Ken, who had a degree in forest management and years operating in that realm. I had little interest in being the potential successor to a job I only knew part of.

Ken had anticipated this, and rapid-fired his response. "Neither did Andy when he took the job. Most know forestry or fire protection or prevention. They learn the others on the fly. You know two of the three. And you'll have expert staff for the forestry stuff if you have to step in—which you won't, because nothing's going to happen to me."

Red's hair bobbed in agreement.

I crunched on fries, then picked a matchstick out of the box, and played my final card. "And second, I fuck shit up."

They both tilted their heads.

"I'm not afraid of taking chances, so I do. Nine out of ten decisions will be good. But that means in a day requiring a hundred decisions, I'll have ten fuckups. You're used to Andy, who has a more calculated style. The good news is, I'm a master at fixing shit I've broken, because I've done this my whole life. So, my batting average might equal Andy's, but it's going to cause you a lot more grief."

Red looked sideways at Ken. All three of us knew he didn't have a lot of patience. Missteps made him nervous. Insecure. He preferred calm seas. I was letting him know that if he put me at the helm, I'd deliver, but

it would be a choppy ride. I struck the match and we watched it burn to my fingertips.

Red blew it out and advised Ken in her motherly voice, "Ken, you're just going to have to be good with saying, 'Clare, unfuck this.'"

The juxtaposition of her tone and words sent Ken and me into a giggling spree. In moments like this Ken reminded me of my brother, Mark. And my willingness to go from a straight-talking chief to a child made Ken trust me. I was like him. Competent. Fun. Volatile.

We demolished the fries, toasted to good times ahead, and tipped the waitress. I slipped the matchbox into my pocket on the way out, thinking, *It's just twenty-two months.* I assume God smirked, knowing what those months would bring.

CHAPTER 2

BLISTERS

Sandy Point Training Center, 1982

Big Carl banged two metal trash can lids together, jarring us from our bunks at 3:00 a.m. A dilapidated firehouse tucked deep into the Santa Cruz Mountains, just south of San Francisco, served as our training site. The barracks smelled like smoke, mold, and wood—like an old church smells.

We tethered bootlaces and shuffle-ran to the asphalted pad, scrambling into our squads. Swaying with half-awake dizziness, we formed into lines that looked like earthworms uncovered by a gardener's hand trowel.

Big Carl eyed us. "You all disgust me. You're not worthy to be seasonal firefighters."

Even on the dimly lit drill apron, I could see his muscles bulge. At five feet two, I weighed maybe half of what he did, stood more than a full foot shorter, and my feet still had some growing before a size 5 work boot would fit.

"Why y'all standing there? This isn't summer camp. Give me twenty!" Big Carl barked.

We dove to the asphalt. The pitted ground stabbed at my palms. I sucked in the summer night's redwood-scented air as I pushed and dropped and pushed and dropped, hiding a smile.

I loved push-ups. Dad taught me as a youngster: push-ups are the great equalizer. A car crash had severed his left leg above the knee at age twenty-six, so he wore a hinged wooden leg during the day. He couldn't play chase, but he did push-ups with all six of us kids piled on top of him.

That was in Granada Hills—where Weldon had burned. Back then, we lived in a normal house. We even had a green lawn. Future yards browned as Dad became more restless and disenfranchised. "Wars and starving children, and all people worry about is their precious patch of suburban green," he'd rant. But in Granada Hills, he still liked lawns, and us. He'd lie on his back in the grass, inviting an attack. The earth and his St Johns Bay Rum cologne smelled like happiness. His smile spread to our faces—a conflagration of contentment—as we jumped onto his rock-hard abs, squealing. He parried each assault and rolled over. With a squirming mass of two dozen limbs clinging to his back, he pushed up, then plummeted down, then up. We counted with him. "Hun, hwo, hre, hor, hive . . ." He'd learned to count as a Marine. Before he became a monk. Before he married Mom. Before anyone understood the nature of his neurodivergence.

Every night, Big Carl banged his lids at a different time, drilling us on a new fireground skill. Hose unrolling and coupling. Fire shelter deployment. Timed gear-up that gave us one minute to don our yellow Nomex safety attire. At first, it felt impossible to dress that quickly. But within a couple days, most of us could do it in forty seconds or less. Then Big Carl added more tasks with new equipment: drip torches, breathing apparatus, backpumps.

We spent sleep-deprived days in the classroom, learning the basics from captains who delivered monotone lectures on different topics.

"It's called the fire triangle. Fire needs heat, fuel, and oxygen to live. If you starve it of one, the fire will . . ."

A chucked chalkboard eraser woke me. "Sleep on your own time," the instructor reprimanded me as I retrieved the eraser from the floor. He held his hand out. I walked the eraser up to him while brushing chalk

dust off my shoulder. After handing him his weapon, I turned back toward my seat.

"No. No. You're up here for a while," he said. "Before your snoring interrupted us, we were talking about the stages of a fire." He pointed to the board. There were several large bullet points, the first of which had IGNITION written next to it. The rest were blank.

"The books will tell you there're four stages," he said. "That oversimplifies it. The more attention you pay to details, the better you'll know your enemy and how to attack it. So let's break it down further. What happens after ignition but before a fire gets big?" he asked me.

I stared at the bullet points and thought back to my escapade with Fat Pat. I wanted to answer, "the wind blows the flame out," but knew that wasn't what he was looking for. I pursed my lips and dug for the memory. I could see it. After our match heads flared, the flame sputtered, like a newborn trying to fill its lungs with air.

"Struggling flame?" I said, not knowing how to make it sound like nomenclature.

"Why's it struggling?"

"It needs more."

"More what?" He asked, then gave me the answer by writing SUSTAINED HEAT next to the second bullet. Eyes back on me, he asked, "Then what?"

I pictured the matchsticks we lit, when the flame steadied and gave us hope. "Nonstruggling flame?"

He gave a half nod and wrote FREE BURN on the board. "The fire has established itself. It has everything it needs and is burning freely—like our snorer said, no struggle. Now what?"

"The flame moves."

"toward what?"

"Unburned fuel?" I answered, picturing my flame traveling down the matchstick toward my fingertips as I transferred it to the twigs and watched it build into bigger flames.

He smiled and wrote GROWTH on the board. "Next?"

"It moves faster."

He wrote FULL DEVELOPMENT. "This is when fire is happiest. It's devouring everything available to it." He raised his chin, asking me for the last bullet point.

Once our matches ran out of stick, they no longer carried flame. They just collapsed into the twig pile. "Death?" I guessed.

He clapped and wrote DECAY on the board. "Fires have a life span, just like we do. We come in feeble, live vibrantly, then peter out." He set the chalk into its tray. "Time for a coffee break." He lowered his head, looking me in the eyes—commanding me to caffeinate.

<p style="text-align:center">***</p>

I had not yet developed an affinity for coffee. My brother, Mark, had told me about the sleep deprivation. He was a third-year seasonal, had been through the training, and had advised me to acquire a taste for coffee. But it smelled bitter, so I ignored his advice. Now I had to buck up. I found a happy medium by mixing a hot chocolate pack into the brew. Several cups a day worked, keeping me alert during classroom sessions that dove deeper into detail.

We covered weather and fire behavior, extinguishing strategies like pincer action and frontal attack, and basic structural firefighting tactics. We memorized the Orders and Watch-Outs—foundational directives for staying alive in wildland firefighting. We learned colloquial safety constructs like, "Escape into the black, not the green. It's already burnt." And we diagrammed the department's organizational structure: twenty-two units each the size of a medium or large fire department, reported to a regional headquarters, which reported to State Fire Headquarters—an ivory tower I was certain I'd never step foot in.

On the morning of our sixth and final day, we took a comprehensive exam covering the classroom material. Then Big Carl relinquished the stage to his boss CK—a captain. For most of the training, CK had lingered in the back, sipping from a coffee mug emblazoned with the department logo. He wore an easy smile and long sleeves rolled up to his elbows. We felt a charisma that belied his lean frame and lazy right eye, which turned

out to be glass. On occasion, he'd wander into our squad lines, giving quiet encouragement—a you-got-this nod to someone struggling with hose coupling, or a "good job" shoulder slap to someone who passed a previously failed drill. We wanted to impress him. Hell, we wanted to *be* him. We didn't know he'd drop more people in one afternoon than Big Carl had all week.

"Okay, gang," CK said. "All ya gotta do is finish a little hike." He knew what Bill Bryson and Cheryl Strayed would alert America to in the years ahead: there's nothing more brutal than hiking when you aren't used to it. And sometimes even when you are. It's so deceptively simple. One foot in front of the other. But at some point, your feet hurt. Your shoulders ache from the gear pack. And unless you trick yourself, all your mind can focus on is pain.

A few miles in, I felt blisters forming on top of blisters raised earlier in the week. I had clearly messed up with my boot purchase. None of the local work boot stores carried anything in teenage girl size. So, the day before the training, I settled on a pair of boys' construction boots from a children's shoe store at the indoor mall. The cheesy boots were killing me now.

My brother must not have had this problem when he went through the training. He would have warned me. Mark had always looked out for me. He didn't have a choice. Throughout our childhood, I was way more interested in snake hunting, roof jumping, and cap guns than in trying on clothes or suntanning with my older sisters. Besides, it kept everything in order. Mom and Dad had split the six of us down the middle as a divide-and-conquer tactic: "You take the big kids; I'll handle the youngsters." Cathy, Tera, and Bernadette made up the former; Mark, Annie, and me, the latter.

We were each born roughly sixteen months apart—a solid testament to the rhythm method. As the youngest, I felt a world away from the big kids. Mark and Annie consumed my time. Annie had Down syndrome, and Mom raised her and me as twins—until I passed her in size and went to a public school she couldn't attend. Then I shadowed Mark on after-school adventures with his friends, but always promised Annie, "We'll play doctor when we get back. You can be the patient." Annie rocked back and forth to

her music, or worked on a puzzle, or practiced writing our names, awaiting our return and real Band-Aids placed on fake owies.

I would kill for a box of Annie's Band-Aids now, I thought as I trekked in the mountains above Sandy Point. I pressed on, vowing to custom-order a real pair of fire boots if I made it through this day.

<center>***</center>

CK stopped us for a break. "Why do I roll my sleeves up when I'm not on the fire line?"

"Prevents heat exhaustion?" someone guessed.

CK shook his head.

"Looks cool?"

"Well, yeah. But no." CK said with his cocky smile. "Check me. Eighteen percent."

He'd thrown out numbers all week, popping in during a Big Carl drill to guess the relative humidity. One of us would check the actual reading using our squad's belt weather kit. CK either hit it spot-on or fell off by two percent in either direction. We thought he had a cheat, like he'd run his own reading, minutes before.

The guy with the kit took out the sling psychrometer, an instrument with two thermometers attached to a small chain and handle. One of the thermometers had a wick that he wetted with the small vial of distilled water. Then he swung the chain in circles. In a minute, the two thermometers would give him the dry and wet bulb temperatures that would determine the air's relative humidity. "Damn, Cap. Eighteen percent."

CK nodded. "In firefighting, use everything you've got. Your forearms can tell you how dry the air is, a clue to how fast the fire will move. The back of your neck can tell you when there's trouble. Your feet can tell you when you've had enough. Right now, your feet are liars. Let's move."

Five miles in, we stopped for another breather. "You should all feel good right now. Strong. We haven't even got to the fire yet." Two cadets raised

their hands and asked if the four-wheel-drive pickup lagging behind could drive them back now. CK waved the truck forward. Six ended up going back. They were done. Washed.

The rest of us kept at it. I have no recollection of what propelled me forward. A tumble childhood schooling me in denial and perseverance? The years sitting in church pews teaching my mind how to wander to more exciting places? My disdain of failure?

When we reached the summit, CK stopped us. "Circle up your tools." We laid them on the ground, tool heads together and handles fanned out, like Big Carl had taught us.

"Now, you get to be firefighters. Pick a tool. Doesn't have to be what you carried."

Every firefighter has an initial favorite. Some love the nozzle—spraying water on fire, like in the movies. Some are dirt firefighters. They laugh at the luxury of water. They want the brush hook, a brutal chaparral chopper shaped like the grim reaper's scythe. Or, the Pulaski, a classic wildland firefighter axe with a blade opposite a grubbing edge used for trenching. Some like the simple meditative motion of the McLeod, a combo tool with a rake opposite a scraping edge. Some want chainsaws to feel the power of taking down burning trees that could torch a fire across a ravine or widow a spouse by falling on a firefighter. And some want the shovel position at the back of the hand tool line. They're called dragspoons. If the fire jumps the line, it's on them. They like the pressure.

I went straight for the drip torch: a 1¼-gallon canister filled with a diesel-gasoline mix and outfitted with a spout that drips flame. It fought fire with fire. Once I assembled it, CK coached me. "Fire wants to burn in a *V* pattern. Swing the spout in the shape of *V*. *V* after *V*. *W* after *W*. It's the way to grow a backfire that can put out the main fire."

I dripped flaming *W*s onto the grass, and built a wildfire—legally, effectively, and without Fat Pat.

"Let it get momentum," CK told the others. He nodded at me. "Grab that extra Pulaski. Join the line." We waited for the command as we watched fire come at us.

"Go get it," CK said. I could hear glee in his voice. This man loved a good firefight. He'd found the right profession.

We worked in our squads, thinking ahead of the fire. It had its own team: wind, slope, and fuel. Everything we'd learned in the classroom made sense in this moment. Backpumps sprayed to quiet the flame. McLeods scratched at an angle to pull the flame's edge into dirt. Pulaskis followed, using the trenching side to cut a ditch that trapped rolling pinecones so they wouldn't start a new blaze below. Dragspoons cleaned up. I forgot my exhaustion and blisters, focused on the battle.

Once we put the fire out and had a secure dirt line around it, we sat at the top of the charred hill. In our soiled Nomex, we devoured Vietnam-era C-rations, trading like schoolkids, but using fewer words.

"For your peanut butter?" Someone offered a processed meat product.

Wordless exchanges accompanied the sound of depleted bodies renourishing and rehydrating. These moments on burnt knolls with canned calories and dying wisps of smoke would become spiritual for me over the next thirty years—my version of home liturgy.

<p style="text-align:center">✳✳✳</p>

If heaven is sitting atop a smoky knoll after smothering flames, hell is the hike out. My blisters woke up as soon as I stood. And my sweat-soaked gear conducted an unshakable chill down my spine as redwood shade and a falling sun conspired against me. At a good clip, I could expect the distress to last at least 2½ hours. Drawing on my childhood churchgoing skills, I attenuated the pain by concentrating on something else.

At first, I started shyly, humming it. But it didn't distract me enough, so I belted out the words, "Ninety-nine bottles of beer on the wall. Ninety-nine bottles of beer . . ."

The only other gal in the class joined me. Then the guy in front of her chimed in, and the guy behind me, then all of us: "Take one down. Pass it around. Ninety-eight bottles of beer on the wall." Our singing line wove down the mountain, reminding each of us we weren't in this alone.

We arrived back at Sandy Point with seven bottles left on our fourth time through the song. After circling our tools, we collapsed on the apron and listened to magical silence, awaiting a wrap-up speech from CK.

When he walked to the middle of the apron, we stirred, willing ourselves to sit up, to get into squad formation.

He waved us down. "You've earned a few minutes. Take it. Then clean up. And we're done here. You'll each get a certificate, which qualifies you to apply for jobs as they come open in the unit." CK surveyed our sprawled, sweaty, Nomexed bodies, and broke into his cocky, crooked smile. He looked like a baker pleased at the creation he'd just set on cooling racks.

He started a slow clap. *Clap. Clap. Clap.* Someone stood. Then we all did. We clapped in time, then snapped into formation while building a faster rhythm. *Clap. Clap. Clap. Clap.* I knew this hype from playing school sports—the soaring feeling of team, of pushing your limits alongside others who are doing the same to find victory in a place we couldn't get to by ourselves. I stood straight, clapped hard, and clenched my jaw to keep tears from spilling. Our hands sped past the rhythm, and we exploded into cheers. A tear leaked out. I caught it mid-cheek and saw others doing the same. In a week, we'd created what felt like a lifetime bond.

But I would be the only one in the group to stay in the fire service for more than one season.

During cleanup, CK pulled me aside. "We have three current openings. Top three finishers here get jobs now."

My stomach tightened. *Was I one of them?* I bent to the ground to pick up a pinecone and tossed it from hand to hand.

"You got the top score." CK cracked into a full smile.

My eyes went to the ground. I knew I'd earned the certificate, but not the top spot. My brother, Mark, had spent hours quizzing me before the training. We did it as a hedge, so I'd have a better chance at passing. Now it felt like a cheat.

On an outdoor basketball court midway between Mark's crappy apartment and my crappier one, I'd moved around the key as Mark rebounded and grilled me on the Orders and Watch-Outs.

"Third Order?" Mark called out, passing the basketball back to me.

"Act on current and expected fire behavior." I fired off my shot.

Mark didn't mind me taking all the shots. He was a cross-country runner, not a baller, except when the two of us played a version we'd made up as kids, called no-nothing. The only rule was out-of-bounds. We didn't have to dribble, and tackling was fair game. It always ended with a low score and both of us on the ground grabbing stomachs that ached from laughing too hard at well-timed pushes and headlocks.

"First Watch-Out?"

"Fire not scouted and sized up." I'd memorized the words, allowing me to ace tests at Sandy Point. But I didn't understand their real-world application. That would take many fires and a few funerals.

CK stood in front of me, waiting for my elation. I transferred the pinecone from left hand to right and back, not sure how to explain my feelings to him or myself. Years later, I'd identify it as a cousin to my fear of failure—an understanding that failure in this realm would splatter on other females who wanted a life filled with dirt and danger. While I didn't understand the nature of the precipice I stood on, I sensed there was one. And CK was asking me to step forward.

CK intercepted the pinecone. It worked. With the introspective attention span of a teenager, now I didn't care that I was a cheat or coward. I just wanted my pinecone back.

"You can pick which slot you want, but I think Big Creek Station would be best."

I didn't know how to pick a slot, so I nodded and kept my eye on the pinecone.

"It's a coastal station. Couple captains there who can turn you into a good firefighter. One of them is a little crusty, but I'm guessing you can handle it." CK couldn't stop smiling.

He held his hand up for a high-five. I slapped it and he grasped my hand. "You should be damn proud of yourself. I am."

CK was an early believer in me—more than I was in myself. I felt baffled by his pride, so I just said, "Thanks, Cap."

"You know how you can thank me? Never sing 'Ninety-Nine Bottles' again. Ever."

I laughed. "Copy that." My blisters and I limped off, as I hummed the tune aloud and ignored the pinecone chucked at my back.

For fifty bucks a month, I lived in an illegally converted garage apartment in Santa Cruz. It came with a hot plate and teakettle, a small table and wooden chair, an underfilled waterbed, and main-house bathroom privileges. I supplied a toaster, books, worn bedding, and a blue storage bin I used as a pantry.

I put on the kettle and dumped food from my blue bin onto the waterbed. Toast makings and root beer cans sent ripples to my pillow and back. I placed the emptied bin at the foot of the chair. Just before the kettle whistled, I filled the bin with steaming water, then popped open a root beer. Treating it like whiskey, I took a long swig and held it at the back of my throat before stripping off my boots to reveal what I'd expected—stiffened socks adhered to blisters. I tested the temperature with my pinky, then slipped my socked feet into the stinging hot water and let them soak while I read a Kerouac paperback and sipped my soda. Once the socks had softened, I peeled them off with the skin attached. The pain made me wince, then smile. It felt earned.

The next morning, I placed a phone order for fire boots from Minnesota, which would fit if I wore two pairs of thick socks. Then I put fresh moleskin on my feet, donned my best T-shirt and jeans, and rode my twelve-speed bicycle to unit headquarters in Felton, eight miles away. I had to complete paperwork and pick up an official name tag.

I locked my bike to a pole, swallowed my nerves, and walked inside. Shiny floors and buzzing fluorescent lights greeted me. The smell of fresh-brewed coffee mingled with pine-scented disinfectant. Maps and Smokey Bear posters plastered the hallway walls. A big-boned personnel

clerk handed a thick pack of forms to me and to two other guys from the training. She sat us at a conference table to work our way through the documents. My pen stopped at a blank spot asking for my birthdate and admonishing, "Must be at least 18 years of age." I'd just turned seventeen and hadn't considered how to handle this.

CHAPTER 3

COFFEE

Big Creek Fire Station, 1982

A full year before my fire training, I'd convinced my parents to legally emancipate me. They were planning on moving north and I wanted no part of another new town, another new school. Dad's undiagnosed quixotic restlessness had landed me in sixteen different schools by tenth grade. I was done.

Dad looked relieved and started typing a document we'd need to get notarized. Mom and I watched, and she got teary-eyed, so I pretended it weighed heavy on me. But it didn't—at all.

Years later, I'd learn more about how "beautiful minds" work, but at sixteen I thought only about how hard it was to live with one. Dad was a bona fide genius who saw the world esoterically, not practically. His compass: Christ's beatitude teachings. "Blessed are the merciful. For they will be shown mercy" meant Dad would pick up hitchhikers and load them into our full car, even after one had pulled a knife on us. "Blessed are the poor in spirit. For theirs is the kingdom of heaven" meant Dad left his tenure-track professor job at Gonzaga University and we became a food stamp and welfare family.

Dad had many impressive qualities, and I could see why Mom fell for him when he showed up on her doorstep. He'd seen Mom's picture on the back cover of a Christian book she'd authored and illustrated. Enamored, he set out to find her and ask her out. He arrived on her stoop with flowers and a soft, irresistible smile. They picnicked at Chatsworth Park on a plaid blanket and talked theology and children. Mom wanted nothing more than to be a mother. *The Sound of Music* was her model and she had found her Captain Von Trapp in this former Marine Corps pilot, turned monk, turned seminarian. They married six months later.

But us kids, we'd made no such vow. All my siblings except Annie, who couldn't live on her own, had already moved out.

"How will you take care of yourself?" Mom asked on the way to the notary.

"I'm going to get a full-time job to start. Then student loans can get me through college."

"That's two years away. What about your schoolwork now?" she protested.

I shook my head. "They're offering the early grad exam next week." It was actually called the high-school proficiency test, but I spun it to appeal to the side of Mom that went to Stanford and cared about credentials. "If I pass, I can apply to college early." That and promising her I'd come visit on holidays and still go to church got me her signature in front of the notary.

After Mom and Dad pulled out of town, I felt my world open. I laid on the underfilled waterbed in my low-rent garage apartment with an ear-to-ear smile, thinking I could do or be anything. I took and passed the proficiency test, finished my basketball season, quit school, and got two jobs: one at the best calamari-and-fries joint in town and one at a custom T-shirt stand at the Beach Boardwalk. They paid my way up until I went to Sandy Point.

With my pen hovering above the firefighter application at Felton headquarters, I looked at my surroundings. Every uniformed person had an

Adam's apple and a moustache. I didn't want to be more different than I already was. I didn't want to have to explain "emancipated minor," so I left my birthdate blank, hoping no one would notice as they assembly-lined us through the hiring process. It worked.

Name tag in hand and a report day two days away, I walked outside, grinning. A balding captain with bright teeth stopped on the walkway in front of me, blocking my passage. A sling held his right arm at an angle above uniform shirt buttons struggling to stay closed at the belly.

"You the one going to my station? Big Creek?"

"Yes, sir." I glanced at his name tag: PETERS. CK hadn't told me the names of my captains, or which one would cause more distress. To Peters's credit, he didn't keep me guessing.

"I won't be out there for a bit. Ladder. Fall." He moved his slung arm like a wing, in case I didn't understand. With his good hand, he pointed at me, like he was holding a pistol. "I've never had a girl I haven't fired."

I swallowed, looked him in the eye, and said, "I hope to change that, Captain Peters."

He raised a skeptical eyebrow. Then he looked past me, signaling he was done. I pivoted out of his path.

In the wake of a court consent decree ordering the department to improve its "underrepresented" statistics or risk sanctions, Peters must have thought higher-ups imposed my assignment to his station. In an instant, affirmative action became more foe than friend. To me, it meant everyone except my brother and CK would presume me incompetent and think I was a mandatory hire, incapable of cheating my own way in.

"Hey," Peters beckoned. I turned back to face him.

"What's the first thing you do when you get to a fire?" he quizzed me.

Big Carl had drilled this into us. Captains can't have rookies freelancing. "I wait to be told what my assignment is."

Peters looked at me longer than seemed normal. I sensed an internal struggle. I'd given him a perfect response with no hesitation, no sign of the doubt that filled me—no sign of my proclivity toward being argumentative, or stubborn, or scared. He turned and walked away.

A slight wind blew. I felt the air on my forearms. *Twenty-four*, I guessed cluelessly at the humidity. My grin returned. At least until Peters had a shot at me, I was going to be a firefighter.

My brother, Mark, had known what he wanted to be since age two. Mom had locked herself out of the house with him inside. She watched through the front window as Mark jumped up and down on the couch clapping when the fire truck pulled to the curb. From that day, Mark drew lots of pictures of fire trucks and those firefighters. He added himself to the tailboard, knowing he would be just like them—kind men with prominent brows and chiseled jawlines.

Despite my big chin and bold eyebrows, I never saw myself on a tailboard. As kids, we'd both learned our career options from Mom's first children's book: *ABC and 123*. "A is for Artist alone by the sea, painting a picture of 1 lovely tree. B is for Baker. Your nose tells you when he takes from the oven 2 gingerbread men!" And so on through Z. In her book, F was for Fireman. The only women she'd drawn into the book left me with four options: Homemaker, Librarian, Teacher, or X-ray nurse.

As a kid, Mark reinforced the typecast. By eight, he'd deemed himself a chief and assigned me as his secretary, saying, "Girls aren't allowed in the ranks." But weathering five sisters evolved Mark, and after his second fire season, he pressed me. "You'd love firefighting. And it would love you. At least try it for a summer."

So here I was, trying it.

On my first day, Mark dropped me and my gear at a training burn. He had to. I didn't have a car. "Go get 'em, Klotchum." None of us remember how he came up with this childhood nickname. But I liked it; it felt endearing and enduring.

I retrieved my gear bags and waved as he drove off. Firefighters and engines milled about at a ranchette where the owner had agreed to let us burn a ramshackle structure. I found the check-in area and geared up. The incident commander pointed and gave assignments. He aimed two split fingers at me and a tall guy in a red captain's helmet, "Entry team."

Already in our breathing masks, we couldn't see each other's faces. On the front porch of the burning house, he nodded me forward. I entered, crouched low with my hand on the nozzle's bale—the lever that controls water flow from OFF to FULL BLAST. The captain kept a soft grip on the back of my turnout coat collar, guiding me into a darkness I'd never seen.

Structure fires are nothing like how they are portrayed in TV shows and movies—sets lit with controlled pyrotechnics and firefighters having full conversations. Real footage would display a black abyss and nothing but the sound of respiration and heartbeats.

We inched forward, searching for the cunning fire hiding behind its own curtain of smoke. I entered what must have been a bedroom. Orange embers flickered and low-lying fire spit intermittent flames up a wall. I opened up, gunned them down, then shot water into the air before closing the bale. Big Carl taught us this technique: blast the seat, then create steam that becomes a moist blanket over remaining embers.

We sank into a dark, muggy heat that penetrated our protective gear. I sensed the fire thinking. Studying the floor, I tried to figure out where it would reawaken. It tricked me. Violent and quick, it flashed in a massive fireball across the ceiling. I felt the captain's grip tighten. He waited a moment, then tugged at the back of my collar. Locked in my power struggle with the fire, I didn't respond. A second tug almost landed me on my ass. We backed out. Fast. The ceiling collapsed. It would have pancaked us.

Daylight blinded me as I lifted my mask. When he raised his, I saw a silhouette backlit by white sun, producing a well-deserved halo. As my eyes adjusted, I couldn't stop staring. Who knew the face of God belonged to a six-foot-three leather-skinned captain named Norm, with an Abe Lincoln profile and a missing front tooth.

That evening, I stood at the barracks door, my arms filled with a set of stiff white sheets, one thick wool blanket, and a flat pillow. Built in the late 1970s, Big Creek Station sat fifteen miles north of Santa Cruz in a small town called Davenport. It met the most modern standards for a firehouse. Basically, it was a large ranch home with a kitchen, dining area, living room (which we called a *dayroom*), and a shared dorm instead of bedrooms. The oversized garage housed the fire engine, tool rooms, and a captain's office. And there were two bathrooms. One for me. One for them.

"Pick that one over there." Scott pointed to an unclaimed bunk near the back door. "It's the second farthest from Norm's cigarette smoke."

Norm began every morning by fishing a cigarette from his nightstand drawer, striking a match, and taking a deep draw. Then he'd unscrew the cup top off his Stanley thermos and pour it full of hot black coffee brewed the night before. He finished his first smoke and coffee before rising from his bunk.

"Mine's the furthest," Scott bragged. Sandy bangs fell across Scott's forehead, and dimples emerged with a closed-mouth smile hiding Skoal-speckled teeth. His build and country good looks betrayed a high-school football history—running back or slot receiver maybe.

I looked to James, the other firefighter, for his thoughts. "They're all pretty much the same," he said, providing zero help. James wore a rope bracelet around his wrist; dark, shaggy hair barely within the grooming policy; and a vibe that nothing bothered him. Ever. If someone put me in charge of casting him, I'd call twenty-year-old Keanu Reeves.

James had started two months ahead of me. But this was Scott's second season, so I decided to take his veteran advice and carried my bedding to the far end of the barracks.

"Do you know how to do hospital corners?" Scott asked.

I shook my head.

"C'mon. we'll show you."

I made and unmade the bed a few times to lock in the skill and make the bunk my own. It reminded me of all the times I had set up a desk or

locker as the new kid in school. All those new starts had made the unfamiliar familiar and taught me to not flinch when tossed into new circumstances, even if terrified. Maybe that's what CK saw in me: I'd spent so many years pretending to be unfazed that I came across as brave.

At lights-out, I tucked myself in. The near-death firefight, the stress of being the new kid, a heavy wool blanket, and a nonliquid mattress drove me into a deep firehouse sleep. So when the alarm bell sounded late into the night, it didn't wake me. Scott and James toppled my mattress to get me up. When we got back from the call, a false alarm, we all headed for our bunks.

"Oh no you don't," Norm said in a soft voice. Somehow, the quieter his command, the more forceful it played. I cocked my head to the side like a dog. He pointed at the bed across from his, the one right under the bell. I couldn't argue. I moved my pillow and blanket, and in the morning put fresh sheets on my old bunk so someone else could have it. I never slept through another call. I've had insomnia ever since.

All seasonal firefighters worked five days straight (120 hours), then went home for two—unless days off were canceled because of fire activity. We were the ground-pounders, the infantry responsible for hoses and tools and doing what we were told. The first-level officers were engineers. Their primary responsibility was driving and operating the engine. But if a captain wasn't present, the engineer was the officer in charge. They worked three days (72 hours), then went home for four. Captains were in charge of the station and everyone who worked there. They worked the same schedule as the engineers. Battalion chiefs were in charge of a battalion, which typically consisted of four stations. They worked four days, with three off, but slept at home instead of in the barracks and only got called out for larger incidents needing a higher command level.

Big Creek, a one-engine station, had two captains, a floater engineer who covered open shifts at more than one station, and three firefighters: Scott, James, and me. We worked staggered schedules that intersected on some days. I landed on the Saturday-through-Wednesday shift, which

30

made me happy. Weekends were busier, and it meant I overlapped mostly with Norm.

My first few weeks brought minor vehicle accidents and fires originating in other parts of the county, which left us with mop-up duties or cover assignments at stations closer to the action. I itched for my first real fire. On a sunny, dry, windy afternoon, I got my wish: an initial-attack grass fire where we'd be the first engine in by miles.

Red lights and a siren soundtrack accompanied us as Norm navigated the engine through ranch roads, onto the hillsides, and past the power lines. I stared over the hose bed from my seat on the back, marveling at the mushrooming smoke's aspirations. The training fire I'd lit back at Sandy Point had covered a half acre at best and there were twenty of us to put it out. But this was a bona fide fast-moving wildfire. Angry. Hungry. As ready to fight as I was.

At the fire's edge, Norm gave us our tasks, pointing to Scott, then me, then James. "Nozzle. Hose pull. Backpump." Scott turned the nozzle to a wide fog pattern, knocking fire down in front of us. Then he adjusted it to a straight stream, cooling flames ahead as we advanced alongside the rolling engine. I fed hose to him, making sure to pull at a rate that kept Scott from being jerked back by it and Norm from running over it. James trailed behind with a backpump—a five-gallon water tank worn like a backpack with a pump nozzle allowing a low-volume squirt to extinguish rekindled flareups. We called them "piss pumps."

The smoke curled thick. Even when it swirled away, providing a momentary clearing, it didn't matter. Its sting defeated my goggles and kept my eyes more closed than open. My face shroud and a bandanna worn over my nose and mouth—wildland firefighting's version of a respirator—helped filter particle-filled air pouring into my lungs. Sweat dripped from everywhere. In wildfire purgatory, I tugged at the hose, protecting it like an umbilical cord to Scott as we progressed toward the fire's head.

We caught the fire before it escaped into a canyon that would have carried it for days or weeks. Standing on the smoky knoll, I savored the contrast between the verdant canyon and the blackened acres under my

feet. Ranchers drove their trucks up the hill to thank us. Norm pressed his index finger against the side of his long nose and blew its contents out the opposite nostril. Then he switched sides. I tried it and blew out my first fire-black snot with pride.

James and I began mop-up. Scott flicked his chew can and dug in for a pinch before joining us. He showed us how to conserve water but still smother every cinder. "Keep the nozzle low. Reduces overspray," he said, wanting us to know what he knew.

We worked our way toward the fire's origin, where Norm waited. He waved us over and pointed at the ground. A dead hawk lay there, cooked. *What are the odds a bird couldn't fly away from a grass fire?* I thought. I looked up at Norm. He said nothing, but nodded to the power lines above and held his arms out in a *T*.

"Whoa," I said, understanding the bird's wingspan bridged two wires, causing an electric arc, and turning the hawk into a flaming vessel as it fell to ignite the grass below.

On our return to the station, I bounced on the backseat of the engine as it crawled down the rutted dirt road before reaching speed on the coastal highway. I felt whole. Somehow it all fit—the focus of the fight, the thankful ranchers, the fire boogers, the fated hawk. Always the newcomer, I'd grown up a chameleon, sure I'd never get a habitat of my own. But here, I'd found it. I hoped a car would come up behind me, giving me a witness. I wanted someone to see my soot-covered face and think, *She belongs there. She's a badass.* No cars came. And it would take me years to realize it didn't matter if anyone but me thought I was badass.

Scott, James, and I spent mornings cleaning the firehouse and maintaining tools. James balanced out the Type A in Scott and me who already finished each other's sentences. On hot afternoons, the three of us sat in the cool dayroom and watched old training slides that required a carousel tray and projector, or Norm taught us knots he'd learned in the navy. On cooler afternoons, Norm took us out for field training.

We passed evening hours taking turns on the landline to check in with family. Then Scott, James, and I played two-on-one basketball. Whoever had the ball tried to score against the other two. I held my own with scrappy, irritating defense and a good point-guard long shot. Scott was athletic, but too footbally, so he played an unintended hard defense and scored few baskets. It reminded me of the no-nothing basketball I'd played with my brother. James had long, spidery arms and the grace of God, so he made it a tight game. He high-fived whoever scored, as if he were on the same team. Almost everything James did impressed and irritated me.

Norm left us to scrap with each other, opting to spend his evenings with a favorite hobby: macramé. He kept his latest project hanging from a hook fastened to the ceiling in the dayroom. With big, grease-cracked fingers, he wove and tied tiny knots, sculpting thin rope into flower baskets, wreaths, and purses. It was such an unexpected juxtaposition seeing the most macho man I knew lacing together a handbag. But the more time I spent with Norm, the more I understood why macramé suited him. It required precision, patience, a love of knots, and a desire to craft something out of nothing. He treated his macramé projects just like his firefighters, twisting and shaping raw product into something useful.

After basketball one night, I saw Norm's latest project suspended from the hook, half-done and looking vulnerable. Over nighttime hot chocolate and cards at the kitchen table, I suggested to Scott and James that we replace Norm's project with an abandoned bird's nest James had found behind the station. James nodded and we both looked at Scott. He balled and released fists, pumping up his forearms to help him decide if this was a good or bad idea. I guessed some football locker room pranks flashed inside his head. He thought about it, then displayed his dimples. "Let's do it."

The next day, we executed the plan during morning cleanup. All afternoon we waited for Norm to notice. He didn't say a word. We were certain he hadn't seen it until we went inside to prepare dinner and saw a perfectly tied noose dangling from the hook instead of the nest. Eyes bulging, we scrambled to get his macramé project back in place.

With dinner in the oven, I called my brother for a quick check-in. He was on shift at Corralitos Station, a busy two-engine house in the southern part of the county.

"Yeah, we should have known better than to mess with Norm and his knots," I said, after telling Mark about the nest and noose.

"Sounds like you're having fun," Mark said.

"So far. How's things there?"

"Great. Except"—he lowered to a whisper—"there's one dipshit who's driving me—"

Dispatch tones interrupted. We each heard it on our station speakers and through the phone receivers. "Victim trapped on the beach, north of Shark Fin Cove. No reported injuries."

"That's us," I said.

"Load 'n' go, Klotchum."

Norm pulled the engine out and waited for us to gear up and buckle in. Siren blaring, he turned left out the driveway toward the cliffs for a typical coastal station call. Inane or inebriated beachgoers often waited too long before ascending to the trailhead, which disappeared at high tide, leaving only sheer-faced cliffs as a way out.

Norm slowed at the dirt entrance to a Brussels sprouts field, then accelerated south. "There's a cove below these sprouts. Sounds like that's where our friend is," he explained. "Looks like they just irrigated, though. Might be too sticky to cut through." He paused and added, "We'll go around. Tide's still filling in. Should give our friend some thinkin' time."

Norm was right. The victim stood trapped in the unnamed cove below the sprouts. Norm, Scott, and James set up a pulley system while I made a seat harness from webbing straps so they could lower me, the lightest one. I took a spare harness, hooked up the victim, waited for them to haul him up, then caught the re-lowered rescue rope for my lift out.

We packed our gear as the humbled victim walked toward his car, waving thank-you.

We waved back.

"What an idiot. Who lets themselves get stuck?" I whispered, holding myself out like a veteran already tired of cliff rescues my first season in.

That's when I saw Norm eyeing the irrigated dirt road through the sprout field, probably thinking it a more expedient route back to the dinner table and worth the risk. Norm liked his dinner on time.

"We oughta be able to handle this," Norm said, talking to the fire engine and not us. Scott, James, and I shrugged "why nots" at each other. We knew Norm could get our two-wheel-drive engine many places four-wheel-drive engines wouldn't go.

He turned onto the muddy lane. A few yards in, the wheels started slipping and Norm began to work his magic, selecting the right gear, RPM, and steering wheel positions required to move forward—until we didn't. The tires spun and spewed, digging us deep into a predicament.

Norm pursed his lips and made the notification to dispatch. "Engine 5283 on delayed response. Mechanical issue."

We climbed out and watched Norm assess while the sky hued into electric orange and pink over the darkening ocean. A high-volume sprinkler tapped back and forth a few fields over, punctuating the quiet. The balmy air smelled like brine and crops—to this day, one of my favorite combinations of smells.

Norm gave us directions on digging here and piling there. We bled air from the tires and pumped water from the engine's tank, spraying it on a far reach of drier land. The farmer would be pleased. Then Norm cranked the engine and rocked the apparatus back and forth on the berm we built. Voilà! It climbed right out.

Norm steered through the remaining sludge, docking on dry ground near the highway. Scott, James, and I hiked up to meet Norm, clapping as we approached. We'd just learned how to unstick an engine, and save face.

Norm radioed in. "Back in service. Mechanical problem resolved. Low on water. Returning to quarters." Only those who had pulled the same trick would know "low on water" after a cliff rescue meant the engine had been stuck, and they weren't going to say anything.

★★★

It wasn't just dinnertime; Norm took the whole work schedule as seriously as you can when alarms blow it all to hell. He was a stickler for two midday fifteen-minute breaks the union had negotiated—one at 1000 hours and one at 1500 hours. I gave two shits about a fifteen-minute break in the middle of my five-day shift. They interrupted my momentum. But Norm had spent time in the navy and in masonry work. He knew the difference between non-union and union shops. So whenever he saw me blazing through break time, he scolded me.

Late that summer, I was in the supply closet, finishing the monthly inventory. I heard him come in from the captain's office, settle into his chair in the dayroom, and strike a match to his cigarette. I worked quietly, hoping he'd think I was in the tool room with Scott and James, who both followed the break rule.

"For Chrissake. Sit down and have a cup," Norm said.

I rolled my eyes, emerged from the supply room, and went to start a fresh pot of coffee before plopping into the chair next to him.

"Who's cooking tonight?" Norm asked.

"Scott. Any special requests I should relay?"

"Yup. Brought some house-made sausage from the Corralitos Market."

"Oh, heck yeah. I'll tell him," I said, pausing before I asked, "Hey, why don't you transfer to Corralitos?" Norm lived two minutes from the Corralitos firehouse, where my brother worked, but a full forty-five from Big Creek.

"Trying to get rid of me, eh?" He grinned, exposing his missing tooth.

"No, really, why not?" I pressed. It seemed like a no-brainer to me. He could walk to work if he wanted. This was big in my book. I traversed the fifteen miles to Big Creek from my garage apartment by hitchhiking or riding my bicycle. Norm couldn't stand that I hitchhiked, and I didn't have the sense to grasp his fear.

"Not sure you'd get it," he said, exhaling smoke through his nose.

The coffeepot hissed, signaling it was ready. "Try me," I said, grabbing Norm's mug off the kitchen counter. I poured fresh coffee into it for him. No one ever drank out of Norm's mug. It was seasoned with layers of stains; a surefire way to piss him off would be to wash it. It would be like

ruining someone's sourdough starter. Retrieving a clean mug from the cupboard for myself, I made my cheater's mocha and carried both mugs back to our chairs.

I handed him his cup and sat back down. He nodded thank-you and peered at my concoction. "You should take your coffee black. It's a simple way to say, 'I'm no priss.'"

I shrugged and took a sip of my delicious mix. He took a drag from his cigarette. "It's too close," he said, then fell silent. We both sipped until he wanted to add more. I was learning to operate at Norm speed. "When the call comes in for an injured kid, I don't want it to be mine."

Norm's nickname was "Ironman." He never put on long sleeves because he didn't get cold. On the fire line, he scooped raw C-rations from the can while the rest of us heated them over fire embers. His favorite coffee came from a tin pot we kept on the engine, filled with water and grounds, and set on top of embers until it reduced to a thick high-octane syrup. A Vietnam vet, forged and impervious, he never complained about aches or harsh conditions. But I began to see Norm had an underbelly, and wanting to separate his children from his jurisdiction told me he understood this about himself.

"I get it," I said.

Before returning to the supply room, I dumped my polluted coffee and gave myself a fresh black pour.

CHAPTER 4

VERMIN

Big Creek Fire Station, 1982

At the end of our twelve-hour shift on a massive wildfire along the coastal range in San Luis Obispo County, I opened my fire shroud and took my helmet off. Norm looked at my face and asked, "That poison oak?"

We'd spent all afternoon on progressive hose lays. Uncoil a hose roll hiked from the engine to the nozzle. Apply a hose clamp behind the nozzle. Remove the nozzle. Attach the new length of hose and put the nozzle on the other end. Unclamp. Chase the fire's flank toward its head while battling through thick chaparral laced with the toxic oak, which had swollen my left eye shut.

"No, sir," I answered, because the policy stated that anyone with a severe reaction to poison oak couldn't be a firefighter.

"That's a relief," Norm said, winking before showing me how to take care of it.

After that I became an expert at identifying the poison plant and treating my skin and equipment with special counteracting soap. Poison oak would be my enemy for as long as I fought in the wildlands, but it taught me early on: no matter how much you love the job, there are parts of it that will pummel you.

This proved itself in a different way the following shift back at Big Creek. Norm found us at the wash rack, scrubbing char from cotton-jacketed fire hose. "Follow me." He walked us to the engine and pointed to tiny turds next to a front tire.

"We got this," Scott told him. Norm nodded and headed into the captain's office.

A fire station garage stall is called an *apparatus bay* and its floor, *the deck*. The fire service adapted it from maritime nomenclature referencing a ship's deck, the place needing all hands. Originally, it meant work and in many cases death, as it was safer to be quartered above or below a sea's crashing waters. I'd grown up thinking the opposite, that decks were a place of leisure and play. On this day, the deck served all purposes.

Scott showed James and me what to do. We pulled the engine outside, then dry-mopped the concrete floor, pressed electrical tape down in the shape of a goal box, and set a peanut butter-and-cheese bait ball at the deck's center. Scott suggested we employ the same rules as our two-on-one basketball games. James and I nodded in agreement.

We hung our uniform shirts on a neat row of wall hooks. Scott and I tucked our undershirts into place. James didn't bother. Brooms at the ready, we waited for the puck.

Our setup felt cruel. It's not like I was a mouse advocate, but until now I'd managed to avoid direct involvement in the violence. As a kid, we lived in a few places that required mouse traps. Dad bought Victors—the kind with the spring clip designed to guillotine a mouse on top of a tiny wood plank printed with a big red *V*. On chore rotation, I would bait and set the traps or dispose of tripped ones. Sometimes the mouse got away with the bait and its life. I respected that. "Nicely done, buddy." But sometimes the spring won. Before carrying the trap out to the garbage, I'd cover the stiff mouse with a paper towel—a proper burial, I told myself. But really, it meant I never had to look at the little guy's fixed and dilated pupils.

"There!" Scott yelled and pointed to the deck. Stiff broom bristles and long handles flashed, while the scampering firehouse mouse tried to redirect its propelled body away from harm. The mouse looked like a motorized lint ball, but surprised.

"GOOOOAL!" James, or maybe Scott, raised his arms in victory, holding the broomstick above his head, like Gretzky. I'd only gotten a few swats at the puck and was embarrassed. Apparently, my basketball skills didn't transfer to mouse hockey.

But my ineptitude wasn't the real reason I stood motionless for longer than I wanted to. Reluctantly, I lifted my head to look at the mouse lying dead in the goal box, or maybe still twitching. A red drop of blood on its head stared back at me—still does.

Norm didn't help, watch, or object. Maybe he hated rodents shitting on his deck. Or maybe it was his way of exposing us to death a bit at a time.

<p style="text-align:center">***</p>

A few weeks after the mouse hockey, we got dispatched to a suicide. The evening call came in as a "vehicle over the cliff." But when we arrived at Greyhound Rock, the dusky sky revealed a car still teetering on the edge. Norm told us to stand by while he assessed the scene.

When he came back, he said, "Scott, hook a rope between the engine and car. James, tape off the lot and keep looky-loos back. Clare, pull a hose line, but stay next to the engine."

Why wouldn't I pull the line closer to the car? I studied Norm and the scene for clues.

A sheriff's deputy came, then the coroner.

"What the hell, Scott?" I asked when he came back to the engine.

"Suicide by shotgun. The guy rigged his car to go over the cliff *if* he missed. He didn't. It's bad." James heard Scott's answer, did an about-face, and checked on his perimeter tape job.

I waited for Norm to return to the engine. "Shouldn't I take a look?" I asked, thinking I needed to absorb as much as possible as a rookie and that it wouldn't mess me up me because I didn't even know the guy.

Norm shook his head. "Not this one. You'll see more than you ever want to in this job. This is the worst I've seen. Wish't I hadn't seen it."

I resisted the desire to say, "Well, Scott saw it." Norm allowing his more seasoned firefighter to make the choice about whether to look differed from

encouraging me to burn an indelible image onto my brain a few months into the job. And he was right; the next thirty years burnished plenty of slides in my tray—many I wished I hadn't seen. These are the ones I still see—the ones that jump into my consciousness without warning, reopening wounds inflicted by people I didn't even know.

Norm drove the engine back to quarters, his lips pale and still. After a sleepless night, he called for relief. I heard it was his first sick day ever.

<p style="text-align:center">***</p>

Instead of the relief guy, Captain Peters pulled into the parking lot. Scott's eyes got big. "He's back. We need to change the hose bed." James and I tailed Scott. He pulled the engine out of the bay and instructed us. "Norm likes the flat load. But Peters wants the horseshoe."

Scott got on the radio. "Engine 5283 on ten-minute delayed response for mechanical."

We hung our uniform shirts on the hooks. With Scott in the hose bed and James and me on the ground, we hand-jacked the hose off the engine, then laid it back in on its side in the preferred pattern.

Scott put us back on normal response. Peters rounded the corner with his gear bag as we finished tucking our shirts in. James missed his back tuck. I poked him to let him know.

"What are the three of you standing around for?" he said. "Looks like you didn't even start morning cleanup."

"On it," Scott said. James and I followed.

I cleaned the toilet and shower in the female restroom while James and Scott cleaned the larger, male restroom. My bathroom served as a place of solace, but it also caused me anxiety. There was a segregated feel to it. I worked fast to finish my bathroom so I could help with theirs. When I walked in, they pointed at a container filled with cellophane-packaged white tablets the size of hockey pucks. "You can take care of those," Scott said.

My eyebrows narrowed. I looked from the pucks to him and back.

James laughed. "Not your thang, *huh*?"

"You don't know what those are, do you?" Scott said.

"Not a clue," I said.

"Urinal cakes. They help disinfect and deodorize," Scott explained.

I scrunched my face. "Why would you need . . . Don't you guys flush?"

"Look. Sometimes, you have to make a judgment call," Scott said.

"About?"

"The person who might have flushed before you . . . and which hand he used . . ."

"Ohhh. I get it. You think pushing the flush lever is like touching another guy's dick."

James and Scott shrugged admissions.

I peeled back the plastic wrap. An overwhelming fake-cherry scent watered my eyes as I pinched the puck into a urinal and watched it spin into place. By the third urinal, I felt like a puck pro, no longer an outsider to this place where men made deals and feared cooties.

The radio squawked. "Wildfire, Warnell Truck Trail."

"That's us!" Scott said. We donned gear and climbed on the engine. Scott had the cab seat. James and I rode in back. Peters wailed the siren and pulled out of the station.

On the long, dusty climb into the Santa Cruz Mountains, I scanned the ridgelines for a column of smoke. I saw thin strands, wisping, not billowing— a slow-moving fire. The morning air and hillside grass still had moisture.

Peters stopped the engine next to low running flames. I double-checked my shroud and goggles and waited for Peters to come around to the back of the engine. I saw Scott testing the nozzle's water flow. Peters pointed at James and signaled for him to pull hose for Scott. I looked through my goggles, awaiting my signal. Peters turned away.

Was I supposed to go help? Was assigning James the same as assigning both of us? I stood and watched James and Scott knock the fire down. It was small, maybe an acre. Peters stayed tucked near the engine's pump panel to monitor the hose pressure output and water level. I shifted, fidgeted, and double guessed myself. *Was Peters going to fire me for not fighting fire? What the hell were James and Scott thinking? That I was a coward? That I was lazy?* Big Carl's training and my first conversation with Peters convinced me to

stay the course, but I was a wreck. I felt my back soaked in sweat—from fret, not fire.

James and Scott returned to Peters, who sent them out with hand tools to scratch a line around the still smoking edges. Forty-five minutes after we'd arrived at the fire, Peters wandered to the back of the engine. He lifted his goggles and undid his shroud.

"Fire's out. Where the hell were you?"

"Waiting for my assignment," I mumbled through my still-closed shroud.

"Take that shit off. I can't hear you."

I unfastened my shroud and lifted my goggles. "I'm waiting for my assignment, sir."

Peters dipped his head and shook it. When he lifted it back up, I saw a brilliant smile I didn't think him capable of. "Congratulations. You're the first one who's passed this test. Put your goggles down. We're heading back to the station."

And that was all it took. For the rest of this season and the next, Peters became my champion, defending me when other captains asked him if I was any good. "Wouldn't trade her for any of yours," I heard him say over and over, loud enough for me to hear it.

✳✳✳

My second season at Big Creek brought my first firefighter funeral. Captain Marlboro had gone up the coast in his small fishing boat, planted his feet in a bucket of wet cement, let it dry, and flung himself overboard—at least that's the story I heard. It tracked. Marlboro kept a fishing pole on his fire engine in case he ran across an irresistible stream. And rumor had it he never married because he couldn't love any person more than fish, or fire, or beer.

I'd worked with Marlboro on a few occasions while covering his station. He struck me as complex, with weathered skin but boyish eyes below thick red hair graying at the temples. I could feel his command presence. Everyone could. No one asked who was in charge if Marlboro was there.

At Marlboro's wake, I stood beside Norm on a boat dock at the Santa Cruz harbor.

"Do you see my brother?" I asked, knowing Norm's vantage point fared better than mine.

"What's he wearing?" Norm joked, straight-faced in our crowd of uniforms. "There he is."

"Hard to spot you people," Norm ribbed. Norm favored country music, but occasionally whistled Randy Newman's "Short People" when I walked into the dayroom.

He waved Mark over. Uniforms lined the dock and broke into a salute as Marlboro's ex-girlfriend carried an urn and battered red captain's helmet onto a tethered fishing boat. Some close friends loaded in behind her. One of them said a few words—something like, "Marlboro would've wanted a party. So that's what we're gonna do to honor the dude. We'll be back. Change out of your uniforms. Party starts in an hour."

Headed out the channel, Marlboro's red helmet bobbed, staring at me just like that drop of mouse blood. I couldn't look away.

Most changed into Hawaiian shirts and beach shorts—Marlboro's preferred off-duty attire. Norm went home, not wanting to celebrate the loss. Mark and I retreated to the harbor cliffs, where we each cracked open a Coors hijacked from the clubhouse cooler. We weren't old enough to drink alcohol but felt the occasion entitled us to a waiver.

Dangling our flip-flopped feet over the water, I asked Mark, "Why do you think he did it?" A wave crashed against the harbor rocks.

Mark took a swig. "So fierce. It's hard to understand. Heard he was trying to work on things. Maybe he opened the lid on Pandora's box too quickly."

"Guess he could tame anyone except himself," I said.

We looked to the tumbling surf, waiting for it to explain the whole thing to us. For years, Mark and I drank a Coors at the cliffs on the anniversary of Marlboro's suicide, until we just stopped—probably because other suicides tired us of trying to find the meaning in his. Back then, I had no clue how easily depression could swallow a life. Over the years, one body at a time, including my oldest sister Cathy's, I'd learn.

The season raced by. Fires, vehicle accidents, and beach rescues started to look familiar, blending together instead of each creating its own memory. Then fall came. Cooling trends blanketed Big Creek, but Southern California's annual Santa Ana winds—the same winds that had pushed Weldon toward our cul-de-sac when I was four—created red-flag conditions.

The National Weather Service issues red-flag warnings to alert the public to extreme fire danger based on forecasted strong winds, low humidity, dry fuels, dry lightning, or some combination of these. Here, their forecasts were spot-on. Fires began popping up everywhere in California's Southland.

We headed down in strike-team formation—five engines lead by a battalion chief in a pickup truck. Each engine carried an officer and two firefighters. A relief officer named Orco drove our engine, Scott rode shotgun, and I took my rightful rookie place on the back. I loved sitting in the open air and watching our red caravan. Like connected train cars, we tracked behind one another, moving as a single unit. Travelers stared as our fleet passed. I could sense their thoughts. *Where's the fire? What's the trouble? Is that a girl?*

When we stopped for coffee and fuel in a dusty gas station town, I realized how numb my glutes were. The seat cushions on the back hadn't been padded for skinny butts on long-distance hauls. Orco asked, "This next stretch is long. Wanna ride the hump?"

"Yes, please," I said. I'd miss my back-of-the-engine world, but my cheeks needed a break. Turns out, I should have declined.

We rode three across on the bench seat. Hot sun created miraged highway puddles that lulled Scott into a drooling slumber. Orco went somewhere that kept him awake—somewhere other than on the Interstate. I felt alone, still energized by the large black coffee I'd downed at our fuel stop. I stared over the hose reel and into the rear window of the engine in front of us—Hogan's engine.

Hogan had twenty years in and could be described with one word: oversized. It covered his mustache, appetite, and ego. His shotgun firefighter's

head sleep-bounced like Scott's. His second firefighter, Pam, had the same two rookie seat choices as me: on the back, or in the middle up front. But she was nowhere in sight. And Hogan seemed wide awake, jittery even. *Maybe he drank a lot of coffee too,* I thought before making an assumption I didn't want to make. My stomach sank as I watched Hogan twitch. I shook the thought out of my head and told myself Pam must be riding on another engine.

I looked out the passenger window and concentrated on thoughts about my changed plans—trading an intended bachelor's degree and collegiate basketball for the local community college fire science program. When my head questioned my new life strategy, my heart shut it down. *Stop. You found your calling.* The next time I looked straight ahead, Pam's *Flashdance*-style spiral-perm curls filled the middle of the frame and Hogan had settled down.

The Tehachapi Mountains spat us into the Southland's balmy, smoky air. We navigated the quagmire of freeways and pulled into a headquarters station, where we'd rest for the night before deploying in the morning.

We changed into shorts and T-shirts and entertained ourselves at the station's pool table, taking turns calling next game. On my turn, I sunk a few balls, then scouted the table. With no easy shot left, I bent and stretched, trying to find an approach, which is when I felt a pool cue sneaking up my leg. The cue traced over my inside thigh. When it registered, I jerked away, leaving my leg with a right-angled blue chalk streak.

Even before I spun to face him, I knew who piloted the cue. Hogan. He mistakenly thought himself irresistible. Even without man boobs and twenty years on me, he wouldn't have been a prize. I was no beauty queen but had enough self-respect to think I was out of his league, and that he was a predatory creep. Vermin.

"That's harassment." I chose a matter-of-fact tone. I have no idea how I knew to say this. In 1983, it wasn't a commonplace firehouse phrase.

"Only if I stop." Hogan winked. He held his cue like a fishing rod, waiting for an easy land. My face curled into the position it does when people ask me if I like beets. I hate beets. Everyone stood around the pool table, frozen, waiting for the drama to unfold. Even Pam.

I stared at Hogan, then posited a riddle. "Do you know how to tell how many wrinkles a big prick has?"

Hogan cocked his head, trying to figure out my aim.

"One, two, three . . ." I pointed an index finger at his face and began counting his wrinkles. "Sorry, Boss, could you hold still? This is gonna take a while. Four, five, six . . ."

The pool players erupted into laughter.

Hogan stood his pool cue down. "Take your shot. You're slowing the table."

I moved to the other side, took my shot, and missed. Still, I felt victorious.

The next morning, we deployed. Dispatched to a fast-moving grass fire, all five of our engines attacked. The battalion chief pulled in ahead of us and directed, "First two engines on the left flank. Next two on the right. Last one handle the anchor point—make a line around the heel, give the flanks something to tie into."

Our engine worked with Hogan's. We pulled hose lines and sprayed as the fire tore through the grass, heading to a brush line. That would be our spot to catch the fire. Fire slows when it goes from light flashy fuel into heavier fuel, which retains more moisture. But it's a short window.

To get through to the brush, we had to cut a barbed wire fence. Hogan instructed me to slice through the wires even though Pam stood closest to the best cut point. I brushed past her to get it done. I didn't even look at her.

I didn't blame him for his poor self-assessment. I blamed her for feeding it. I expected more from Pams than Hogans—maybe because I'd learned as a kid to rely on Mom, not Dad, to hold everything together. It would take me too many years to understand how unfair I was. And it would take a national movement to out the problem. Pam had snared herself in a double-standard trap she didn't see. It would cost her; after that fire season, I never saw her again. Somehow, I knew about the trap, but never told her. Sorry, Pam. Sorry to all the Pams over all the years. I mean, get your shit together and stop disrespecting yourself. That's part of the movement too. But I am sorry.

Back in the fog at Big Creek, Scott, James, and I climbed into our bunks. Our heavy wool blankets guarded against the late season coastal chill. I

grabbed a paperback from the stack I kept in my locker, which I refreshed regularly from the used inventory at Bookshop Santa Cruz. It stocked what I liked: books with beatniks, road trips, extreme adventure, and lives that interrogated theology.

About fifteen minutes in, Scott asked, "Okay if I kill the lights now?" James and I nodded. Scott looked at me funny as I set my book down. "*The Electric Kool-Aid Acid Test*? What the hell is that about?"

"LSD," I said.

Scott hit the light switch, then climbed under his covers. "Because who wouldn't be reading a book about LSD at a firehouse," he said. Then the three of us jabbed at each other in darkness until we began to fade. That's when Norm flipped the lights back on, popping the tranquility like a pin to a balloon. We sat up, trying to figure out why. With the dispatch radio silent, we knew it wasn't a call.

Norm folded back his wool blanket, stripped down to his boxers and T-shirt, crawled into bed, and said, "Smokey's getting cold out there."

It took a second for us to get it. Norm called the bear on the California flag "Smokey." The flags were supposed to come down before nightfall. This night, we'd forgotten.

We looked at each other from our bunks and went straight into a roshambo. I chose scissors and lost. I pulled on my turnout pants, opting to brave the cold without my jacket.

"Grab yer flashlight in case there's a live Smokey out there," Norm said.

I did and headed to the flagpole to retrieve Smokey and Old Glory, unaware that years later I would present the station's flags to Norm's widow.

<p style="text-align:center">✳✳✳</p>

Late autumn rain brought a sense of relief and lazy-day schedules, but successive days brought the gloom of an ending fire season. We began battening down the station for winter. This involved sharpening and storing tools, inventorying food staples, waxing floors, and checking the rain gauge—hoping two inches hadn't fallen. That's what sent seasonals home for the year.

Norm sipped his 3:00 p.m. coffee. "I'm calling game time," he said.

I grabbed Monopoly. James set out a bowl of tortilla chips. Scott tuned the radio to Norm's favorite country station.

We claimed our pieces and started rolling dice. A navy tattoo of an anchor peeked through the bottom of Norm's short-sleeve uniform shirt. "Did it hurt?" I asked.

"Shit, kid, I don't even remember getting it. Your roll."

As "Pancho and Lefty" played in the background, we reviewed our best and worst moments while buying Marvin Gardens and Park Place. Norm hoarded the railroads.

"Funny shit when Peters told you biking to work didn't count as PT," Scott said to me. "You looked so dejected. And tired."

"Peters was right," Norm said. "Bikes don't do anything for bulk. Keep lifting weights."

"I will," I promised, then said, "Hey, James, remember when you almost lit—"

"Yourself on fire?" Scott finished, already laughing. Working on a pre-scribed burn to reduce overgrown grasslands near the University of California, Santa Cruz, we'd burned six-foot strips at a time. James took the flame thrower, which he hadn't used before, and pulled the trigger. He was so enthralled with the spewing fire, he spun in a circle and created a fire cage around himself. Norm watched, letting enough time pass to turn into a lesson, then walked over and pushed James out of the fire circle with a long-handled McLeod tool.

"Ha, ha. At least I didn't forget to put my goggles down and burn off my eyelashes," James said, looking at me.

"They grew back." I batted them to prove it.

"And I didn't get fired." James reminded us about Norm's vacation week, when a new officer with a Napoleon stature and complex covered Big Creek. Scott and I took an instant disliking to him. We figured out ways to push back. When Napoleon ordered me to crawl under the engine to determine which fluid leaked onto the drip pan, I did it, and accidentally wiped a streak of bright pink transmission fluid onto his clean shirt. When he demanded we label the engine compartments to help him find things

quicker, we labeled everything. Steering wheel. Radio. Hammer. Window. It took us all day.

We finally broke him the next day when he caught us mopping floors while issuing ridiculous orders with our hair propped into the same pompadour he wore, using gel he'd left in the bathroom. He fired us. Scott and I went into the barracks to pack our stuff, but really to call Norm and Peters. They both told us not to leave until relief was available, which would be in the morning, which was also when Norm would be back to rehire us.

Rain slapped against the dayroom windows. "You think we were too hard on Napoleon?" I asked, after landing on B. & O. Railroad.

"Nope." Norm said, backing the course he and Peters had taken. "He'll be working for you one of these days. Hopefully, you won't be as brash. That'll be two hundred bucks, please."

I forked it over, knowing I was going to lose the game and the rain gauge was full.

II.

SUSTAINED HEAT

When I was five, we moved to Santa Fe, New Mexico. I'm not sure why. We stayed two years. My memories from that time are mostly spotty recalls of firsts in my life. My First Communion, where I scrunched my face at the priest with his cannibalistic offer of "the body of Christ." My first taste of beer, snuck from the teacher's lounge at my school. My first pet, a rat named Gerald, who eventually escaped his cage.

But one first stands out with more vivid detail. It's my first memory of experiencing rage. Mark, Annie, and I were at a park. It was Annie's turn on the slide. Her Down syndrome didn't preclude her from moving fast, she just had no sense of urgency when ice cream wasn't involved. Relishing her turn, she wiggled her foot into place on the bottom rung of the ladder. The boy in line behind her fidgeted. I looked away, scanning for Mark, but a thump and yelp swiveled my head back to the slide. Annie was on the ground. The boy had pushed her aside.

I charged at him, not giving one whit that he was bigger and I might take on damage. The boy's mother got there first and held my flailing little body at bay. Fuming, I grabbed Annie's hand and rushed to find Mark. "He shoved. She's hurt. Then his mom . . ." I explained to Mark in a single breath while displaying Annie. But the swing set ahead had already replaced the upset in her eyes with a broad smile—which I couldn't understand because I was still so heated.

Years later, I'd learn the nomenclature. *Flashpoint. Fire point.* The first is the temperature at which something is hot enough to create a fleeting flame—the ignition. The second is the higher temperature required for continuous burning—the sustained heat. Annie's blood flashed but never caught. Me, I still blaze when I think of the boy, and all the stares over all the years from everyone who hadn't seen a face like Annie's.

CHAPTER 5

ROODS

State Fire Headquarters, Still 22 Months Left

Outside the Shady Lady, I hugged Ken and Red good-bye and I headed upstairs to my loft. An edgy developer had converted a brick bakery into twelve second-story walk-ups, which sat above street-level bars, burger joints, and hipster hair salons in Sacramento's regentrifying midtown. I lived there during the workweek and drove home to Bud on weekends.

As soon as I shoved my key into the lock, I could hear Brody. When I opened the door, he pressed puppy slobber onto my pants. His thick black muzzle set off a red-fawn coat that made him a showstopper. Bud hadn't wanted me to get him—didn't think a bullmastiff puppy went well with my demanding job and tiny urban loft. But I had irrefutable counterpoints: "It's a lazy breed—won't need walks. Plus, the place is made of puppy-proof brick. Indestructible."

My phone buzzed as I hung keys on their hook and rubbed Brody's velvet ears.

"Hey, Andy," I said, topping off Brody's water.

"Ken said you kicked a bit."

Andy was the one leaving the vacancy I'd fill after shadowing him for a few months. I'd known him since Harbor High School but hadn't spent

any real time with him until he became my boss at headquarters three years earlier. In school, Andy was a year behind my brother Mark and a year ahead of me. All three of us lettered in athletics but in different sports, requiring separate cliques. Over the next three decades, we'd leapfrog each other across the state and through the ranks. The long-banged, cocky football jock I'd once known still had a square chin and bright smile, but his eyes had deepened, seen more, and he now wore a hairline and wisdom that reminded me of Norm.

"Yeah, I kicked. But then he got me extra-crispy fries."

"Fries are fair play," Andy said. "Anyway, welcome to the job you never wanted."

I nodded, then spotted splinters on the floor at the bottom of the loft's spiral staircase. On closer look, I found an entire chunk of wood missing from the bottom stair. "Shit."

"You'll be fine," Andy said.

"No, I didn't mean 'Shit!' to you. Brody ate half a stair."

Andy laughed. "You know, being chief of Fire Protection is a lot like having a puppy; you can't begin to guess what it'll throw at you. Expect the unexpected."

"I've spent my whole life doing that," I said, thinking about the repetition of this theme over the years. Somewhere along the line, it wasn't Dad's fault anymore. I'd fully adopted his penchant for chasing dreams and adrenaline. I could hide behind the crispy fries or accept that I still fed off dares. My biggest yet, I'd be going from commanding a few statewide fire programs to all of them: wings and wheels, command teams, mutual aid, fire cops, civil cost recovery, command center operations, crew camps, training, safety, research and development—all the fun stuff. We joked about the difference between Fire Protection and Red's Admin shop: toys vs. turds, glory vs. guts, shine vs. shit. It wasn't spot-on, but we liked the alliteration, and it acknowledged that the non-uniformed part of our force did dirty work too.

When Andy and I signed off, I scooped kibble from bin to bowl and swept up splintered wood, wondering if the hickory in Brody's stomach would end up in a vomit pile next to my bed.

After gobbling his food, Brody led me to the door, ready for his walk. At six months, he weighed seventy pounds and still had climacophobia: fear of stairs. We were working on it, but in the meantime, I carried him down to the street, let him pee, then hauled him back upstairs.

I hung his leash, then fished the Shady Lady penny matches out of my pocket and flipped them onto the coffee table, an antique steamer trunk I called "Charlotte" after Bud's mom, who had given it to us when she passed.

After changing into sleep shorts and a T-shirt hijacked from Bud, I made a cup of tea and plopped onto the couch.

"C'mon, Brody." I patted the seat next to me. He leapt up and started circling into his spot. "Absolutely a not-on-the-furniture dog," I'd promised Bud. "There's no way I'll give in to it." Brody pushed his nose into the leather cushion and his butt into my thigh as I surfed through guilty-pleasure reality shows, away from Bud and his sci-fi. I settled on *American Idol*, sipped my tea, and matched my breathing to Brody's.

<p style="text-align:center">✳✳✳</p>

A set of three-star collar brass waited for me on my new desk in a small office across from Andy's. I set my backpack in the corner, put on the brass, and acquainted myself with the coffee protocols. Andy ushered me into my first executive staff meeting, a weekly briefing with Ken and his top team.

I remember three things from the meeting. The weather patterns tended toward red-flag conditions throughout the western states. A coms guy tired of directing questions to "Clare and Andy," so he dubbed us "Clandy." And doggie daycare called in the middle of it all to let me know they were kicking Brody out and they'd like me to pick him up "as soon as possible."

At lunch, I drove to the daycare. "What did he do?" I asked the polka dot–shirted guy at the front counter.

"He doesn't play in a size-appropriate manner. I'll go get him for you."

I looked through the glass window at dogs playing together. Off to the sidelines, a fenced area labeled PENALTY BOX contained a smiling Brody.

Polka Dots came back with him and handed the leash to me.

"Is this for today, or . . . ?"

He shook his head. "He can't come back."

"He's not aggressive. He's a puppy and loves other dogs. I don't get it."

"He only has two maneuvers. The takedown, and the pin."

"But that's just play."

"He doesn't let them go. He just lays on them. For a long time. They can't get up."

I sighed, tugged on Brody's leash, and left. I felt like a mom walking her kid out of the principal's office after a fight, secretly proud of the kid's brawn.

I dropped Brody at the loft, made a few calls to daytime dog walkers, and went back to the office for more Clandy work. Andy and I traded off the lead spot, giving briefings, sparring with ops on staffing levels, and keeping the state's national guard from self-deployment on our fires. Troops of fit, bored altruists with a waning mission wanted in on our midseason action as President Obama downsized the United States' presence in the Middle East. When fires reached a massive scale, we needed them. But on smaller fires, too many resources get in the way. And the generals are more sensitive than you'd think, so it took time and diplomacy to back them off. "We really appreciate you reaching out, but we don't have any resource needs at this . . ." "Yes, we're aware of how capable . . ." "No, there's no other force that can do what your folks can, but we're . . ." "Yes, we're sure we don't need to activate. Thanks again for leaning in." And so went the week.

<center>***</center>

Most weekends I made it home to Bud. Fourteen years earlier, we'd purchased a three–bed, two-bath Mediterranean in an eclectic San Jose neighborhood between his downtown deputy district attorney office and the city's rose garden. Bud made it the first house I ever sentimentally attached to when he said, "Counting fire stations, you've probably lived in fifty houses. This may be your first true *home*—a place you never have to move from." The loft in Sacramento made this truer. Every weekend, I couldn't wait to get back to my warm wood floors, backyard basketball hoop, six-burner stove, and Bud's hugs.

"How was your first week as a three-star?" he asked as I unloaded Brody from the back of my Jeep.

"Not too eventful," I said, starting with the truth.

Brody ran around Bud in circles, then went to pee. "How's he been?" Bud asked.

"Piece of cake," I lied.

Bud lowered his chin and raised his eyebrows at me. He could say almost anything with his eyebrows.

"Yeah. I mean, daycare didn't work out, but I got an even better solution. It's all good."

"Didn't work out?"

"Not a good fit. But it's cool. He has an adventure walker now. She takes him on field trips with other dogs during the day. It's the best."

"Adventure walker? Sounds expensive."

"Nope."

His eyebrows moved toward center.

"Well, not really, considering I come home to a tired puppy."

"Has he been chewing on things?"

"Nope."

"How bad?"

"Just a stair and the community couch on the deck. But that's it."

Bud helped me carry my bags inside. Brody leapt into Bud's seat on our couch.

"Whaaat?" I said. "He does NOT do that at the loft."

I don't know if lying came to me naturally or by way of Dad. He was a master. He'd pay for a motel room and sneak in Mom and the six of us kids. For fifteen years, he swore to movie box offices my sister Annie was under five, so she'd get in free. Her Down syndrome made it hard for them to tell—until her breasts gave it away. He'd tell cops he was speeding because his wooden-leg hinge seized up. He'd knock on the leg to show them and, since they hadn't seen that before, they failed to notice he'd knocked on his left leg. Dad didn't call it lying. He called it God's work. He called almost everything he did God's work.

I followed his lead, starting with low-stake fibs, like, "Nope. I didn't eat the cookies." By six years old, I upped the ante, telling Mom and Dad, "My new Sunday School teacher is taking us to Confession." Then, I told the teacher I'd already completed Confession in the town we'd just moved from. She bought it and initialed a box on a form that verified my purity. I figured if God didn't want Dad to pay for things or follow speed laws, God certainly didn't want my first-grade self to crawl inside a freaky confessional booth to tell a robed, dandruffy old dude secrets an omnipotent God would already know.

With Bud, I made my lies obvious, an advanced tactic designed to be endearing. Bud shook his head at me, then went to the kitchen to make us a big bowl of popcorn while I changed into my pajama sweats.

I scooted a sleepy Brody over to make room on the couch for Bud, me, and the popcorn.

All nestled in, Bud found a TV show we both liked and turned the volume up loud enough to drown out Brody's snoring.

The next morning, we did Saturday stuff: errands, home repair, dog park, dinner, and sipping our favorite scotch on the back porch—trying to teach Brody the difference between his chew toys and our drip system.

On Sunday, my phone rang, flashing Sacramento Command Center on the caller ID.

"Chief Frank," I answered in my work voice. My fallen face told Bud it was bad news.

"A hotshot crew? Fuck. Full shelter deployment? Confirmed? Okay. I'll head to HQ." I hung up and told Bud, "A burnover in Arizona just incinerated nineteen firefighters."

<center>*** </center>

Even though these weren't our firefighters, our desks sat at the top echelon of the most wildfire-prone land in the country. There was work to do. Andy and I called our counterpart in Arizona to offer condolences and assistance. Then we supplied Ken with briefing materials. Our chief of legislation, dubbed "Griffin" because that was her collegiate mascot and because nobody messes

with a flying lion, calmed state legislators, who always wanted to know who to blame and how they could fix it with new laws the minority party would hate. Red worked with the firefighters' union to send an honor guard contingent. And Chief of Coms Turbo fielded press inquiries: "Has this happened in California? Could it? What are we doing to make sure it doesn't?"

At the end of the day, we all gathered in Ken's office. Red opened a box of Cheez-It crackers from Ken's stash and poured a pile onto the middle of his conference table.

Ken grabbed a handful and leaned back in his chair. "Gov's been briefed. They just want to be kept in the loop."

Turbo rattled off her report. "I'm feeding the press talking points from Clandy. We can't comment on tactics until Arizona completes a full review of the incident. Our hearts go out to the families, city of Prescott, and Arizona firefighting community. We don't know how drought conditions factored in. Yes, we believe lightning caused the fire. Yes, thunderstorm patterns can shift a fire's direction. No, we don't know if or how many of the Orders and Watch-Outs were compromised. Yes, the Granite Mountain Hotshots were a relatively new crew. Also, there have been twelve hundred thirty-nine shelter deployments since they were invented in the 1960s and only twenty-two deaths up until yesterday." Turbo delivered the information in a single breath while exchanging texts with her staff.

At the pause, we all crunched crackers we'd stopped chewing for fear we'd miss something vital.

"Oh, for fuck's sake," Turbo said, looking at her phone.

We stopped chewing again.

"Some savant in Riverside tweeted that the hotshots shouldn't have left the black."

Ken fidgeted. He hated it when the department's message hadn't been vetted through the Cheez-It group. And it happened all the time. With 10,000 employees and social media, it was inevitable.

Andy jumped on it. "We don't know what happened yet. That little asshat has no business weighing in. Probably a damn first-year firefighter trying to impress his girlfriend."

"A little sexist," I said. "And hetero-assuming."

"I'll buy a case of Cheez-Its from Costco if I'm wrong."

Griffin raised her hand. New to our team, she was still learning fire lingo. But she was wicked smart with degrees from Cambridge and Carnegie Mellon, and she had British sensibilities. "I assume 'black' means it was burnt, and conventional wisdom would have crews staying nearer the black during a weather shift?" Griffin said.

The rest of us nodded.

Turbo made some furtive thumb movements on her phone screen. "Yup. Asshat is a boy firefighter whose first like was from @Lila P."

Andy gave me an I-told-you-so look and dialed South Ops, who would need to rein in independent commentary on what the hotshots had done right or wrong.

We finished the pile of crackers and headed home—and did the same every night that week. Gather. Snack. Repeat, swearing to the governor's office, legislators, the press, our own troops, and each other that we had no opinions about what happened. We couldn't. It was beyond bad form to point fingers when you weren't there and a morgue was involved. But by the end of the week, we all had the same opinion as Asshat.

<p style="text-align:center">∗∗∗</p>

A wall-mounted television in the headquarters lobby displayed live coverage of the memorial service in Arizona. It drew dignitaries from the White House and Capitol Hill, top state officials, and tens of thousands of Arizonans and uniformed personnel. Not since 1933 had a wildfire killed as many firefighters.

I stood at parade rest in front of the television, as if I were there. Center stage, nineteen helmets topped nineteen tool handles footed by empty boots—haunting battlefield crosses. For some reason, it reminded me of the opening lines from William Blake's poem "The Liar":

> Deceiver, dissembler
> Your trousers are alight
> From what pole or gallows
> Shall they dangle in the night?

The only member of the Granite Mountain Hotshots who hadn't died stepped to the stage. The day his crew burned, he'd been assigned as a lookout away from them. Now, he read the hotshot prayer in an increasingly cracking voice that felt like a slow, unstoppable avalanche.

I looked beneath the nineteen helmet brims, where eyes or at least sockets were supposed to be. I knew none of them but had learned a few things over the week. Their leader was forty-three years old. Four others were in their thirties, and the remaining fourteen in their twenties. Avid churchgoers, the crew always had a Bible with them. The ridgetop they'd departed had burned two days earlier. It was black, cold, and safe. They left it and headed toward Yarnell, a small town in the fire's path. The fire picked up speed during a squall and advanced on them, but they couldn't see it from the canyon they were traversing.

Fire loves canyons, which operate like chimneys designed to ensure a hot, clean, fast burn. Water boils at 212°F. If you stick your finger in it, it will blister within seconds. In that canyon, the fire's temperature surpassed 2,000°F. They couldn't outrun it, so they deployed their fire shelters.

Worn on web belts next to canteens and hose clamps, an accordion-folded fire shelter is about the size of a Kleenex box. It's an aluminum-coated tent designed to reflect heat away from the firefighter inside. We drilled endlessly with them. Clear a dirt patch. Ditch your tool. Unfold the shelter with a vigorous shake. Tuck yourself inside. Pray. We were taught to use them as a last resort and called them "shake-n-bakes." They would begin to melt at 500°F.

I'd never had to deploy mine on a fire. The closest I came was pulling the engine's fire blanket on a blaze in a national forest near the Oregon border. Mounted beside the open-air backseats, the blankets provided an aluminum cover, like a fire shelter's, to tuck under if the engine rolled through fire. It had happened in an instant. The fire crowned in timber, then flaming wreckage rained. We cut our hoses and leapt to our spots on the engines. Alone on the backseat, shrouded in the foil blanket, I remember thinking in present tense. *It's hot. This is what cracking timber sounds like. It might fall on me. We're moving. My back is really hot. The air is thick. My back is really, really hot. It sounds like the engine's paint is blistering. I hear gravel under the tires. It's less hot now. It's easier to breathe.*

I didn't pray as fire lapped at my back. I suppose I didn't want to go there, so I forced myself to presume I'd make it out. I wondered if that's how the Granite Mountain Hotshots felt. Surely the God they praised every day would support their decision to travel from black to green. Surely God wouldn't let Lucifer consume them with his most savage tool. But all of them baked in place. Over half were found with their fire shelters stripped off, bared by the fire's stormy ferocity—the youngest burnt in the fetal position.

I asked their eyeless helmets, *Did you know you were about to die?* They didn't respond.

I focused on the first helmet, the leader's. *Why? Why did you make this call? Did you think you could save Yarnell? Would I have done the same, if I saw what you saw?*

I blinked and looked at all of them again. They stared back, looming, like roods—elevated crucifixes in a cathedral. But roods are also acreage measures. In fighting this fire, the hotshots became crosses for acres—roods for roods.

"They didn't have to die," Andy whispered from behind. I had no idea how long he'd been there.

"I know."

"It's about more than them leaving the black. The mistake happened earlier. Two days before this crew even got there, the fire was five acres and suppressible." Andy escalated to full volume. "If you've got triple-digit temps, single-digit humidity, a fire near where people live, and your resources aren't tapped, you don't dick around with it. You fucking smother it. That crew didn't need to be on that fire."

In Cal Fire, it was that simple. We'd expanded our mission beyond land stewardship and received funding and resources to protect people who'd migrated to the wildland. Our ongoing goal was to catch ninety percent of wildfires at ten acres or less. We wanted one hundred percent, but we were realists.

Standing with arms folded across our chests, Andy and I watched the remainder of the memorial service—feeling like we saw things with the self-righteous clarity an older sibling has. The feds and most states,

including Arizona, hadn't shifted as much weight from forestry to fire. We shook our heads, wanting and waiting for our fellow firefighters and states to grow up, to move past a bygone era that just cost nineteen lives.

At the same time, we both knew it was more complicated. The suppression goal represented only one aspect of the complex relationship between humans, land, and fire. But the circumstances of seeing brethren converted to crosses turned us into proselytizers. In that moment, we were William Blake's deceivers—marks in perpetuating a lie that all fire needs quick death; that people need to live on a patch of land more than fire needs to burn it.

The worsening drought years ahead would bring this convoluted fire-human relationship to the forefront across the West, then the nation and the globe.

CHAPTER 6

GUM

Soquel Fire Station, 1984

Every winter, the department shrank by nearly a third when it laid off its seasonal firefighters. We came in three flavors: those who weren't recommended for rehire, those who were but ran ski lifts in the winter, and those who'd sign up for a program like Ricochet's.

Ricochet was a fast-talking, gum-chewing battalion chief with an innovative mind. He wanted laid-off firefighters to staff Soquel Station during the off-season, for free.

Built in the early 1950s as a two-man station, Soquel had cramped barracks, a dayroom that barely fit a love seat and two armchairs, a tiny bathroom, and an eat-in kitchen with original tile, which would have been retro cool if it didn't have cracks in it. It was a slow house that sat mid-county. We all thought of it as the buck short of the unit—not necessary, but great for backup. It was perfect for Ricochet's idea.

My brother, Mark, Scott from Big Creek, ten others, and I gathered in Soquel's parking lot, forming a half circle around Ricochet. "Okay, kids. Here's the dealio." Ricochet cracked his gum. "This is a pilot program. So don't blow it. You'll cover the station on nights, weekends, and

holidays—assist the year-round stations with their calls. Vehicle accidents, chimney fires, flood emergencies, yadda yadda."

He surveyed us and continued, "There's no pay, but you'll be on the books as sleepers, which gets you travel costs, fire science credits from Cabrillo College, and training. Ground rules. Work out a staffing schedule. Don't respond to a call with less than two." He chewed and cracked faster. "Questions?"

"Are we all the same rank?" a dude named Dunkle asked.

Ricochet stopped chewing. He hadn't considered we'd need a hierarchy to resolve internal conflicts. Dunkle was the tallest, the oldest, and had the most seasons in. But Ricochet saw more potential in my brother, so Dunkle didn't get the answer he'd fished for.

"Good point. Biz, you're in charge."

Most people called my brother "Biz," a shortened version of our last name, Bisbee. This meant I got tagged with "Li'l Biz," which stuck with me until I made captain.

Ricochet ranked the rest of us, assigning everyone as drivers except for me and a nineteen-year-old who everyone called "Colt." "You two can drive the rig for training but not response until after I check you off at a driver's class."

Colt's jaw tightened. I couldn't tell if he really wanted to bust through red lights or didn't like being lumped in with me—a year younger and estrogen laden. Plus, he was growing sick of a nickname he couldn't shake because he didn't need to shave his face any more than I did mine.

"Anything else?" Ricochet asked.

"Cool if we hang out here to study or train even if we're not on shift?" someone asked.

"Yeah. Yeah," Ricochet said. "That's the whole idea."

A guy we called "Schmidt" leaned toward Mark and me and whispered, "Gonna be cozy if everyone hangs out here. Thirteen of us and a one-holer." Schmidt nodded toward the bathroom. He had a Christian Slater inflection, a surfer demeanor that kept him from getting riled, and casual good looks everyone noticed except Schmidt.

"Schmidt? Question?" Ricochet asked.

"Just making a wisecrack, Chief. Not worth repeating."

"Good. We're done here." Ricochet turned to leave, then spun back around. "Obviously, no alcohol at the station. And Biz, get me that staffing schedule."

Ricochet rushed to the next place he had to be. We circled around Mark, forming into shifts that accommodated part-time jobs and school schedules. I landed mostly with Schmidt and Hanlon. Hanlon had wavy brown hair with a matching moustache, and olive-toned skin that highlighted his lean muscles. I crushed on him but didn't dare let on. I already had a boyfriend with wavy hair and a matching moustache—but he was a redhead.

"This place is a shithole," someone said.

Hanlon scanned the room. "Just needs some TLC." The most domestic of our baker's dozen, he cared about things like wall colors and cookware. The sole vegetarian, he was the best cook among us. He had to be. If he wanted meals without meat, he had to make them. And he cooked well enough that the rest of us ate whatever he made.

Mark finished the schedule, then got to work on our station T-shirts. Mark had inherited Mom's illustration skills. He could draw or paint anything. He sketched a cartoon of our tightly packed barracks bunks with firefighters sleeping in helmets, at the ready, then added SOQUEL SLEEPERS in a block font.

Mark and I got to work our first shift together. In our new Soquel Sleepers T-shirts, we cleaned the station, then went for a Saturday morning drive. I navigated with the map book as he wove the engine through tree-shaded back roads. We tested each other on details: hydrant and water tank locations, nearest truck trail, fastest routes to the major highways.

Together, we made a great team. What had started in childhood, me handling the administrative needs of my eight-year-old fire chief brother, had evolved into this partnership on a real fire engine. I sank into the moment. All the childhood moves had taught me there's little value in sentiment, but I knew to savor this ride. Except as sleepers, we could never

be assigned to the same station because of nepotism rules. We'd see each other on larger fires, but riding shoulder to shoulder only happened a few times in our firefighting careers.

I fished a Hubba Bubba cube out of my pocket, unwrapped it, twisted it in half, and handed one side to Mark. The gum-splitting habit came from Mom, who could make a pack of Wrigley's last twice as long with six kids in the car. Now that I bought my own gum, I picked the brand with the best bubble-making capability. It was a thing for firefighters—like ballplayers with chew. We had contests: bubble within a bubble, within a bubble. I won more than I lost.

Sun streamed through the tree canopy as we blew bubbles and waved to oncoming traffic.

Dispatch broke in, "Engine 5279, confirm you're still on area orientation."

I grabbed the mic. "Affirmative." It was an odd inquiry. We hadn't been out that long. Mark and I looked at each other, shrugged, and continued with our bubbles.

Dispatch came back. "Confirm staffing."

"Bisbee and Bisbee," I said.

"Felton copies. Landline when you're back in quarters." The dispatcher held his tone, but we heard laughter in the background.

As soon as Mark pulled into the driveway, I got out to call dispatch. "Hi, it's Soquel. You guys wanted a call when we got back?"

"Yeah. *Uh*, while you two were out there, we got three separate calls that two kids were joyriding in a fire engine. Something about cartoon T-shirts and bubble gum."

"Bubble gum?" I lied. They knew it.

I went back outside to tell Mark and see if he wanted help backing into the tight apparatus bay, but he'd already expertly parked the rig.

A week earlier, Schmidt hadn't been as skilled and took a chunk out of the garage's wood frame and deep-scratched the engine's back corner. A bunch of us inside heard it and rushed outside, letting the screen door slam loudly behind us. The hinge springs were out of whack, so the door made a loud cracking sound if you didn't hold it back.

We looked at the engine, then at the wall, then at Schmidt.

"Yeah," he said. "This was a cool program while it lasted, eh?"

We milled around the damage, assessing, thinking about options. The phone rang. Mark rushed inside to answer, letting the screen door bang behind him.

A minute later, the door banged again. "Ricochet's gonna to be here in twenty minutes."

One way you know you're meant for firefighting is you become way more effective if there's a crisis. With all the time in the world, none of us had a plan. With twenty minutes, we wordlessly filled roles. Scott grabbed paint: light green for the siding, dark green for the trim, red for the engine. Schmidt retrieved a handsaw and started his wall repair, squaring off the splintered fragments. I measured and called out numbers to Hanlon, who laid a plywood board from the scrap box under the chop saw blade. Colt buffed the engine with rubbing compound. Mark followed with his artist hand, deftly feathering paint so it would blend to the eye. Hanlon rushed the fresh-cut piece to me. I placed it in the hole. "Just a hair off this corner." I roughed the cut with a carpenter's pencil. Hanlon sawed and Schmidt slathered the notch with quick-dry adhesive that had the same consistency as my chewed gum. I pressed the new piece into place.

"Whoever's free needs to make a fresh pot for the chief," someone yelled. Everyone was at full speed and thinking of everything.

"Five minutes," Mark called. Schmidt painted the bare wood. "No time for primer."

Scott grabbed a hair dryer from the bathroom and someone else pulled an extension cord for him. Scott blasted the red first, then the green. The plywood grain bled through.

"Two minutes."

Schmidt brushed a second coat over the still tacky first coat—a risky move.

I pulled hose rolls off the rack, stacked them in the driveway, and unrolled one.

"What the fuck, Li'l Biz?"

"We're training. Right? We need to distract him from the fresh paint."

Schmidt hid the paint cans and brushes without cleaning them while everyone else gathered around the hose rolls.

We spotted Ricochet's pickup hood cresting the driveway.

Someone tossed out the next hose roll.

Ricochet pulled into his parking spot. As soon as he neared the engine, he railed at us. "What the hell, guys?"

We were astonished he saw it so quickly.

"Gloves! Nobody's wearing any goddamn gloves!" Ricochet hollered. "You think you're going to unroll hose on a fire with no fucking gloves on?" He shook his head and walked inside for his cup of coffee, letting the screen door slam behind him.

The screen door has since been fixed and the engine went to auction years ago. But if you go to the station today, you can still make out the patch job on the garage.

The Soquel Sleepers got a smattering of calls, but we spent most of our time training, cleaning the station and equipment, and completing coursework for fire science degrees. I carried an eighteen-unit load, plus an auto-shop class I thought would come in handy.

On a quiet Sunday afternoon, I had my head in a textbook when I heard tires crunching on the gravel driveway. Others looked up from their books and we all shrugged, thinking Ricochet would catch us in a moment when we weren't doing anything wrong.

The screen door slammed. We looked up to say hi to Ricochet and instead saw Grady, one of the training captains. He held his gear bag in one hand and a suitcase in the other.

"Hi, kids," he said glibly.

We shifted our eyes to one another, looking for someone who knew why Grady was here.

"Been sent to keep an eye on y'all. Which bunk is open?" he said, leaving out the truth.

Tall with remnants of handsome, he wore his graying dirty-blond hair with long bangs. He'd acquired a head flick tic, clearing them from large,

droopy Saint Bernard eyes. They betrayed his damage. He'd worked as one of the first paramedics for the department and had seen too much carnage too quickly. I'd figured this out in his first-aid class last season, when he told us, "By my second year as a medic, I saw bodies no different than a butcher sees a cut of meat."

Grady had a quick brain, and he came across like an intellectual, throwing out philosopher's names and multisyllabic words. The chiefs took this as a sign he could handle thorny issues, so they put him in charge of random programs they didn't know how to deal with—like the Equal Employment Opportunity program. Grady studied up on it and figured out the department needed to deliver training to every employee. He went to each station in the unit and gave the same spiel, summarizing the EEO regulations.

"Look. We're embracing the existential concept of inclusiveness by hiring women and minorities. Get over it. If someone can't do the job, fire him or her. If they can, it doesn't matter what kind of bigot you are— and trust me, every human is a bigot—you can't fire the person. Deal with your personal implosion off duty. Talk to your therapist or whiskey bottle or fucking drum circle. Oh, and one more thing. Thomas Hobbes was right, and Jean-Jacques Rousseau was wrong. We are human scourge. Which means we always want to have sex. If you couple on duty, I'll watch 'til you're done, 'cuz that's the kind of sick fuck I am, then I'll fire you both. Keep your pants zipped at work. Got it? Any questions? Didn't think so. Sign the roster and I'll make sure the training office sends you a certificate."

Grady set up his bunk, then took off for the afternoon. Ricochet stopped by for a cup of joe and gave us the scoop. "Old lady kicked him out." Ricochet chewed at a rapid rate, sucking the last bit of flavor from his gum before spitting it into the trash and taking a draw from his coffee mug. "Boss said he could stay with you sleepers since the station is open anyway."

Divorces were never a secret in the fire service. Almost a requirement, they worked like a rite of passage. I'd hear hallway banter: "Heard the word, Bro. Sorry. First is the hardest. Gonna sting for a bit. But welcome back to the free world." The counsel changed if it was a fourth or fifth divorce.

"Heard the word, Bro. Sorry. Another bite out of your retirement. Guess you're staying on longer than you thought."

This was Grady's first divorce, so we knew he'd take it hard, and we felt bad for him. But we didn't like that he was at Soquel. We knew it would change the chemistry of what we'd built. We feared constant oversight and parenting. We didn't know we'd be the parents.

Turned out, Grady was spiraling into a serious alcohol problem. He'd spend his off-duty days at the bar, then drive to Soquel and collapse in his bunk long after we'd tucked in.

Like a classic movie scene, the quieter he tried to be, the clumsier and louder he was. He'd catch the screen door from slamming but miscalculate its speed and crush his fingers. "Son of a bitch!" we'd hear in place of the wood slap. Then a knee bump on one of the dayroom chairs would elicit, "Fuck!" Next, he'd limp to his bunk and plop onto the squeaky springs. "Shit." He'd manage to pull off his boots and shuffle to the bathroom for a sloppy open-door whiz, then back to his bunk, where he'd stub a socked toe on the metal foot of the bed frame, whereupon he'd lose it. "Aw, fuck y'all. Fucking pansies, going to bed same time my gramma does." We lay awake, hoping for a callout before he fell into his raucous, inebriated snoring.

When the snoring came and the call didn't, I slipped on my sweats, grabbed a book from my current stack of paperbacks, and settled into an armchair in the pitch-dark dayroom. I didn't turn the light on. Instead, I thought about my sister Cathy. Was she as broken as Grady? Worse? I wanted to help her but didn't know how. We'd already done the tearful pleadings, the tough interventions, and Yellow Pages research on programs. She hadn't listened to any of us since she was seven and wasn't going to start now. Mark and I always thought about her, but seldom gave much conversation to it. We didn't have to. A look here or a nod there said as much as a lengthy circular discussion ending with, "She has to be ready for help."

I put my socked feet onto the chair cushion, hugged my knees into my chest, and rocked. *How can I be a firefighter and not be able to help my own sister?* I woke before dawn with a stiff neck and a more painful ache inside.

In early spring, Ricochet announced the EVOC training—Emergency Vehicle Operations Course. It covered engine pumping and driving maneuvers. If we did well, Colt and I would be allowed to graduate from driving Code 1 (no urgency) to Code 2 (urgency but no lights or siren) and Code 3 (lights and siren). Colt was super-excited. He couldn't wait—literally.

A week before the class, Colt broke the rules, and I was his accomplice. Scott and Colt worked most shifts together. On this day, Scott was running late. I'd ridden my bike to the station to study, but then a call came in for a vehicle accident.

"Let's go," Colt said.

"We can't. We don't have a driver," I said.

"The class is in four days. Four days don't matter if someone is dying and we don't go help them. Besides, we can call Scott and tell him to meet us there. He'll drive the engine back. No one will even know."

"I don't think this is a good idea," I said as I climbed into the engine. I knew better and should have stopped Colt but wanted to respect the assumed hierarchy. He was a year older.

Colt eased the engine out of the tight bay, then floored it out of the driveway and flipped on the Code 3 switches. He drove too fast for the mountain road. I kept stomping on an imaginary brake on my side, like drivers' ed. teachers did in high school. Colt loved every second of it. I didn't think his smile could get any bigger until we broke onto Highway 17.

"This is the real deal," he said, as cars peeled to the right for him.

"The turn's coming up, you gotta slow down," I said.

Colt wasn't about to let me ruin his fun. He stayed at speed.

"It's the next left," I said, more urgently.

"I know!" He sounded irritated.

"You're going to miss—"

"Stop telling me . . ."

The turn lane appeared. Colt switched from accelerator to a hard brake, and we skidded toward the center divider. The engine came to a halt inches before we hit it. The seat belt bit into my waist. I reached for the controls, cutting the siren, and scaling the lights back to rear ambers so no one would careen into us from behind. Colt wanted to balk but caught himself.

"Move the fucking truck to the shoulder. Now," I said, no longer deferential or guessing who was to blame—me. Colt didn't know better. It's why his nickname fit.

We got to the accident, which didn't even require an ambulance. Scott met us there and drove the engine back to quarters. I drove Scott's truck. I'd let Colt try to explain everything to Scott on their ride. But I knew I'd have to be the one to tell Ricochet. This was different from the Schmidt cover-up: higher stakes and potential witnesses.

My gut felt tight going into the meeting. The last time I felt this way for a wrongful driving incident was two years earlier, a month before my emancipation.

My parents had made me my own set of keys for their olive-green boat of a station wagon as a congratulations gift for passing my driver's test. Dad hated how suburban wagons were, but made an exception because AMC called this one Rebel.

I could only drive it with permission, so technically it was car theft when I took it to the store after they'd left on their bicycles to go see a movie. I wanted junk food to accompany the junk TV I could sneak in when they weren't home. *Love Boat* was on in an hour.

I bought chips and cookies, and parked Rebel back in the exact spot Dad had left it. When I got out, I saw lights in the house I hadn't left on. *An intruder? A sibling seeking refuge?* I snuck a peek around the side yard and saw their bicycles, home two hours early. *Shit.* I stashed my junk food in the bushes and grabbed my basketball. Maybe they came in the back and hadn't noticed the car missing from its curbside spot. I started shooting free throws. Maybe they'd think that's where I'd been. I didn't let myself go in until after I sank eight out of ten.

I took my basketball inside with me. "Oh, didn't know you guys were back."

"Yeah, they changed the movie, but forgot to change the listing," Dad said.

They'd gone to see *Chariots of Fire* and it ended up being a replay of *Midnight Cowboy*, which Mom and Dad had walked out of ten years earlier

because it had edgy sex scenes. I think Dad would have stayed, but feigned indignance for Mom's sake.

"That sucks. Well, how about we catch something on TV? There's this show I've been wanting to see about a ship and its crew," I said, trying to appeal to Dad's naval roots.

Mom looked at Dad, who nodded.

It was working. They didn't have a clue. As soon as the show ended, I decided not to press my luck. "I'm going to do some homework then go to bed. Night."

"What about the keys?" Dad said.

"What keys?"

"The keys we need back because you violated our trust." He held his hand out.

My heart sank and my stomach met my throat, like at one of those freefall amusement park rides. I looked at him, then Mom.

"I just went to Thrifty to get cough drops. We didn't have any and I haven't been feeling that great. You weren't here to ask, so I thought it would be okay."

It didn't matter if Dad believed me. To him, any excuse was irrelevant. And Mom knew I was full of shit. She hadn't heard one cough during *Love Boat*, and no smell of menthol emanated from me. I dug the keys from my pocket, handed them to Dad, and went to my room feeling shackled, pissed, and stupid for having been caught. Plus, I was hungry. I had to wait until they fell asleep before I retrieved my snacks.

★★★

At the meeting with Colt and Ricochet, I spilled most of the details, refraining from ratting out Colt on the near-miss crash. Colt could jump in if he wanted. He didn't.

Ricochet cracked his gum. "What the fuck were you two thinking? I should kick you both out of the program. But I like that you didn't try to hide it." He chewed and squinted at us.

"Look, you can still go to EVOC training, but I have to give some thought as to whether I'll clear you for *any* driving. I'll give you my answer after the training."

Three days later, I showed up to the training on my skateboard.

Ricochet shook his head. "That's your ride?"

"Yeah. I don't have a car."

"What? Why am I finding this out now? How the fuck can I let you drive a fire engine when you don't even drive a car?"

I wanted to ask him if he could ride a skateboard, which I didn't think he could and which I thought took more skill than driving a car. But I scaled it back. "Norm and Peters have been teaching me engine ops for two years. And, I haven't had any trouble with 5279 all winter." I shut up before saying, "which is more than I can say for a couple of other sleepers."

Ricochet gave me his I-don't-know-what-to-do-with-you headshake, then said, "You can drive Code 3 *if* you pass the training, and *after* you buy yourself a goddamn car."

I ended up buying my ex-boyfriend's car—the redhead's. Evidently, he wanted a new gal *and* a new car. He felt bad for breaking up, so I got a screaming deal: twelve hundred bucks for a Honda Civic in top shape. I drove it to Soquel for my last shift before sleeper season ended and the next fire season started. Ricochet looked over the rim of his coffee cup and gave me the thumbs-up. I had this day only to drive Code 3. We had no calls.

The next morning, I packed my gear. Even without a Code 3 run, I felt like Soquel had cultivated me—readied me for the upcoming season. I'd decided to leave the cocoon of Big Creek and Santa Cruz County and throw myself into the fray of the busiest initial attack station in the region.

CHAPTER 7

SKIVVIES

Sunol Fire Station, 1984

My new captain, Garrison, pointed to a space blocked off with a yellow curtain in the middle of the barracks. "You get your pick between the two female bunks in there since you're the first one we have this season."

I looked at the ceiling above the curtain. A horseshoe-shaped track, like the ones in a shared hospital room, held a full-length cotton fabric panel. It looked hand-sewn.

"What's the curtain for?" I asked.

"Privacy. Set your stuff down, I'll show you how the bathroom works."

I was pretty sure I knew how a bathroom worked but followed him anyway. He led me to the bathroom door and stopped, pointing to a contraption mounted at eye level—a wood block, about six inches wide and eight inches high. It had grooves to slide a small wood door from one side to the other. If you slid the door to the left, the jack of clubs would appear on the right. If you slid the door to the right, it would cover the jack and reveal the queen of spades on the left.

"When you need to go in here, switch this to the queen spot. That way we'll know to wait until you come out. Just be sure to switch it back to jack when you leave."

"How will I know when there's no jacks in there? Is there an 'Unoccupied' option?"

He looked at me. "That hasn't come up. You'll figure it out."

This is how most fire stations throughout the state handled the issue of shared-gender bathrooms. Big Creek was new, so it had two bathrooms. Soquel was old and small, so no one shared. If the door was open, you went in. If closed, you stayed out. It was foolproof and truly gender-neutral. Sunol was neither. Like the cards, it felt like a game of chance.

But Garrison was right. I figured it out. Every time I had to go to the bathroom, I cracked the door without looking inside and asked at volume, "Anyone in here?" I'm sure it caused a few stray droplets for those trying to urinate in peace, or hastened heftier projects in the stall, or interrupted me-time implied by the *Penthouses* stacked on each toilet tank. When I first saw the stacks, I wondered how the guys reconciled their bathroom entertainment with their fear of flushing urinals.

After Garrison completed my how-to-use-the-bathroom orientation, he showed me the engine I was assigned to. The station ran a squad with year-round two-person coverage, and two wildland engines and a bulldozer during fire season, giving us a daily staffing of nine, plus a battalion chief who went home at night.

"This is your third season, right?" he said.

"Yeah. Plus, I worked as a sleeper last winter."

Garrison tilted his head to the side. I read it as a let's-see-how-this-goes tilt. "Well, I guess that means you're the senior firefighter. Set your gear in the cab."

In his late thirties, Garrison looked like a quintessential captain. Slightly receding hairline. Check. Well-groomed moustache. Check. Eyes that could be kind or harsh. Check. Strong jawline. Check. And a beltline losing a hole a year. Check.

"What time is PT?" I asked.

"You'll need to do your cardio and weights before breakfast. You a volleyball player?"

"I played in high school, but only for a year."

"Why only a year?"

"I can dig. But I'm short and can't set. Which means I rode the bench a lot. And I don't have that kind of patience."

"We play here every day before dinner if we're not on a fire." I could tell from his tone it wasn't an optional activity. I knew a lot of stations throughout the state took their firehouse volleyball seriously. But single-engine houses like Big Creek couldn't field enough players, so this was my first taste of mandatory VB.

"Looking forward to it," I said.

He let a smile slip out. I guessed he liked that answer. "One more thing," he said. "Are you a union member yet?"

"Yes, sir," I said.

He unwillingly smiled again. "Don't ever call me 'sir.' "

"Copy that, Cap." He nodded and headed to the captain's office, satisfied he'd given me a sound orientation. I spent the day introducing myself to new station mates and the equipment.

Just before dinner, we got a fire on the Altamont Pass. Volleyball would have to wait until tomorrow. It was a mobile-attack grass fire, like the first wildfire where I'd pulled hose for Scott. This time I took the nozzle, and someone pulled hose for me.

The fires moved quicker here, in hotter air without coastal moisture. But the terrain was much easier to navigate, rolling hills instead of mountainous canyons and redwoods.

Being at the nozzle on a fast-moving fire gave me the same thrill as riding in the front seat on a roller coaster with no one blocking my beautiful view of the danger. We caught the fire, mopped it up, blew out our fire snot, and returned to quarters.

After dumping the dirty hose at the wash rack—we'd wash it the next day—we filled the water and gas tanks and loaded on clean hose from the storage racks. Good to go, we converged on the kitchen for an after-fire meal. This meant a free-for-all since the fire sabotaged the cook for the day. Boxes of cereal, bread and peanut butter, and Tupperware containers full of leftovers hit the counter. We all carved out a spot in the kitchen, made our meal, and ate it standing up. I didn't realize I'd made a critical error in following along with this station routine.

I sat on my bunk, sooty, happy, and full of Raisin Bran, but tired of waiting for my turn at the shower and feeling closed off by the curtain. I opened them and made a plan I'd employ for the rest of my time at Sunol. I'd beeline inside when we came back from a fire or drill no matter how close we were to mealtime. First, I'd switch the sign to queen, then I'd grab my stuff out of my locker. I could tell the guys were terrified of opening the bathroom door with the queen staring at them. But I felt justified. There were nine of them and one of me. And I was considerate enough to rush my business. I became a master of the quick bathroom trip. I'd be in and out in under five minutes. Then I'd enjoy a leisurely bowl of cereal at the table while they gussied themselves in front of each other.

That first night, I emerged from the bathroom in clean shorts and a T-shirt, bra-free. The guys milled about their bunks, readying themselves for lights-out. I caught a few of them staring my way, not at me, but at the curtain, like they were waiting for me to close it.

I found first nights at stations needed careful navigation around the nightwear conundrum. We all set our bunkers (fire boots tucked inside turnout fire pants) next to our beds at night—a practice that would be outlawed several years later due to the toxins off-gassing from all our safety gear while we mindlessly sucked them down in our sleep. The guys slept in their underwear, no shirts. When the alarm went off, they swung their legs around, stepped into their boots/pants, pulled on a T-shirt, and adjusted their suspenders on the way out the door. At Big Creek, I felt like I should emulate them as closely as possible without making things weird. So I slept in cotton Jockey bikini briefs and a white cotton T-shirt, no bra. I risked getting stuck for hours on a call that might prove more comfortable in a bra. But sleeping in a bra every night guaranteed discomfort, so I played my odds.

At Sunol, the effort at female accommodation made everything palpably awkward. I decided to leave the curtain open, keep my shorts on, and bury myself in Orwell's *Nineteen Eighty-Four*.

A captain named Briggs bunked across from the yellow curtain. He had a Clint Eastwood demeanor, using squints to communicate, speaking only when necessary. "Closing your curtain will save you from knowing what kind of skivvies we all wear," he said.

"No offense to anyone, Cap. I'm more interested in my book."

"Suit yourself." He stripped his shorts off. I couldn't help but peek past my book's pages. *I'll be damned. Briggs wears boxer briefs.* I totally wouldn't have called that. It was the first time I'd seen boxer briefs outside of a catalogue.

Until that moment, I'd categorized guys as tighty-whitey or boxer dudes. It's more difficult than it sounds to guess. In high school, I thought I'd found a predictable correlation. Jocks wore tighty-whities and stoners wore boxers. But then I went out with a guy from the water polo team, and he wore boxers. So I looked to music for answers. I found some good data that country music and tighty-whities went together, which Scott confirmed at Big Creek. But then Norm blew it to hell. The truth was, my sample set was too small. I'd only dated a few guys and had just a handful of fire stations as my Petri dish. And now, Briggs introducing a third underwear type made my study exponentially more complicated.

I stared at Briggs's boxer briefs longer than I should have. There was something I really liked about them. They had everything: the secure hold of tighty-whities, but the aesthetic appeal of boxers. A perfect hybrid. They would remain my favorite long after I abandoned trying to guess what a man wore beneath his pants—giving up when an engineer introduced a fourth option: commando.

✳✳✳

Sunol's call volume was as promised: fast-moving grass fires, earlier every day as the month moved on. We'd jump on them, finish mop-up, and hurry back to the station for volleyball. Whoever had cooking rotation made dinner. The rest of us would shower and change into shorts, T-shirts, and tennies. Fires left us far stinkier than volleyball, so that's what we did.

Someone would call out the team makeups. "Squad versus Engine," or "Blonds versus Brunettes," or my favorite, "Brass versus Ass," where firefighters would take on the higher ranks. We had youth, they had strategy.

If one doofus engineer was on duty, the rest of us could count on him saying, "Shirts versus Skins. Bisbee, you're with the Skins." The first time

was mildly amusing. After that, I let everyone tire of it along with me. Garrison broke first. "You need new material, dude."

Doofus missed the hint and started in the next day. "Shirts versus—"

Briggs gave him a stronger hint. "If you finish that sentence, I'll rip your fucking head off and shit down your neck."

Not gonna lie; it was kind of hot. And it stopped Doofus.

Doofus avoided me for a couple of weeks, until just the two of us were in the barracks one day. "If you didn't like it, why didn't you tell me instead of lodging a complaint?"

"I don't know what you're talking about."

"The Shirts versus . . . Ya know," he said, still too snakebit to say the whole tired phrase.

"I didn't fucking complain."

"Well, I don't like the double standard. You can sit here and cuss, but if I say something 'off color,' I get jumped. We got you a curtain, and you keep it open. It all feels like a trap."

Suddenly, I missed Grady's homespun spiel, which this guy would benefit from.

"I don't know what to tell you. I'm here to fight fire, like you. And I didn't complain."

"They wouldn't have said anything if you hadn't. This whole thing wouldn't have happened if you weren't here."

"Dude, yes it would have. You're tone-deaf. That's the problem."

"What's that supposed to mean?"

"It means nobody gives a shit if you say something stupid once. But you have to mix up your lines. Develop a repertoire. Like, if I were going to hurl insults at you, I wouldn't just call you a dipshit day after day. I'd switch it up. Dipshit. Birdbrain. Crapstain. Dingleberry. Fartlicker. Mouthbreather. Puss sucker. See?"

His jaw tightened. "What's wrong with you?"

"That's a list we don't have time for, my friend." I walked out of the barracks, leaving Doofus with his mouth open.

<p style="text-align:center">✳✳✳</p>

Mid–fire season, I met Mark and many of the Soquel Sleepers in the parking lot outside of San Jose's largest high school. The department contracted with large venues in cities across the state to hold the written portion of its promotional exam for engineer. Passing the written exam and a fitness test would provide a shot at a temporary summer promotion. But a high enough score would secure assignment to a rigorous two-month academy, followed by a permanent year-round job.

"Everyone ready for this?" Mark asked.

We shrugged "maybes" at each other. We'd studied but knew these exams could be tricky.

"How's it going at Sunol?" Schmidt asked.

"Pretty good. I love the fire activity. And it's a VB house. But the station life is so-so."

"Remind me to not transfer there. I suck at volleyball," Schmidt said.

"Dude. It's the best," Hanlon argued, sweeping his arm into an overhead spike.

"Jerk captains?" Schmidt guessed.

"The captains are pretty cool. Some of the others are still trying to figure out that a firefighter with tits is the same as a firefighter without them."

"Yeah. Not sure that's true, though," Schmidt said. "I'm working for a captain right now. Has tits. And he can't keep up. So . . ."

I missed these guys. I never felt they presumed me less capable than them.

We heard a voice from across the parking lot. "Line it up!" Hundreds of us shuffled into alphabetical lines, A through F, G through L, and so on.

They checked our picture IDs. We found seats in a gymnasium filled with long lines of tables and plastic chairs. Proctors passed out test booklets, careful to repeat the A, B, and C versions in sequence. Each version had the same questions, but in a different order, so we wouldn't be tempted to eyeball the Scantron next to us for a hint.

The test covered basic reading, writing, and math skills—like an SAT. Then it veered into more job-specific questions. It addressed firefighting fundamentals by naming tools and asking their main purpose. It tested mechanical aptitude with pictures of gears where we'd have to determine

the end output. And it probed the depths of our station care and maintenance knowledge, asking questions about proper water temperature for washing dishes and the correct ratio of water, sand, and concrete when mixing mortar.

After the test, none of us had a clue as to how we did. I spent the drive back to Sunol switching back and forth between "I maxed that bad boy" and "Oh well. Chalk it up to experience. I'll try again next year."

I passed with a score that wasn't high enough to get a first-round academy slot but was high enough to get sent to the physical abilities test so I'd be cleared if a temporary spot opened.

On the day of the physical test, I dressed in my running shoes and sweats. I was and wasn't worried. I'd been lifting weights ever since Norm and Peters nudged me, and could complete triathlons on a whim. But this was a new test. Experts designed it to mimic job skills I'd already performed, but rumor had it women were tanking.

The test had four performance stations: weighted hose pulls, a dummy drag in a tunnel, a hose tower climb followed by lowering and raising hose from the fourth floor, and a smoke ejector hang. I'd need to complete each back-to-back within the allotted time.

I made it through the first three stations with enough time left on the clock to catch my breath at the smoke ejector—a big fan designed to get smoke to flow out of a building so occupants could move back in. Three feet wide, three feet high, and two feet deep, the ejector weighed about sixty pounds. Two four-inch chains welded to the top ended in hooks I'd need to secure onto a pull-up bar set at six feet eight inches high—the standard height of a doorframe. I heaved it above my head, held it at a diagonal to get one hook as high as I could, grabbed the hook, and swung for the bar. I missed. I was too short. On my next attempt, I grabbed the bottom of the chain below the hook, giving up accuracy for inches. The trajectory was good, but the hook barely tapped the bar. I needed another inch.

"Three tries is all you get," the proctor told me.

I set the ejector down, took a deep breath, and decided I had to jump with the ejector above my head while slinging the hook toward the bar.

I hoisted it back onto my shoulder, angled it, grabbed the bottom of the chain, and jumped to release the hook. It was high enough, but the hook turned parallel when I jumped and clattered off the metal bar.

"That's a fail," he said, making a check mark on the sheet clamped to his clip board. "Take this to Table One. They'll process you."

I was numb. Then pissed. Pissed at the test. Pissed at myself. Pissed at the six-foot-tall dude who wasn't affected enough by my failure to even look at me when he handed me the scorned score sheet. And pissed all over again five years later, when wind tunnel tests proved smoke ejectors were far more effective if operated at ground level.

A big-haired gal with press-on nails gave me the speech at Table One. "We know this is a tough day for you, but we believe in you. You're allowed one test retake. It doesn't matter which portion you failed, you must retake the entire test. You're permitted two weeks to retrain. I can schedule your retake if you'd like."

"Can I retake it today?"

"Oh, that's not a good idea. We want you to pass."

"Can I?"

"There's nothing that says you can't. But, Sweetie, don't you think you should try again after some rest and practice?

"When's your next opening?"

"We have a few slots open with the one o'clock group."

"Sign me up."

Part of the problem with Scottish-Irish heritage, or me being "fire, fire, fire," is my fuse. Its length is unpredictable. But the way to instantly shorten it is to tell me I can't do something.

I helped myself to two free Gatorades from the ice bins near the candidate tables, walked back to my car, sat in the driver's seat, and downed them. Then I took off my running shoes, put on my logger-heel wildland boots, which added almost two inches, and got back in line.

The good thing about my temper running hot is it left no room for self-doubt. I didn't give a shit that everyone else had track shoes on, or that my sweatpants looked ridiculous with wildland boots, or that other candidates and proctors looked sideways at me.

At "go," I took off. The first stations proved more difficult in boots, and I'd already taxed myself, so I felt behind. But I still made it to the ejector with enough time for two attempts.

The proctor looked at me funny, as if to say, "Didn't your sister just go through this?"

I nodded to him, indicating my readiness. He nodded back with his clipboard in one hand and a stopwatch in the other. I snatched the ejector, rotated it to a diagonal with a firm grip at the bottom of the chain, and swung the first hook around the bar. Then I grabbed the second hook without any weight on it and jumped it onto the bar. Done. I clapped my gloved hands together as the signal. He hit the stopwatch.

He checked the PASS box. "Good job. Take this to Table One. They'll process you." He still had a funny look on his face.

I accepted my pass certificate from the dazed lady at Table One and lifted two more Gatorades. Still pissed, it took the drive home and an increasing need to pee to redirect my hot head. I willed my bladder to not leak until I made it back to my apartment and into the bathroom. My own fucking bathroom, with no playing cards on the door.

CHAPTER 8

POP-TARTS

Pescadero Fire Station, 1984

A few weeks after I'd passed the fitness test, I got an offer for a temporary promotion to engineer—what we called a "limited term," or LT, assignment. After twelve days of basic fire engine operation training, I landed at a two-engine station in San Mateo County—a place I immediately wanted to leave.

Pescadero Station sat inside a perennial fog belt that discouraged wildfires but caused corrosion in transformers, making power line fires along the coast highway a recurring event. Plus, rugged cliffs brought occasional rescue opportunities, and a small eccentric town provided a smattering of medical calls and occasional structure fires. But for the most part, Pescadero was a sleepy firehouse that invited its occupants to catch up on the classics.

And they did. The core crew chose this station on purpose, priding themselves on being laid-back middle-aged beach types—old-school surfers and trawlers embracing the fog and slow call volume. The day's project might be driving the engine to Duarte's Tavern, which promised "the world's best cioppino." On cold summer days with a biting onshore wind, it was.

While they read novels and napped, I filled my time studying map books and training myself on the equipment. One apparatus was a standard wildland engine: short wheelbase for off-road operations, 500 gallons of water, 1,200 feet of 1½-inch hose, 800 feet of 1-inch hose, firefighting tools, rescue ropes, first aid bag. I could already operate it and everything on it with my eyes closed. The second apparatus was a new, specialized municipal engine with a more complex pump panel, larger diameter hose, and a monster three-section 24-foot ladder I'd never seen before. The pump panel wasn't a problem, but I spent hours trying to master the heavy ladder. After two weeks, I could wrestle it off the engine and raise it into place, but it exhausted me. Laddering happens early at an incident. I'd be useless before the real work began.

Several sessions in, I plateaued. With no improvement, doubt consumed me as I stowed the ladder back on the engine. I stripped my gear off and slid to the cold cement floor, leaning against the rear tire. *Maybe I can't do this. If it's not a smoke ejector, then it's a ladder. If it's not a ladder, it'll be something else.* I stared into mid-space and fought tears off. *Not here,* I told myself. *Never where they might see you.* I wondered if I'd have to step down from engineer. Or out. What would I do if I couldn't be a firefighter?

I don't know how long I sat on that floor beating myself up—maybe an hour. Then I shook my head, stood tall, and went inside to pretend I was their equal.

"You know that's a two-person ladder, right?" one of the captains said. "Risney is the only one who can do it by himself. He's a beast. I'd throw my goddamn back out."

My jaw froze, clenched from vying emotions. Anger flashed crimson behind my eyes, like a red ink jar had exploded inside my head. *You motherfuckers let me* . . . But then blue flooded in, a swell of relief at having not failed—the kind of relief that rushes at you and urges tears. *Don't you dare,* I reminded myself. I fought to bring back the red, knowing ire could keep my eyes dry. I settled on purple, which allowed a deep breath and unlocked my jaw.

"Good to know," I said, hoping he hadn't noticed the gravel in my voice. I grabbed my jacket from the wall hook by the door, planning to walk laps around the station until the colors and the headache they'd created went away.

"Service is due on that engine tomorrow," the captain said without looking up.

"On it," I promised, then headed out to the fog, where misty eyes couldn't be seen.

<p style="text-align:center">✳✳✳</p>

I knew the basics of engine service: a simple oil and filter change, battery cleanup, air filter check and replacement if needed, Zerk fittings lube, tire pressure check, fluid top-off for brakes, power steering, and window washer. It was meditative for me. I donned my coveralls, put the engine on "delayed response," and got to work. While the oil drained, I disconnected eight cables from the four batteries it took to power the electrical on this engine, careful to hash mark each with chalk to match its battery post—a trick I'd learned in my auto-shop class. I sprayed and cleaned the inside of each terminal, then let them air dry while I finished other tasks. Clean oil, new filter, everything done, I reconnected the cables according to the hashmarks, missing that I'd smeared the chalk on one of them, causing me to misread it and connect it to the wrong post.

I closed the battery tray, radioed us back on "immediate response," cleaned the tools, and stowed the dolly back into its slot next to the rollaway Snap-on toolbox. Halfway out of my coveralls, I tied the arms around my waist and degreased my hands with sandy shop soap while apologizing to myself. *Sorry about the meltdown. I know you can do this job. Let's start the engine up for good measure.* I dried my hands on a clean shop rag, flipped on the battery switch, then turned the key. The assault was instant. Snapping, acrid burnt-plastic smell, and an arc show attacked all at once. I dove to shut off the battery switch.

Fuck. When I pulled out the battery tray, I saw molten terminals and connectors. *Fuck. Fuck. Fuck.* I had no choice. I ran inside and interrupted the captain's novel.

"I screwed up. The engine is out of service. I can call it in and gear up the reserve engine, but do you want to look at it first?"

"What did you do?"

"I shorted the batteries."

"What the hell?" I couldn't tell if he was more irritated at having to put his book down or at our compromised response capabilities.

He followed me outside. I pointed to my welding job.

"Yup. That's a hot mess, sister. Call it in."

He went into the office to tell the other captain. The two of them talked freely, without shutting the door, as I switched everyone's gear to the reserve engine.

"She blew the alternator," novel-captain explained.

"Geezus. That engine is brand-new. Is she going to fucking pay for it out of her check? Guess we got ourselves another Pop-Tart," the other captain said, comparing me to a female engineer assigned to the opposite shift. I didn't work with her, but the only nice thing I ever heard anyone say about her was, "Well, at least she's not hard to look at."

I doubted anyone muttered the same flattery about me. I had small tits and a unibrow that seemed to attract more women than men. But years later, after I made captain, the is-she-going-to-fucking-pay-for-it captain proved me wrong. I wasn't as hard to look at as I'd thought, at least not at a conference. A group of us had settled at the bar after the first day of workshops. He sidled up next to me. Curly blond hair, good eyebrows, and dimples made him handsome by anyone's standards.

He flicked his eyebrows up and smiled to show off perfect teeth.

I looked down at his wedding ring, then back up to his face.

"Oh, that. Gotta love the conference rule, though. Right?" His eyebrows went up again.

"Not a fan of it," I said.

"C'mon. Just because my wife is married doesn't mean I am," he argued.

"Wow. Has that line actually worked for you?"

"Not gonna lie. I usually don't have to work for it." He winked, deepened his dimples, and cocked his head to the side. He looked adorable. And I reveled in the irony. He'd just presented himself as a yummy treat with no substance—a Pop-Tart.

I shook my head, put on my sweatshirt to go for a walk, and left him to charm someone else. To his credit, he treated me like a captain from that point forward.

<p style="text-align:center">***</p>

As an LT engineer who'd damaged a brand-new engine, I had to work hard to prove I wasn't a Pop-Tart. I trained by myself, working on pumping drills and with my enemy ladder. I volunteered to do shit tasks around the station and made it clear I'd accept any amount of grief dished my way about the batteries. But hard work and denigration isn't what they wanted from me. They wanted me to chill out and adopt their rogue beach-paced style.

The crucible moment came after one of the crew members made a uniform shirt–off evening trip into town, returning with a brown bag the size and shape of a small whiskey bottle.

They passed it around in the dim dayroom while a movie we'd already seen played in the background. The bottle never left the bag. *Is that their plausible deniability?*

When the bag came my way, they all watched. I knew it was a show of trust to offer it. My guess was that they never gave this test to my counter Pop-Tart. She didn't even cuss.

I had enough confidence to keep people from fucking with me too much, but not enough to call out the crew or be open with them about not wanting to drink on duty. Hell, I still wasn't old enough to drink *off duty*. It would've been so cool if I'd been that brave—brave enough to not care if I fit in. But I wasn't.

I took the bag, put the bottle to my lips, and kept them closed as I tipped the bag up. Then I shook my head, feigning throat burn.

"Atta girl." As far as they were concerned, I was now one of them—my battery sins forgiven—and a member of a club I didn't want to belong to.

Once I was in, they opened up. I heard about their worst calls—the ones they wished they'd never seen. I learned about their rotting marriages, addictions, aging parents, troubled kids. This crew didn't help me with anything related to the technical skills of being an engineer. But they schooled

me in an important, prevalent aspect of the fire service. Both Marlboro and Grady had tried to show me, but I thought them anomalies. They weren't.

Before Pescadero, I saw firefighting as my way out of dysfunction. It was supposed to fix everything—my oldest sister Cathy's addiction issues, Dad's restlessness, my own self-doubt. It was supposed to ensure I had a grounded path to follow. But now I knew firefighting could break as much as it could fix.

<center>***</center>

Corralitos Fire Station, 1984

The battalion chief from Corralitos, McFlay, called two months after I'd arrived at Pescadero. My brother had accepted a job in another county, making Corralitos an option for me. "I've got an LT spot here and didn't know if you'd be interes—"

"Yes. Yes. I'll take it." I realized I'd cut McFlay off and tried to cover my tracks. "Sorry, Chief. It's just that up here . . ." I didn't know how to finish the sentence.

"I get it. There's a lot of rust in all that fog," McFlay said.

He'd said it perfectly. Neil Young wrote the songs for his *Rust Never Sleeps* album at Broken Arrow Ranch, fifteen minutes from Pescadero. A few of the old-timers had responded to emergencies at the ranch and reminisced about it. "He's a goddamn genius," they said, as if they agreed with Neil's philosophy. But they didn't. They found comfort in Pescadero's fog, hid in its haze, sought numbness from its cold. Antithetical to Neil's iconic advice, they preferred to fade away rather than burn out. Not me. That's why I had to get out of there.

The only problem with Corralitos was a captain named Tommy. In his early forties and on his third wife—all with the same first name—he spoke with a nasal affectation and tic that made him start every sentence with "Yeah, o-kay." Word had it he was trustworthy on fires, but also that station life made him batshit paranoid. He combatted the affliction by staying on the offensive, always looking for fault with how others completed daily

tasks. Eventually, you could prove yourself and, after two or three years, he'd let up.

I inadvertently devised a Tommy strategy on my first day. After station cleanup and equipment checks, I went into the office to read station logs. I took a small memo pad from my breast pocket and jotted down notes on call types and locations. When Tommy came in, it surprised me. He'd given no audible clues with his sneak-up-and-blast-in approach. My shoulders jumped and for some reason, I slammed the note pad shut. That caught his eye.

"Yeah, o-kay. I saw you missed the generator on the volunteer engine." He hadn't told me that was part of my equipment check duties. It felt like what I'd been warned about.

I bit my tongue. It was too soon to be a smartass with a guy like this. He'd reacted to the note pad, so I decided to go with that. I grabbed it, shoved it into my breast pocket, then shifted my eyes. "My bad. I'll go check that right now."

For the rest of the shift, I took the note pad out of my pocket when Tommy wasn't in the room, and as soon as he walked in, I stashed it back in my pocket so he'd think I was keeping book on him. He gave me a wider berth the following shift. Whenever I felt him closing in, I upped the frequency of my note-taking. I even bought different-colored note pads, so he'd think I was filling them up.

A few weeks in, we got a ripping wildfire. It threatened homes, a rural power grid, and a retreat center. I sent firefighters up a hill and ran fresh lengths of hose to them as they advanced on the fire. Tommy handled the pump panel and directed incoming resources. He placed them perfectly, getting shuttles in for an uninterrupted water supply, helicopter drops for flare-ups, and more firefighters on the hose lay.

My legs shook as I forced them to climb the same incline over and over, each haul a little longer as firefighters up top progressed. The steepest segment had the rise of a ladder, but no rungs. I tossed the hose rolls in my hands up ahead of me, to a shelf at the top of the mini cliff, then pulled

myself up with two more hose lengths strapped to my back. My goggles slipped on my sweat-drenched face. Ashen air stung my eyes. But if I didn't keep moving, the effort so far would be for nothing, so I dug into the mountainside with my boots again and again. We caught the fire. When we got back to the station, I weighed in. I'd lost eight pounds in one afternoon.

"Yeah, o-kay. *Uh*, good job out there today," Tommy said.

"Thanks, Cap. You too."

We nodded at each other the way world leaders with mutually assured destruction plans do when they also have respect for one another.

<p style="text-align:center">***</p>

McFlay extended LT engineer assignments beyond fire season for budget reasons I didn't understand. He had a nerd vibe—spindly, spectacled, and amicable. He'd graduated at the top of his academy classes, even at the elite law enforcement crossover academy. It earned him the right to arrest arsonists and forest law violators, and to wear his bulletproof vest every day. In a few years I'd learn what that vest covered up. But at this point, I thought he was a smart and kind man. And I was happy I didn't have to go home in November when the rain came.

Corralitos had a respectable off-season call volume that kept us busy. We went to medical aids, vehicle accidents, chimney fires, rubbish fires, gas leaks, and so on. The station's cast was also varied, and because I filled the relief spot, the position that has to fill gaps in the schedule, I worked with everyone.

Wayne read Louis L'Amour during the day and cooked the same meal every night: a skirt steak with mushrooms and onions sautéed in red wine. It was his excuse to bring wine into the station, which no one addressed. He was exceedingly nice to me, and I got a free steak every time I worked with him.

Jimmy, the mechanic, stayed in the shop. We'd go days without seeing him. He had a microwave and a coffeepot out there. We'd do welfare checks on him. As soon as he heard footsteps, he'd bellow, "I don't have time for

your petty-ass horseshit today." This told us he was breathing. We'd do an about-face and check on him next shift.

Dennis was Tommy's co-captain. Stern and intelligent, he'd been my brother's Norm. Rumor had it that Dennis's wife ruled the home front, which is why he unleashed at the station. He started every sentence with, "Goddamn it, I thought I told you." But on long drives or quiet station spells he talked God and philosophy, and always asked, "You doing okay, Kiddo?" And you could answer honestly.

Sherrie worked opposite me, so she and I ended up getting an apartment together. This gave each of us a place to ourselves on our days off for half the rent, but started a rumor we were gay lovers—which didn't make any sense because we spent almost no nights under the same roof. Less shy than me on these matters, Sherrie took it on herself to dispel the chatter by dating the unmarried novel-reading captain from Pescadero. They lasted a year.

Dave, who we called "Radar," had every radio frequency and tone memorized, and could fix anything that had an antenna. He worked hard, had a captivating smile, and loved to watch figure skating at night. He was gay but felt he couldn't own it. Born the same year as me, he died of AIDS at thirty-six, never seeking treatment because that would be an admission.

My favorite person to work with was Celia. We had the same build, dark hair, fair skin, freckles, and swagger when walking in fire boots. But our communication styles differed dramatically. I banked on smart-ass commentary filled with inference but delivered with levity. Celia kept a knife in her boot and spoke without a filter. No subtext. No manipulation. It worked for her because she didn't give a shit what anyone thought. I envied the naked honesty and confidence. She wouldn't have caved to the Pescadero whiskey pressure. If she sipped from the bag, it would have been because she wanted the burn.

I learned about her blunt tendencies the first shift we worked together. We finished our breakfast and headed for mops and buckets.

"Yeah, o-kay. You two ladies gotta take care of the men's bathroom too. Everyone's the same here," Tommy said.

I was ready to say, "Okay, Cap. But we gotta make sure to spread that word, 'cuz the ladies from the last shift, Wayne and Dennis, didn't clean both bathrooms."

Before I got it out, Celia said, "Look, Tommy. I'll carry more than my fair share. But the guys don't clean our bathroom. And while we're on shift, you're the only one using the other bathroom. And you're going to go sit in the captain's office and come out right after we clean it and take a twenty-five-minute shit that leaves a crap stain in the third stall. So, it doesn't even matter if we clean it, but you're the boss."

Tommy laughed, *"Heh, heh."* I couldn't tell if he was proud or embarrassed that everyone knew his bathroom habits. He turned toward the office. "Yeah, o-kay. I'm going to make a call right now. See why Dennis and Wayne didn't clean both bathrooms."

Celia and I looked at each other and shrugged in agreement. We cleaned both bathrooms, scouring everything—except the third stall. Tommy never said a word about it. Either Celia's knife, or my note pad, or both kept him from pushing the issue.

<p style="text-align:center">＊＊＊</p>

In late spring, the seasonals came back on board. Now, bathroom cleanup fell to them. After station chores, I took them out for area orientation. Threading the engine onto a narrow truck trail that would spit us at the top of a ridge, I quizzed the firefighters. "Which of the Orders and Watch-Outs would apply if we were responding to a fire on that slope right there?"

The quickest of the lot got the answer right, "All of 'em."

I nodded, then downshifted to make the engine climb a steep incline.

"How long did it take you to learn to drive an engine?" one of them asked.

"My first-year captains taught me. I kept practicing. A little over two years, I guess."

"What's the fastest you've gone in an engine?"

"Not sure," I said. "But at my LT training, I got up on two wheels on the lane-change course." I had set the record for the second-fastest time and regretted not pushing harder.

I had a little Colt in me that didn't respect the danger of constantly pushing limits. When you do that to an engine, you'll find its edge and roll past it. Which I did later that summer.

It was on a day assignment to Burrell Station, about fifteen miles north of Corralitos. I loaded my gear on the engine and did a quick walk-around before saying hi to the firefighters. I knew one of them. He'd been around for a while. The other was new. This was his second day.

I grabbed a mug and poured myself a cup of joe to take out with me for a more thorough equipment check. Before my first sip, the bell went off. "Wildfire. Old San Jose Road."

"Let's go." I put my mug down. We geared up and I blazed out, Code 3.

At an oddly banked S-curve, the steering wheel began to shake. I remember correcting the wheel. That's when the whole front end of the engine broke loose and bounced off the ground, stripping all power from the steering rod. Then everything converted to slow motion and my inside voice took over, muting everything in the background. *I have no control. We're all wearing seat belts and helmets, so we should be fine. Why can't I hear anything? Did someone turn off the coffeepot? I'm fairly certain this isn't how I die. I wonder how long will this last.*

My audio returned to the screech of metal on asphalt and rattling items settling into place. The engine completed its skid with the driver's side on the pavement and the wheels spinning toward the western morning sky.

"You guys okay?" I asked.

"I'm good," one said. "I'm here," the other one said.

"Don't move until I check things out."

I called it in and treated it as I would have if the accident had not involved me. Patient care for my firefighters. Road flares. Fire extinguisher. But as soon as the first unit arrived, I went into shock.

The wildfire, put out by a slower engine, caused zero damage to anything except two acres of dead grass. I'd totaled the engine, carved a three-inch

gash into my thigh, and scared the new firefighter so badly he quit to join the Marines the next day. The other firefighter was fine—happy to add a war story to his résumé.

The exploit earned me inexplicable allegiance from Tommy. "Yeah, o-kay. Make sure you take a union rep to the investigative interview. And, *uh*, if they ask me, I gotcha covered. You've always done a good job here." By this time, I'd ditched the note pad habit. He must have noticed. And now we were at a point where we still cut the cards but enjoyed working together.

On the day of the interview, the union representative told me, "Don't admit anything."

But we all knew the facts. The Model-12 engine I'd rolled had an unstable design with a light front end. And a loose U-bolt had allowed the leaf springs to unstack during my drive, dropping the back and making the front buck. But engines don't roll themselves.

I knew not owning my shit would be a Pop-Tart move. So I told them, "I was going too fast for a Model-12, especially for a mountain road banked for drainage, not driving. Plus, I probably overcorrected the steering, and if I'd done a more thorough check at the outset, I might have caught the loose U-bolt." I ended up with a three-month pay cut and the nickname "Flipper." And shortly afterward, the department discontinued Model-12s.

After a week off to ensure any concussive effects from the rollover subsided, I loaded my gear onto the engine. Tommy suggested I take a drive around the block, to "check the equipment," which meant my mental status. A little trepidation gripped me going into an S-curve, but I navigated it fine. The real test came later that day on a Code 3 run to a grass fire. My leg bounced as I pushed on the accelerator. I eased up, gun-shy.

I drove too slowly to calls for at least two weeks. Then we got a call that reset me.

"Potential drowning. Backyard pool."

I flipped on the lights and siren and eased out of the barn. This was a medical, so I needed to be less cautious, but still safe.

Dispatch updated us. "Reporting party says victim is a two-year-old."

The part of my brain, of anyone's brain, that engages when a two-year-old is in peril overrode any lingering hesitation. I stood on the accelerator, back to my old habits.

It didn't matter. The toddler died anyway. I drove back to the station in silence because in the last hour I'd had to pry a tiny, cold, blue body from a mother's clamped arms to attempt CPR. Most toddlers feel like loosely connected rubber parts. This one felt cold and fused and had furled fingers. I blocked out the mother's screams with a mantra I'd learned in my emergency medical technician class. *Patients aren't dead 'til they're warm and dead. Patients aren't dead 'til they're warm and dead.* I said it in rhythm to my futile compressions.

On that day, I realized there are two ways to get past trauma, at least temporarily. The first is to usurp it with a greater trauma. The toddler supplanted the distress from flipping the engine. The second is to let a triumph displace the trauma, which happened when I got back in quarters.

Tommy was waiting for me. "Yeah, o-kay. We picked you to go to the engineer academy. Starts in two weeks," he told me with a big smile. This was huge. If I could pass the academy, I would have a permanent spot at Corralitos—a full-time career punctuated by calls that might impart greater trauma than the one I'd just come from. I couldn't have been more excited.

III.

FREE BURN

At age seven, I packed my belongings again. This time, I knew why we were leaving. As religious leftists, Mom and Dad believed only God should take a life. This meant we went to antiwar protests, and that we had to move when Mom and Dad learned our kids' dorm-style bedroom in Santa Fe had previously housed a discreet abortion clinic. Anywhere in the state was too close to the shock of it. We landed one thousand miles away, in Ventura, California.

When a fire gains ground and finds its direction, it enters into the free burn phase. That's what Ventura felt like. The ocean. Our own rooms. A teaching gig for Dad at the college. A new book contract for Mom. We all found some direction there.

I began to realize who I was, other than a daughter and a sibling. I loved basketball, books, animals, God, and shoplifting. I hated dresses, vinegar, sitting still, and getting caught in one of my lies. Also, I'd determined my future did not include motherhood.

I broke this to Mom on my eighth birthday. She'd given me a large doll in a flowered box with MEET JULIE stamped on the front. I thanked Mom and took Julie outside to play. Mark and I tossed her about like a football, tucking her under our arms after a good catch.

Mom spotted us and dashed outside. "Stop throwing her!" she yelled, trying to muster a harsh tone. But even riled, she had a ridiculously warm tenor. "You need to nurture her; practice for when you're a mommy."

"I'm not having kids," I blurted before launching a Hail Mary pass that fell short, popping Julie's head off when she hit the ground.

After that, Mom began hinting at the only viable future I'd left myself. "Wouldn't this be a nice life?" she said, showing me pamphlet pictures of a llama farm run by Benedictine nuns.

CHAPTER 9

REMAINS

State Fire Headquarters, 16 Months Left

Curbside at Sacramento International Airport, Bud grabbed my suitcase while I hugged on Brody. "Be good, Little B-Man." I turned to Bud. "It's just five days. Please don't kill him."

Bud gave me his I-can't-make-you-that-promise look, which I returned with my oh-hell-yes-you-can stare. We hugged and kissed good-bye.

"Oh yeah," I said. "He howls whenever you drive over forty miles an hour. Love you." I wheeled my suitcase to baggage check.

Once through security, I found Andy at the gate.

"Last hurrah, *huh*?" I said.

"Yup. Final meeting of my career."

"You picked a doozy to end with."

We were heading to Phoenix, Arizona, for an annual meeting of the National Association of State Foresters. Once a year, higher-ups from all fifty states met in whichever state's turn it was to host. For the better part of a week, we'd talk forest management and fire policy while sitting in hard chairs at white-clothed conference tables over a dizzying carpet. Andy came for one reason: to say good-bye to his counterparts from across the

nation. When this trip was over, he'd collect the few belongings still left in his office and move to Idaho. I was there for three reasons: to meet my new counterparts, share California's hits and misses from last year, and pick up my sister Annie's ashes.

A month earlier, I had come to Arizona for Annie's fiftieth birthday. Annie lived in a group home close to my sister Bernadette. All the siblings, everyone except Cathy, who had passed thirteen years earlier, rented a big house near the group home to throw Annie a party. We knew it was likely her last. She'd been in steady decline with seizures, respiratory issues, and early-onset Alzheimer's from accelerated brain aging common with Down syndrome.

We spoiled her all day: a coat of fresh polish on her ten tiny fingernails, a new Band-Aid every twenty minutes, bright balloons, ice cream, cake, and her most cherished music tracks.

As early as I can remember, whenever Annie heard her favorites—Cat Stevens, Simon & Garfunkel, Elton John, and later Tom Petty—she'd dip back and forth in a patented rocking-horse dance style. Whoever was around joined in. We dipped our heads toward the center of a circle. The more of us, the bigger her smile. All of us had a special connection to Annie. I won't try to explain it for the others. But Annie and I were inseparable from the start. Dressed as twins, we kicked in unison from our high chairs, blew dandelions in the wind, and pretended to read—pointing out interesting passages to each other from books unknowingly held upside down. Sometimes we just sat and leaned our heads together. We still did that. Maybe that's how it happened. All that is good in my head and soul, she put there.

Now confined to a wheelchair, she danced by bending at the waist, back and forth, to "Benny and the Jets." When Petty came on, she couldn't hold it in. She pitched the empty cake plate from her lap and reached one foot outside the wheelchair brace. I saw it in slow motion, my optical nerves playing it in still frames. Steadying herself with one arm, she pushed with the other, shaking, stubbornly extricating her second leg. In tiny steps she'd been incapable of for months, she shuffled forward. The rest of us filled in to form the circle. We dipped our heads in time with Annie's beat. A tear

dripped past her unbound toothless smile as we rocked back and forth, running down a dream—dancing together for the last time.

At the conference in Phoenix, I stared at the carpet's gauche pattern, trying to find a face or animal within its scattered swirls while I mindlessly twirled a pen in between my fingers. Someone at the table droned on about the Granite Mountain Hotshots accident report. But the droner couldn't say what he wanted to, which was that Arizonans, some of whom were in the room, had made mistakes. We could tell our state hosts were still raw from their loss, so Droner meandered to avoid making his point too bluntly.

I whispered to Andy, "Maybe Arizona should have passed on hosting this year."

"Yup. Too soon for them to have this talk. They still have that thousand-yard stare."

"That's a good way to put it," I said.

"By the way, so do you," Andy said.

I thought I'd been hiding it better. I swallowed. "I go get her tomorrow. I'll miss the morning session."

"What time you leaving?"

"Crack of dawn. I'll be back by lunch. You can catch me up over a burger. My treat."

"I gotcha covered."

The next morning, the sun peeked over the horizon as I deposited my backpack in the rental car's rear seat and climbed behind the steering wheel. The passenger door opened. Andy ducked his head in.

"Andy? What's going on?" I asked, wondering why he was up this early.

He loaded in and buckled up. "This isn't something you let a friend do alone."

It put a lump in my throat that lasted for sixty miles. Andy rode beside me silently, letting me sip my road coffee and drive with my thousand-yard stare into the past.

I'd picked up a sister's ashes before. I knew what to expect: remains that fit inside a box about the same size as a folded fire shelter. With my oldest sister Cathy's, I'd felt a general sense of sadness, but also relief for her and the rest of us. She'd tried a million ways to make life work and kept gravitating back to "broken." Picking up her ashes was an act of closure. With Annie, I felt part of me was gone.

Andy and I stopped for sodas, got back in the car, and spent the second half of the drive talking religion. He was a born-again Christian with deep faith in the New Testament, and passage recall almost as good as Dad's. I had bad recall, but a broad read of spiritual texts and travel to religious places. We tossed theories back and forth until we landed on a spot of complete agreement: we gain, not lose, significance once we turn to dust. It put me in the right mind-set to pick up Annie.

"Welcome. Welcome to Angel Valley Funeral Home and Crematory," a man said in a syrup-slathered whisper—the kind of fake verbal hug responsible for keeping me far away from yoga studios. The man seemed so very tired of his painted-on half smile. I told him my name and he went to the back to collect Annie for me. He returned with an aqua paper bag outfitted with white twine handles.

"Here she is," he said.

I took the bag. She weighed less than Cathy. I paid and walked to the door. Before I pushed it open, I spun around. "How hot? What temperature do they use?"

He hesitated, fighting off a look of surprise. *Why would she ask such a question? Poor girl.* His face fell into an authentic expression. He finally looked sorry for me.

"Just under two thousand degrees," he said in his real voice.

I stared at him. That was less than the heat that had consumed the Granite Mountain Hotshots.

He must have felt compelled to fill my blank stare, so he fed me more. "Only the bones are left. Everything else gets vapor . . ." He stopped himself.

"Vaporized? Makes sense at that temp. Thanks." I raised Annie in her Easter-colored bag as a wave good-bye and walked out the door.

"Hey there, Annie Banannie," I said, before zipping her inside my backpack and placing her in the backseat with a double tap—a way to tell her, *"I got you. I'll always have you."*

"Let's ride," I said to her and Andy. Andy had switched to the driver's seat, but otherwise our trip back was a repeat: silence for the first half, then soda and God for the second.

<center>✻✻✻</center>

I have no recollection of the rest of the conference. My next cogent memory is going through security at the airport with Andy. He glided through ahead of me, but TSA stopped the X-ray belt when they saw bone dust in my backpack. A stern man asked me to step aside. He assigned a female officer to me who ran her wand and swabbed my fingers for gunpowder and explosives residue. Then she hustled my pack to an inspection station.

"Hey! That's my sister. I don't want her out of my sight."

"Procedure, ma'am."

"I get it. Do what you need to do, but I have a right to keep the remains within my sight," I said, as if I knew a rule they didn't. She let me follow her to the inspection station, where she opened the box, but not the plastic bag. She sent me on my way with a "condolences" nod.

When I made it to the other side of security, Andy was waiting. "Got Annie?" he asked.

I reached behind me and patted my backpack twice—my new version of us leaning our heads together.

Andy nodded. "Let's ride," he said.

At cruising altitude, I held my backpack on my lap and looked at the sky outside my window. Bright clouds formed a haloed porthole. *Wow*, I thought. *I guess she's showing me where her soul went. Maybe this is how she felt when I left her by insisting on my emancipation.* I plugged in my headset. "Knocking on Heaven's Door" piped into my ears and flooded my eyes with both kinds of tears—happy ones for her and sad ones for me.

Through blurry eyes I saw the flight attendant making her way down the aisle behind a beverage cart. I couldn't stand the thought of missing

a free beverage, so I wiped my eyes with a shirtsleeve and pulled the tray table down in front of me. It reminded me of our high chair trays. Side by side, Mom would give Annie and me a midday snack: milk-filled sippy cups and cubes of bread. When Annie sipped from her cup, its circumference hid me from her peripheral view. I'd reach over and steal a piece of her bread. She was a slow eater, and I, an opportunist.

"Normal" babies have 46 chromosomes. Down syndrome occurs in babies gifted with a 47th. Study upon study reveal this causes cognitive delays and impairs fine-muscle control. None of the studies mention how it benefits its carriers by neutralizing the greed, senseless rushing, and spite imparted to the rest of us.

I read somewhere that once an older couple produces a Down syndrome baby, a subsequent baby like me is seven times more likely to have it. The world had it so wrong. My whole life, I'd tell people Annie had Down syndrome, and they'd say, "Oh, I'm so sorry," not understanding *I* was inferior to *her*—*I* wasn't worthy of that extra chromosome.

After Arizona, I put on a Winnie the Pooh T-shirt lifted from Annie's stash once my siblings and I packed up her room—the second time we'd had to categorize a sister's paltry belongings into three piles: Keep, Discard, Donate. I'd don the shirt once a week and listen to "Knocking on Heaven's Door" on a loop while driving home with Brody in the Jeep. Brody stopped howling when I played the song. He made room for my grief the way only dogs can. Our drives together provided me time to process Annie's death.

<p style="text-align:center">✶✶✶</p>

Every year, the first week of May is dedicated to Wildfire Awareness Week, WAW. The Cheez-It team travels the state, preaching preparedness and warning of fire in the months ahead. WAW kicked off with a press conference at our McClellan Airbase in Sacramento. Over the years, the governors always attended. They liked giving a speech in front of our sharp red-and-white fleet of air tactical planes, airtankers, and helicopters. The backdrop made even the nerdiest governor look badass.

The previous year, the Cheez-It team spent hours on a presentation for Governor Jerry Brown before the presser. My staff printed color-coded wall maps with greens, tans, yellows, oranges, and reds of varying shades that indicated heightened danger. Overlay layers provided details for the entire state: fire history, drought conditions, fuel models, ecosystem sections, jurisdictional boundaries, fire station locations, air base response times, and a measure gaining significance—the energy release component— which calculates how much energy a flame front can produce, based on how parched the fuel is.

Ken had distilled the posted information into a fifteen-minute soliloquy for Brown, who was always in a rush. When Brown walked in, he looked at the maps, then at Ken, and summed it up without a briefing. "So, red isn't good, right? Let's go tell them that." And that's what Brown said to the press. "I've seen the maps. The whole state could turn red. Red is bad." Then he and his entourage left to go handle some other important state matter.

This year, we put the maps up but didn't bother with particulars Brown wouldn't want. When he walked in, he said, "*Hmm.* Still lots of red." He scanned the map, looking for details in one area. "How's Colusa County looking?"

"Not good. As you can see." Ken pointed right to some hot spots in a small county sixty miles northwest of Sacramento. Ken knew the state's geography as well as anyone.

"What if someone wanted to have a big campfire there?" Brown asked.

I don't have a poker face, and Turbo captured a photograph of Governor Brown, Ken, Natural Resources Secretary Laird, and me. Hands on hips, I have a look that says, "No, you can't have a bonfire on your family ranch, dipshit." Brown might have been one of the most intelligent men I'd stood in a room with, but his was the kind of intelligence that occasionally impaired common sense. He regained it by the time he buttoned his suit jacket and went outside to stand in front of airplanes, cameras, and bone-dry hills. His message to the people of the state of California: "Don't do something stupid."

But people missed the message. They didn't change how they normally worked or behaved—at least, some of them didn't. So when a heat

wave and dry winds swarmed Southern California a week later, twenty human-caused wildfires took off. They scorched 26,000 acres and cost over $60 million.

Handling the siege was easy for us. We'd trained for it. Hell, we lived for it. With Cheez-Its in front of us and North and South Ops on the phone, we did our thing.

"Any issues with tipping the table?" I asked North Ops.

"Nope. Strike teams are heading south now."

"After the orders are filled, can we pre-position some resources, maybe mid-state?" South Ops suggested.

Ken said, "Yup. Yup," and I nodded. It was always a guessing game. Northern California was dry too. But our team agreed: let's fight the fires we have first, then the ones we expect.

Turbo, Red, and Griffin sat at one end of the table, listening, but also admiring Griffin's shoes. She had a fabulous collection.

"Sorry," I said to both Ops guys on the phone. "What you're missing is gushing over Griffin's new Mary Janes."

"Those aren't Mary Janes," Ken corrected me, garnering looks of approval from the end of the table.

I shook my head and wrapped up the call. "Sounds like we have a plan. Let's check in tomorrow. Same bat time, same bat phone." I hung up the con call. Ken, Red, Turbo, and Griffin all stared at me.

"Mary Janes? Really, Chief Frank. I know Doc Martens are all the rage, but you ought to expand your portfolio a bit then. Beyond combat boots."

Ken laughed and pointed at me like a sibling watching another sibling getting in trouble.

"I have flip-flops too. And Chucks. And *whoa!* running shoes; don't get me started."

My phone blew up. Six messages from Turbo with various shoe descriptions and pictorial attachments for future reference. The others got up, scraped the Cheez-It dust onto paper towels, and began packing their bags to go home. I'd just been shoe-shamed. I missed Andy. He would have been on my side.

We worked the siege, taking lighthearted shots at each other as opportunities allowed. All of us rowed the same direction, handling our tasks with an ease that comes from trusting each other. We didn't notice it seemed too easy. But the cosmos did, and sucker-punched us on a Friday morning with an event we weren't prepared for.

Our phones wouldn't stop buzzing, and news banners on every local channel carried the story. One of our battalion chiefs was missing. And his girlfriend had been murdered the night before—stabbed and strangled—in the home they shared. We scampered into Ken's office, wondering if one of our own could have done this.

CHAPTER 10

FOOTBAGS

State Fire Academy, 1985

A key in the door signaled my academy roommate's arrival. I'd already unpacked, hospital-cornered my bed, and put on my running shoes for a jog.

"Hi. I'm Lenore." She smiled, dumped her bags on the empty bed, and held her hand out.

"Clare." I shook her hand, which she didn't hold firmly enough.

She surveyed our cramped, sparse dorm room, which held a desk, locker, and bed on each side. "This is cute. Where'd you drive in from?" Her voice had a pleasant quality, like it didn't know darkness. I pegged her at around twenty-three. Perfect brown curls framed flawless skin. She looked like a soft-focus prom photo. I couldn't help but judge her for it. Curling irons and helmets didn't go well together. I wondered if she'd make it through all eight weeks here.

"Santa Cruz," I said.

"Isn't that where all the hippies landed? Well, there and Berkeley?"

"Pretty much." I laughed.

She studied me and my hospital corners. "You have pretty short hair for a hippie."

"I got it cut for this adventure. I like bohemian lit and Bob Dylan, but otherwise, I don't fit the bill." I finished tugging my shoelaces tight. "See ya. Gotta jam before I lose my mojo."

"Okay, Santa Cruz," she said. "I have more questions," she called down the hallway.

The outside air smelled of gravel and dry grass. I ran along dirt roads winding through the grounds and back acres. Leaning into a hill, I sprinted to its top and caught my breath while taking in a view of the world I was about to get sucked into. Near nothing but oaks, cheat grass, Mule Creek State Prison, and a creepy boarded-up reform school called Preston Castle, the academy's lonesome 420 acres were perfect for loud drills and training tower fires. This remote spot in the middle of the state served as the department's glue—the one place we all had to endure before scattering to assigned locations somewhere in the state of California.

From the hilltop, I oriented myself. Classrooms, a cafeteria, dorms, offices, a weight gym, a massive apparatus barn, shop buildings, and intimidating training props splayed across the campus. Excitement and nerves wrestled with each other in my stomach as I descended back toward the dorms, questioning whether I had any better shot than Lenore. Could I pass the endless battery of tests this compound held cocked and ready? If yes, I'd have my dream—a profession I'd already fallen in love with. If no, I'd have nothing. No job. No path. No purpose. Just three lost years and a tally mark in some column used to prove "women can't hack it."

The last quarter mile lay in a straight stretch, begging me to sprint. I did, then walked in circles catching my breath and shooting snot out my nose.

Lenore peppered me with questions as soon as I returned. My answers led to more questions. "You didn't finish high school? You aren't old enough to drink? You've already been an LT?" She held out open palms at me. "How does this happen?"

On my end, I found out she came from one of the hundreds of towns all sounding alike in Southern California. She'd worked one and a half fire seasons there, already missed her boyfriend, squeezed her toothpaste tube from the middle, and yes, she'd brought her curling iron.

In the morning, all the cadets met in the main classroom, each wearing a pressed uniform, tie, and polished black shoes. Name cards dictated our seats. We swiveled our heads, assessing each other. There were twenty-nine of us: sixteen white guys, seven non-Caucasian guys, five white women, and one Latina. Everyone was in their twenties, except a few who had made it to their third decade. A small group stood out the most. Despite having the testosterone to grow moustaches, four guys had chosen clean-shaven upper lips. They looked wildly out of place.

Our class coordinator, Battalion Chief Boran, swaggered in, chewing on the end of an unlit cigar. He leaned on the podium and surveyed his new crop. Thick muscles and deep facial lines made him look like a seasoned military officer, someone Tommy Lee Jones would've played at the time.

Boran removed the cigar and welcomed us with a speech he'd delivered a hundred times, mastering a tone and expressions that provided subtext. "We're here to help you pass." *A bunch of you are going to fail.* "When you leave here, you'll have the skills needed to serve as first-line officers in the department." *You won't be prepared for what's coming your way.* "Apply yourselves, and we'll get through this together." *I'll be in my office doing important shit, so don't bother me unless you or one of my instructors is dying.* He handed the class over to our primary instructor, Captain Ebert.

BOILING LIQUID EXPANDING VAPOR EXPLOSION, Ebert wrote on the classroom whiteboard. He put the pen in the tray and began pacing in front of the class. I stared at his flattop, bushy moustache, and belly. It strained his uniform's shirt buttons.

"Anyone know why we care about this?"

No one raised a hand, but it didn't matter. Ebert's eyes stayed focused on the floor as he pivoted into an about-face. "A simple grass fire can burn hot enough to ignite the liquid inside a propane tank. Which means what?"

Hands went up, but his head stayed down. Pace. Pivot. "It's the explosion," he revealed. "Boiling propane expands. The tanks explode, blowing off the ends. Boiling. Liquid. Expanding. Vapor. Explosion. BLEVE." He stopped right in front of me and looked up. "In other words, *Ka-Boom.* It's how popcorn works."

I couldn't stop staring at his bulbous abdomen. *If those threads don't hold, any one of those buttons could put an eye out. Ka-Boom.*

Ebert resumed his pacing and continued answering his own questions about ignition temperatures of various fuels we'd encounter, should we make it through these eight weeks.

At the first break we clustered into small groups, asking each other, "What unit are you from? How many seasons have you worked? Were you an LT?" This is how we sized up who we would and wouldn't want to study with.

By the time Ebert called us back inside, several study groups had formed. One of them already had a name: the Olympians. They had revealed an intent to achieve the highest class scores, earning them one of the coveted top three slots, and therefore had quickly found each other. Forever memorialized in the academy's hallways, top three finishers got their names engraved on a gold, silver, or bronze plaque praising them in perpetuity. I wanted to be in that sea of overachievers lining the hallway. I was the kind of person who gave a shit about those things. But instinctively, I knew better. As the youngest, shortest, and lightest person in an academy for the brawniest of professions, I didn't need to disadvantage myself more by adding stress. So I steered away from the Olympians. It was my way to reduce the pressure—avoid a BLEVE.

That afternoon, we headed to the drill grounds for an outdoor lecture and practice session on ladders. This was how most females failed out— lack of shoulder strength. The instructor had a completely different style than Ebert. He wanted us to call him "Stan," not "Captain." A tall, skinny chain-smoker, he emanated warmth and made us feel like we could nail this. "Maybe not at first. It takes some practice. But there's no reason y'all can't pass ladders."

We lined up for our first run-through. I was the first female in line. A few guys ahead of me had obviously handled ladders before. Each raised and lowered it in turn with an ease that made it fun to watch, like martial artists performing katas in a neighborhood park. Others relied on muscle instead of technique, which looked awkward and wasn't good for their backs.

Then all eyes focused on me. I could feel their doubt. *She's so small. I wonder if she'll even be able to stand it upright. There's no way. Too bad. She seems nice enough.*

Thanks to the damn three-section ladder at Pescadero, this standard two-section felt light and easy. It wasn't martial arts pretty, but I left some mouths open. And Stan would remember me in the years to come when our paths would cross at Sacramento headquarters. "I honestly didn't know if you'd be able to do it, but you nailed it," he admitted twenty-five years later.

<center>✳✳✳</center>

Lenore caught me studying by myself in our room after dinner.

"Study with us," she offered. She'd joined with three other gals.

"I'm a lone studier," I said, which was true but not the whole reason for staying at arm's length from the all-female study group. I wanted to tell her they were harming the cause. You can't integrate by segregating. But that wasn't my real motivation either. Two of them had serious problems with the ladder, and my twenty-year-old self thought the best strategy was to distance myself for fear I'd be associated with their weakness.

"Are you a closet Olympian? You know Nadine is going for top three. That's why she won't join us."

"I hope she makes it. But not my deal. I can't handle top-three pressure."

"You have to have some social life here or it's going to feel like a boot camp."

"I like boot camps."

"A hippie who likes boot camps. You're funny."

"I'm not a hippie."

"Whatever you want to tell yourself, Santa Cruz," she said, eyeing the hacky sack on my study table. She grabbed a sweatshirt and headed for the door. "I'll tell the gals you said hi."

<center>✳✳✳</center>

During the first few weeks, all the cadets except the Olympians and I met after night drills at a place I still couldn't get into: Tilly's Bar. It was just as well I liked studying alone. But this also left me by myself during class breaks as groups huddled together. I brought my hacky sack, a small sand-filled footbag, to entertain myself. I kicked it in the air, counting the number of times I could keep it alive, then tried to get a higher count next go-round. Within a couple of minutes a few others joined. We tossed the sack to each other with our feet, collectively going for a high number. Lenore shot me a knowing smile, pleased I'd found my people.

Someone bought more hacky sacks during a store run to the nearest real town. The lawn in front of the classroom filled with growing circles of footbaggers tired of discussions about hydraulic calculations and last night's follies at Tilly's.

It was a welcome break in hamster-wheel days that began blurring together. Cold mornings with damp chamois rags wiping already spotless engines led to sunrise. Wet cafeteria trays with plates of steam-table scrambled eggs and limp bacon sat alongside canned fruit and cold toast. Class lectures on hazardous materials, advanced fire behavior, and centrifugal pumps tested our eyelids before a mess-hall lunch with last night's repurposed dinner. Afternoon drills followed. They always involved getting yelled at. "That's not gonna cut it, Hopeful!" All the instructors except Stan called each of us that, knowing our futures lay in the balance. Evenings brought workouts, a dinner bell at 1800 hours, night drills, showers, then homework and/or Tilly's. After a few hours of sleep, the chamois were back in our hands.

✳✳✳

The academy was easier for those of us who'd held LT assignments. But everyone struggled with something. With ladders behind me, I didn't know what would trip me up until I realized the academy fleet had no map books, which I needed for the stake-side driving test.

Every unit had one of these old flatbed trucks with removable sides, called stakes, which formed a walled cargo area behind the cab used to haul

supplies. The truck scared most cadets because of its archaic square-tooth gears and split-shifter. These posed no problem for me. An old-school captain, Art Adams, had taught me how to shift it when we worked a project together during my winter at Corralitos. He showed up in the stake side with his Stanley thermos and pack of cigarettes. I buckled into the passenger seat, kept my window cracked while he smoked, and watched him operate the split-shifter. Hill coming up, let off the gas, pop up the knob, increase the RPMs. As the grade steepened, let off the gas, clutch in, rev so the gears match, downshift, clutch out, split shift down, crest the hill.

Every day, we followed the same routine. He smoked a morning cigarette, then quizzed me. "What kind of clouds are those?" He pointed with a tobacco-stained finger.

"Cumulonimbus."

"What are the air patterns that form them? What does that air pattern do to a fire?"

I carefully poured coffee into his thermos cup top as I answered the questions. If I didn't know the answer immediately, he'd give me a beat. "Don't give me a book answer. Tell me what makes sense."

After one cigarette, one cup of coffee, and one fire behavior lesson, we arrived at the site. We'd do it again on the way home.

One afternoon, we finished early, so he said, "You're on this side."

My eyes widened.

"You've been watching me for days. Now, it's your turn."

I climbed in and the problem presented itself. The stake sides were so old, the bench seat didn't have a slide-forward option. I was too short to fully disengage the clutch, so I took the map books and stacked them behind my back.

Art waited while he smoked his return-trip cigarette. "Stay parked. Show me first gear."

I put it in first.

"Split it up," Art said.

I popped up the red split-shifter.

"Second."

I found second.

"Split it down."

I pushed the button down.

Sitting in the parking lot, we ran through the gears, before Art said, "Let's get 'er on the road." Art poured his own coffee, careful to underfill it. He knew it would be a jerky ride home. It was. But by the end of the project, it wasn't.

At the academy, Ebert called out our assignments the evening before our first driving day. "Bisbee. Stake side."

When I reported to the stake side in the morning, I brought a pillow from my dorm room.

Ebert carried a clipboard, a cup of coffee, and a scowl. "You planning on a nap, Bisbee?"

"No, sir. It's for my back."

"You're not going to be carrying a pillow with you all the time. You can't use it."

This was one of those times in my career where the filter should have kicked in but didn't. I actually said out loud, "You have one, sir. It's just that yours is in front."

His face reddened. I tried to recover by making it seem I meant it in a comical way. I scrunched my face and tilted my head. "Not funny, sir?"

"Get you skinny ass into the truck. You better figure something else out by test day."

With the pillow in place, I familiarized myself with the gears at a stand-still, like Art had taught me. Then I released the brake and eased onto the rural highway. By my third or fourth split shift, Ebert braved moving his cup to his lips. Within a mile, he felt comfortable enough to rest the cup on his gut.

"You've done this before," he said.

"Yes, sir. Captain named Art Adams taught me during a work project. Plus, I drove one for a couple of weeks on a fire logistics assignment as an LT."

"Tell me you didn't carry a pillow with you."

"I used the map books."

"*Huh.*" He pursed his lips, then took a sip. "You wouldn't believe how much coffee I spill these first few weeks."

"If this had been my maiden voyage, sir, you'd have two drops left in that cup."

Ebert laughed, then admonished me, "Watch your hands."

I'd relaxed and let one hand slip low on the wheel. I corrected it. Ebert surprised me by settling in, happy to sip in silence. I spent the rest of the drive wondering how I'd do this without a pillow or map books.

During practice hours, I tried it with nothing behind my back. Sitting at the front edge of the seat, I held myself upright with a firm grip on the steering wheel and core muscles. It was about a thirty-minute loop with constant shifts and turns, which meant I couldn't rely on holding myself up by the steering wheel. After ten minutes, I was exhausted and turned around early. My abs and obliques needed more endurance to make it through the course with no back support. I added twist sit-ups to my mornings and nights and practiced driving the beast every chance I got, forgoing time on the more fun engine courses I already knew I could pass.

<p style="text-align:center">✳✳✳</p>

While academy hours dragged, somehow the weeks whizzed by and Ebert announced, "Today is late-term reviews. Chief Boran and I will meet with each of you to discuss your performance. If you aren't in review, you'll be in here studying for tomorrow's exams."

He went alphabetically, so I was up early. "Hopeful Bisbee. Front and center." With a key chain dangling from a clip on his suffocating belt, Ebert escorted me to Boran's office. I felt like a prisoner called to the warden.

Boran sat in his swivel chair, half his face hidden behind boots up on the desk, the other half shaded by striped shadows from window blinds. He smoked a cigar and looked at the paper in front of him—a report from the instructors about me.

Ebert sat in a comfortable upholstered side chair and motioned for me to sit in the hard plastic one in front of Boran. I had an excellent view of Vibram boot soles.

"Looks like you're getting by, Bisbee."

"Yes, sir."

Boran lifted his boots off the desk, squared his shoulders, and leaned forward. He took a final draw on his cigar, then stubbed it into the aluminum ashtray that came with every state desk. Blowing his exhale at me, he said, "Captain Ebert and the others tell me you can do better."

"Oh," I said, not understanding what he wanted from me.

"They believe if you applied yourself more, you might have leadership potential." He nodded at Ebert, who opened a manila folder and began to read my stats, none of which I remember except that I was hovering in the top half of the class.

"Nadine is in slot number four right now," Ebert said.

"That's awesome," I said. It wasn't the reaction he was looking for. Perhaps he thought it more humiliating for me to be behind another female.

He shook his head, sighed, and put down the folder. "Look, Bisbee, a little less hacky sack is what I'm saying. It doesn't seem like you're taking this seriously."

They both stared at me, waiting for my response.

I bald-faced lied to them. "I'll try harder."

The sunlight hit me as I emerged from Boran's cave. I squinted and shook tension from my shoulders out my arms. I should have been flattered by their push. Instead, it fired me up. My hacky sack and I *had* shown leadership. We'd fostered teamwork and relieved stress. Pescadero had taught me: without hacky sack, people in these jobs eat, drink, and smoke too much. Those who don't die of heart attacks or cancer or the bottle have shit attitudes, failed marriages, and no mojo. I knew my best bet at getting through the tests here and a career handling other people's drama and trauma was to stay the course and continue footbagging.

<p style="text-align:center">✦✦✦</p>

Black Wednesday. That's what our cadet predecessors had dubbed the eighth Wednesday of the academy. Stacked with ladder, pumping, and driving tests, this Wednesday always eliminated cadets the day before graduation.

"Final push, folks," Ebert told us. "We've brought in proctors from outside to ensure fair testing. You'll get one retake for each station. If you can't pass in two tries, you'll be released to pack your things."

Bundles of nerves, we reported to our respective testing stations. I easily passed the driving tests, even the stake side. I don't think the proctor knew I had to do a thirty-minute isometric hold. He just checked PASS and sent me to my next station because I didn't spill his coffee. I also got passing but not perfect scores on my first four pumping tests.

One last test stood between me and my destined profession: the tank-to-hydrant test. Critical for structural firefighting, it had more steps and caused more failures than the other pumping evolutions. When an engine first arrives at a building, it holds enough water in its tank to last a minute or two. The engineer has to tap into a hydrant, connect a large-diameter hose to the hydrant then to an intake port on the engine. The important part is next: simultaneously closing the tank valve and opening the hydrant valve, so water comes from the endless supply instead of the finite one. The switchover must be smooth to prevent a water surge that could toss a firefighter at the nozzle.

I'd done it several times in the field, but on engines where the two valves lay closer together. On the academy's newer test engine, the valves exceeded my wingspan from the ground. I couldn't move both at once. The first time I tried it during our practice sessions, my body knew what to do. I climbed onto the sideboard step, opened the low valve with my calf and closed the high valve with my hand. It took a few tries to make it smooth.

I did the same for the test, performing all the steps in order with a safe water transfer, completing the evolution well within the time allotment. Holding up my hands to show I'd finished, I looked at the proctor, hoping I'd earned the elusive "one hundred percent."

"Fail. You can't stand on the sideboard."

This time my filter worked. I changed "Why the fuck not?" to "None of the instructors had a problem with it, sir." I didn't actually know if any instructor had witnessed it. They roamed while we practiced, and it might not have caught their eye.

"It's a safety issue," he said.

I swallowed hard and took my time responding. Stripping every bit of smartass from my tone, I said, "It's a sideBOARD, sir—means available for boarding, standing on, right?"

He glared at me. I felt he needed a way to save face because I was flat-out correct.

"I know it's unorthodox, sir. I could see where it would surprise you, but nothing in the cadet-opens-hydrant-valve instructions dictate it has to be with a hand, not a leg."

He squinted at me and rechecked the instruction sheet, scanning for anything that would make him right. He shook his head, made marks on my score sheet, and handed it to me without eye contact or words. I looked at the sheet. He'd circled 100%.

<p style="text-align:center">∗∗∗</p>

Cadets who'd finished testing polished the equipment for display at the next day's graduation. I arrived at the apparatus bays, high-fived those already there, and popped a cassette tape from my car into a boom box. We brushed, scraped, and polished to Phil Collins, waiting to high-five other cadets as they finished their tests.

When "I Don't Care Anymore" came on, I turned up the volume and started singing out loud. "I don't ca-are any-mo-oo-ore." *I don't care that I almost failed out because a dipshit proctor made his decision about me before I'd had a chance to prove myself. I don't care that fire equipment isn't designed for me. I'll work around it. I don't care if people don't appreciate the value hacky sack brings. I don't . . .*

Something clipped my ear. A locker room towel-snapping brawl had broken out. I twisted my chamois, loading it to return fire. We whirled, and whipped, and drenched each other with bucket water while belting out the refrain in a dance that released eight weeks of tension.

When the tape switched sides, the mood turned somber as we mopped up our mess, realizing the now-shaded apron outside the bays meant time had run out on retakes, and five of our classmates were packing their bags.

By the time the cadre released us for dinner, the cadets who'd failed had already cleared out.

I sat on my bed and stared at Lenore's stripped mattress. If you'd have asked me on the first day which five would fail, I'd have put money on four of them: Lenore, one of the gals who struggled with the ladder, and two of the moustacheless guys. I no doubt had been in others' first-round failure picks. But on this side of it, I understood we all owned a piece of anyone's failure. Would Lenore have passed if I, if any of us, had expected her to? When I refused Lenore's study-group offer, I'd chosen self-preservation over solidarity as if both couldn't exist in the same space. Yes, I'd brought a hacky sack, but failed a truer leadership test. I'd been unwilling to risk my own standing to help others succeed in a career that trumpets service above self.

The next morning, I choked down the last bite of academy food. One of the things I missed most while sequestered at the academy was a proper piece of toast. Correctly prepared, it was my all-time favorite food. I made plans for a toast blowout when I got home.

After breakfast, we lined up with our polished shoe tips, waiting for ceremonial bagpipes and certificates issued in front of spotless engines.

Boran, cigarless and looking sharp, called out, "Bisbee, Morgan, Ruiz. Just got word. Your station assignments have changed. You're all going to Belmont." Then he called us to attention and commenced the ceremony. The three of us didn't have time to exchange what-the-fuck looks. Belmont was known as "the Zoo" for its size, chaos, and pranks. As I recited the oath, I tried to imagine what hijinks had created three immediate openings at the station where I would need to complete my three-year engineer apprenticeship.

CHAPTER 11

VERTEBRATES

Belmont Fire Station, 1985

Mule called us to the colossal dining table. Only a few other stations in the state needed tables this big. Belmont quartered four engines, a bulldozer, and a half-dozen administrative staff who worked a normal schedule and went home in the evenings. That still left at least thirteen of us for dinner during fire season.

Instead of family-style platters plunked onto the middle of the table, Mule had plated our dinners individually. Lemon and sage wafted from the glazed chicken. Roasted garlic cloves peered through silky mashed potatoes. And bright peas added a pop of color. No matter what I'd heard about him, in this moment it didn't matter. Mule could cook.

He set a special plate at the head of the table, domed with a fancy hotel-style lid. *A peace offering*, I thought. Mule and Captain Ricky had been at it all day. They were opposites—Mule was tall with sunken eyes from low body fat and tours in Vietnam and had no desire to promote, while Ricky was short, baby-faced, and had just promoted to captain.

Ricky sat at the head of the table, smiling at the conciliation. But when he lifted the lid, he found his badge pinned to a dead blue jay propped on mashed potatoes and peas. Ricky shook his head and took the plate into

the kitchen. I heard a rustled reclaiming of the badge, a thud when the bird landed in an empty garbage bin, and cereal poured into a bowl.

Mule's eyes hadn't followed Ricky into the kitchen, they'd bounced between Morgan, Ruiz, and me. This wasn't about Ricky. It was a test for us—or at least a forecast. The next three years would cover shit they don't tell you about at the academy: mules, skydiving, lung scar, homophobia, group showers, house triage, death tolls, and constant pranks.

<p style="text-align:center">✶✶✶</p>

Morgan, Ruiz, and I knew enough to not flinch at the dead bird, so Mule gave us another test the next morning.

"You three youngins are so cute," Mule said. "We'll see if you're A-2 worthy."

A-2 was the alphanumeric map designator for the area the station covered. Mule had turned it into a motto: "A-2. Can do."

"Aren't we here 'cuz A-2 needs to get its shit together?" Ruiz said, referring to "the sweep" that resulted in our last-minute assignment changes to Belmont.

Mule nodded. "Balls. I like that, Hollywood." We called Ruiz "Hollywood" because he wore sunglasses inside to cover black eyes earned at a gym or bar. A fit heavyweight, he had bona fide boxing skills.

"Since you've got such a big pair, why don't you come with me tomorrow? Going skydiving. Always wanted to try it. You in?"

Hollywood laughed. "No way, Bro. Mexicans are too smart for that bullshit."

Mule turned to Ricky next. "Rii-cky? C'mon."

Ricky shook his head. "Not jumping out of a perfectly good airplane, Mule."

"I'll go," I said.

Mule spun his head. "No shit? You'll go skydiving with me?"

"Sure. Sounds like fun." I didn't tell him I'd done it a month ago on a weekend break from the academy with some other guys who'd "always wanted to try it."

Mule pointed his thumb at me. "Engine-rolling Flipper here's making y'all look like pansies," he said.

"Can't," Morgan said. "Wife just served me with papers. I gotta go get a lawyer." Morgan had been quiet at the academy, content to hide behind bolder characters. Prematurely gray with a young, pleasant face, he looked like the start of a police sketch, before the worn and malicious lines are drawn. Maybe the divorce would change that.

"I get ya, Brother," Mule said. "You hang in. And don't give her a dime of your retirement." Morgan had just gotten a pass through the brotherhood of broken marriages.

"If Flipper's in, I'm in," Bull, the dozer operator said. We called all the dozer guys "Bull."

Three others piled on and the six of us caravaned from the station the next morning. We completed the we-won't-sue-you-if-we-die paperwork, a two-hour training session, and climbed inside the plane.

Mule got quiet at altitude. The open plane door made it real. He started a game of roshambo to see who would jump first. Instead of playing, I stepped into the go spot. It had been scarier the first time. The instructor checked my gear, and I was out the door, arching my back and waiting for the shoulder jerk of an opened chute.

On the ground, I gathered my chute and waited for the others to drop in. Mule hollered on touchdown, "A-2. Can do!" Afterward, he hugged me hard. "You're fucking fearless, Tiger." And just like that, I'd earned A-2 status and a new nickname.

✶✶✶

I'd need both on a structure fire call we had a few weeks later. I bled air from the hose nozzle before Hollywood and I made entry. Smoke poured from the suburban house. There were no signs anyone was home, but a toppled tricycle on the front lawn urged Hollywood and me to move fast. The team behind us would conduct the search. Our job was to make it safe for them by extinguishing active flames.

Kids often hide under beds or in closets, so we hurried through the black air toward the back. If fire showed itself, we'd blast it. If it didn't, we'd

make sure the bedrooms were clear for a search. At the end of a hallway, before we reached the bedrooms, Hollywood yanked the hose to give us extra to make the bend, but it caught on something and catapulted him forward. He careened into my breathing tank. The tank jammed into my helmet and dislodged my face mask. I lost my seal. Hot, toxic soot filled my lungs and closed my throat.

I didn't dare take another breath. Shoving the nozzle at Hollywood, I signaled I was out, and bear-crawled past the rescue team as fast as I could, using the hose as my guide. Along the crawl, I kept reminding my lungs to not give in to reflex: *don't breathe, don't breathe, don't breathe.* Splaying myself onto the front step, I sputtered and choked, and gasped, sucking in air that felt like a drink of cold water after a desert trek.

The battalion chief and exterior team rushed at me. "He needs backup," I rasped. The battalion chief said, "Go," and a firefighter peeled off to follow the hose line to Hollywood.

"I lost my seal," I croaked. "I'll go back in when I catch my breath. I'm sorry."

"Tiger, you're A-2. Proven. Stupid tough. Now go get checked out by med."

I sucked on pure sweet oxygen from the med bag. The family—a mom, dad, and little girl—pulled up in front of their hose-filled driveway and blackened house.

I looked at the girl. *What if you'd been inside? What if me bailing had delayed your rescue? I'm so sorry.* In my mind, I'd failed her. I may have. In a hurry to get inside, maybe I didn't snug the mask straps tight enough. Or I did, and the one-size-fits-all mask was too big on my face to withstand a jolt from a heavyweight fighter. A few years, later, manufacturers produced varied mask sizes. It hadn't dawned on me that maybe I could have made it happen sooner by being indignant instead of apologetic.

<p style="text-align:center">✱✱✱</p>

In junior high, I used my allowance to buy a poster of San Francisco's Golden Gate Bridge. I hung it above my bed and declared, "I'm gonna live there someday." Belmont was only nineteen miles away. This was my chance. I put

word out and an engineer named Yvonne from another station contacted me. We got a cool two-bedroom flat in the Richmond district.

Getting Yvonne for a roomie was pay dirt. She had everything: TV, sofa, gadgets, dishes, cooking skills. All I brought to the party was my beloved toaster and half the rent.

"There's no groceries. What on earth have you eaten for the last two days?" she asked when she got home from her shift.

"Toast," I said, summarizing what had become my first-day-off habit of sleeping and eating a loaf of toast. I'd change into shorts and a T-shirt, then toast and butter and toast and butter. Real salted butter, spread to the edges, melted completely. I'd collapse on the couch with my toast tower, a cold root beer, and an inane television show. My loaf of crunchy, buttery goodness lulled me into a blissful late morning sleep.

Calories were not an issue for me. Firefighting, station workouts, and my weekly bike ride to and from the station sped my metabolism. I also took lifeguard classes and played softball for San Francisco City College while I plugged away at general education units. That's how I spent my four days off: toast, pool, school, softball, and waiting for Yvonne to get off shift to perform her magic in our kitchen.

I appreciated good cooking but vowed to never be a good cook. I feared a female-in-the-kitchen stigma might attach, so I cooked when it was my turn, but never got fancy and never made baked goodies. This brought its own stereotyping, which I learned about on my way to the station coffeepot one morning.

A voice I didn't recognize—someone from another station covering an overtime slot—was chatting with Mule. "I know the bitch who rolled the engine is a dyke. But I didn't think Yvonne was. She makes the. Best. Cookies."

I quickened my step. This crapsack needed a hockey stick check. There were a couple of gals at Belmont who were gay. They could tell I wasn't, but I confused a lot of guys. I didn't have a boyfriend and had short hair, weightlifting shoulders, and a San Francisco address. And apparently the clincher: I didn't bake cookies.

I grabbed a mug from the cupboard. "Morning, guys. See that article in the paper?"

Mule squinted, like he suspected it was a setup. Crapsack shook his head.

"It's about how if you eat a cookie made by a lesbian, or a bitch who isn't lesbian, how it can weaken your brain's neuroplasticity and change your hormonal balance, turning you into a latent homosexual. It's fascinating. You should check it out." I filled my cup, then walked out to the apparatus bay, leaving Mule with a big smile.

I heard Crapsack sputter, "I wasn't . . . I didn't mean . . . Did she just . . .?"

"Yup," Mule said. "Tiger called you a sexist fucknut and a fudge packer."

I shook my head, knowing only the second label stung. I understood by then that most firehouse guys didn't give one whit if anyone else was homosexual—male or female—but they were all petrified of being thought of as gay, even if they were—maybe *especially* if they were.

The exchange seemed inconsequential, but it stuck with me for the rest of my career. I'd see a lot of evolution over the years, but the last bastion of open degradation of a protected class in firehouses landed on gay guys. It's why my pal Radar at Corralitos stayed closeted to his death. And by the way, Yvonne's cookies were awesome, but the best I've had were made by one of the lesbians. So there, Crapsack.

San Bruno Mountain sat twenty miles north of the firehouse. A 2,300-acre state park, the mountain caught fire several times a season. Campfires, fireworks, off-road vehicles, power lines, and arsonists kept it ablaze. We named every fire "San Bruno." Dispatch told us when we got back in quarters which number it was for the year. "For the report, that was San Bruno twenty-two."

Daytime fires looked alike. Low-level flames two to three feet high raced across grassy slopes toward brush, trees, and canyons that promised forty-foot flames. We could catch some of them with mobile attack, the engine rolling alongside the nozzle person. But if it got into the steeps,

past the engine's side-hilling capabilities, we'd find a wide spot on one of the truck trails and start a hose lay to back up airdrops. These were low-stakes fires—the houses were at the base, not on the hillsides, where the fires wanted us to chase them. We treated the firefights like super-sets in a weight room. Warm up with initial hose deployment. Blast the flames while climbing the mountain and adding hose lengths. Repeat 5, 10, or 15 times. Cool down with mop-up and loading dirty hose on the engines.

When dispatched at night, we'd let up a bit—let the fire creep in moist, calm air to blacken a few more acres that couldn't be lit by some idiot until next season. We'd come off the mountain and head to Rolling Pin Donuts for a fresh predawn batch. Pure debauchery. The bakers knew us and threw in extra custard holes.

We rolled back into quarters to clean the equipment, then ourselves. Belmont had a main bathroom with a group shower, and a second bathroom with a broken shower. I used my Sunol trick to get a quick shower ahead of the guys. But one night, the ploy didn't work. Another engine returned from a vehicle fire they'd handled while the rest of us were still on the mountain. Their engine was ready to go before mine, so they got to the bathroom first.

I leaned against the engine, inhaling my smoke-and-dirt fragrance. Exhaustion from being up for twenty-two hours, fighting fire on the mountain, then ingesting fried dough made my head drop. I couldn't waste precious sleep time waiting.

I knew I wasn't the first woman assigned to Belmont to say, "Fuck it," and walk into the group shower. And guess what? Nobody flinched. In that way, Belmont's irreverence was enlightened. We were all the same: sooty, naked *Homo sapiens*. Here at the Zoo, showers were to clean tired firefighters aiming to get an hour of shut-eye.

∗∗∗

Still low on sleep, Murphy's Law poked at me the following night with a midnight dispatch. Ninety minutes from Belmont, Pebble Beach had an out-of-control blaze consuming multimillion-dollar homes between a famed golf course and a wooded botanical garden—a paradise thought

safe because of its proximity to coastal fog. But teenagers drinking beer on a mattress in a grove left an illegal campfire unextinguished.

With five engines and a strike team leader, we caravaned south on Highway 1, six light bars flashing red against darkened skies, like an outdoor rave party. As we closed in on the already evacuated neighborhood, our task solidified. We saw homes tucked into the wildland with wood-shingled roofs that thoughtfully matched nature's aesthetic—serene and picturesque yesterday, but a nightmare now.

"Be sure to flag the driveways you've covered. Leapfrog each other. Stay safe," the strike team leader instructed. Each engine had the same job: find the driveway, back down it or scout on foot, then triage—decide whether the house was savable or not. We used shorthand. "It's a winner," in which case we'd deploy a hose line to douse flames and use tools to clear vegetation, then move on. "It's a loser," in which case we'd go to the next driveway.

We operated by headlamps strapped to our helmets. Flames posed the least risk; we could see them. If we couldn't knock down a fire front, we'd shut the water valve, cut the hose at the coupling with a knife to save valuable seconds, then load on the outward-facing engine and make our escape. But at night, everything else was a risk. Rocky terrain threatened ankles. Burnt tree branches—we called them "widow-makers"—threatened necks. Downed power lines threatened electrocution. The next morning, my crew and I emerged intact, but the night fight resulted in fifteen reported firefighter injuries of various sorts.

We fought the fire for seventeen hours. Then it folded to our force, seeming to surrender in an instant, like it had eaten too much, too fast and wanted a nap. The fire had only burned 160 acres and 31 homes, but it set records for the highest-dollar-value destruction per acre. This nothing campfire in a something area made national news, propelling the wildland-urban interface (WUI) fire issue into living rooms throughout the country.

As with all firehouses, Belmont had a unique print to its call volume. Two call types caused me to develop a steady, unhealthy relationship with

death. The first were the calls to Crystal Springs Rehabilitation Center, "The Rehab." It sat two minutes from the station, and staff called us at least once a shift. We lugged our gear inside and braced for the amalgamated aroma of urine, Lysol, and atrophy. Most of the calls amounted to nothing—shortness of breath resolved with a hit of oxygen. I'd tell dispatch to cancel the ambo, then hurriedly pack our gear.

Mule asked me, "What's so urgent, Tiger? Gotta polish something that doesn't need it?"

He'd turn to the patient and nod at what looked like fresh art pushpinned to the wall. "You paint that watercolor?"

It invariably elicited a proud grin. Mule would add a wink for the women and a definitive nod for the men. Until then, I hadn't comprehended Mule's complexity. A mule is half jackass, half horse, and one hundred percent a beast of burden. Mule knew the residents craved attention more than oxygen, and he'd stay in that depressing hellhole as long as they needed.

Each visit taught me more about death's nuanced stages—its smells and colors. Some patients reeked of sweat and had cold clammy skin, but no blue tint. They'd be alright today. Some had just received a sponge bath. They smelled like Jergens and sported pastel pink flesh. We'd see them for several months until they started to yellow. Then we wouldn't.

About once a month we'd be first in on someone who'd left the Rehab for good. Layered in color, their blood pooled to the lower half of their bodies, turning them deep purple on the bottom and a pale blue version of their original skin color on top. It's called lividity—death's parfait. They smelled like whatever their rectal muscle held before it relaxed.

For the ones on their way out, there wasn't much for us to do. Most residents had a DNR taped to their bedside table. Absent a posted DNR, we had to do more than we wanted. On one of these calls, a patient in her late nineties had gone into cardiac arrest and nobody could find her DNR, so I had to start CPR. The woman's departed eyes told me she didn't want to come back. I remember brittle bones, fragile as a quail's, cracking under the heels of my lifesaving palms.

Residents yelled at me, "Stop! She doesn't want it. Stop!"

With every compression, I apologized. *Sorry. Sorry. Sorry.* I choked back tears as I perfused her heart and brain with oxygen and her blue-ashen color pinked up. Now she had the pain of broken ribs, a tube down her throat, and no hope she'd made it to the other side. *Sorry. Sorry. Sorry.*

Vehicle accidents were the second source of death. Situated between a mass of overlapping freeways, the station responded to several collisions every shift. They all blended together, except one, which I remember in high-def.

I pulled Engine 11 to the freeway shoulder above fresh tire marks indenting a grassy hillside. A car rested mid-slope, precariously balanced on its roof. "Keep ambo coming," I told dispatch. We slid down the embankment with medic bags, and jacks and wood cribbing blocks, used to stabilize the vehicle so we could extricate any patients.

Mule saw it first. "Back window."

I shook my head to make sense of the image: a partially shredded body, bent in half, with a rear end poking out the smashed back window—unrestrained by a seat belt. Parts not coated in blood were the color of blue that can't be returned to pink. I reached for a nonexistent femoral pulse, shoving my gloved hand into a sticky mess that smelled of blood and roughed-up turf.

Mist dampened the air, muting the traffic hum above us. A whirring noise and click came from inside the car—a cassette tape that hadn't shut off in the crash switching back to Side A. An unmistakable guitar riff followed. I couldn't believe or bear it: AC/DC's "Highway to Hell."

I knew the song well from high school. All my friends loved to blast it. I'd hated it from the moment I'd heard the demonic refrain, which I knew was less than one minute out.

I tightened my jaw and made eye contact with Mule and Hollywood. "Can you get enough cribbing under to hold me?"

"Go. Stay at the front," Hollywood yelled. The cribbing hadn't been set. But he and Mule had high-lift jacks going. I dove inside to eject the tape. I don't know if I risked being crushed for the dead driver or for us. I didn't want Bon Scott's demons seeping into the freshly released soul. But I also knew: when you add a soundtrack, a bad scene can loop in your head forever.

In silence, Mule and Hollywood finished the cribbing. I radioed dispatch. This would be the first time I'd say it over the air: "Respond coroner's office."

"Never have to unbuckle the dead ones," Mule said as we headed back to the station.

That was the whole conversation. No emoting required. We'd learned to handle—but not process—death. It's a business transaction, nothing personal.

Mom had always told me, "You were the most sensitive of all six. I only had to raise an eyebrow, and you'd be in tears." *I've come so far*, I thought. Turns out, too far.

<p style="text-align:center">***</p>

"I'm climbing Mount Whitney," Morgan announced over lunch at the big table. "Anyone wanna go? Hollywood? Tiger?"

"Nah, man. There's no oxygen up there," Hollywood said.

"I'll go," I said.

Two others, Rocco and Greg, signed on as well. None of the four of us had a clue about scaling the highest peak in the contiguous United States. We were firefighters in our twenties—we didn't need to know anything. With our tents pitched at base camp, we told jokes and decided to do it in a day—an up-and-back. "Easier than taking all our gear," we agreed.

In the morning, we headed out with canteens of water, snack bars, and a first aid kit. By noon, we could see weather coming in at the top of the peak. If it were a fire, we'd have known what to do with that information. But this was just a day hike, so we kept going. Two hours later snow and hail obscured the trail.

Morgan announced, "I'm bugging out."

"I'm with Morgan," Rocco said.

We split into pairs. They headed to safety while Greg and I foolishly pushed toward the summit. Those hours remain a fuzzy memory. More snow and hail, then lightning. Bolt strikes I could almost touch. *This is how a seizure must feel*, I thought.

My singular get-to-the-top focus never wavered. It possessed me. Vaguely aware of how close I was to vulture feed, I remembered: it's just business. *Am I going to die from lightning? Hypoxia? Hypothermia? That's okay; it's better than a slow ride at the Rehab or being ripped to pieces by my own car. This might be a nice way to go.*

It wasn't our time. We touched the inside wall of the summit's stone cabin, checked in with each other as if each of us was okay, then unceremoniously headed back down. Screaming head pain. Altered brain function. Damaged knees. Freezing feet. We arrived at base fifteen hours from when we started. I assume I collapsed in my tent to sleep. I don't remember.

<div align="center">✳✳✳</div>

It seemed I'd lost the respect humans are supposed to have for the Reaper. Maybe I needed a change of scenery. I went to the filing cabinet in the captain's office to retrieve a transfer request form—just to look at it.

Staring at the form made me nostalgic about Belmont. Yes, it was chaotic. But the steady stream of pranks had become music playing in the background, where I didn't always like the song, but preferred it to no music at all.

Forgettable shenanigans happened daily: pinning a name tag upside down on an unattended uniform shirt; filling boots with shaving cream; putting a stray toothbrush in a bowl of water, then in the freezer; loosening a toilet's Sloan valve so refill water sprayed uncontrollably inside the bathroom stall; securing Saran wrap *over* the toilet bowl but *under* the seat.

More exacting strikes had to be earned. Syrup of ipecac—a projectile vomiting expectorant—landed in an admin chief's coffee when he habitually drained the pot without starting a fresh one. A daily spread of fresh-baked sweets appeared on the table when an arrogant captain with a sweet tooth announced he had to cut weight to pass his physical. Raw chicken gizzards rotted inside the florescent light fixture in the prevention chief's office after he ordered the crew to remove the holiday tree because it was flammable. Also, the crew stripped the tree, took it outside, set it on fire, let it cool, brought it back in, and redecorated it.

Then, there were pure Mule moments. One day, he burst into the dayroom during the morning break. "You're not gonna believe this shit! C'mon." He bounced up and down on his toes, waiting for us. We followed him into the main bathroom. He opened a stall door and pointed at the toilet. Three or four heads at a time, we looked then peeled away, groaning, "Aw fuck you, man."

"That's gross."

"You're disturbed."

"I can't unsee that."

"That's the longest unbroken shit I've taken in my life," Mule defended himself.

We filed out of the bathroom, with Mule yelling at us, "I've been training hard for this."

Despite the spirited dysfunction, we made progress. We started a blacklining project on San Bruno Mountain, burning strips close to access points, which cut the fires in half. We remodeled the main bathroom into two bathrooms with single-stall showers. Captain Ricky formed us into a decent softball team for the annual tournament. Another captain got us to train for the world police and fire games, where a bunch of us medaled. We worked the calls and helped each other move through off-duty life.

I opened the filing cabinet to return the transfer request form to its folder. From the captain's office, I heard the division chief interviewing a new battalion chief candidate.

The candidate asked, "I know the reputation here. Are there still some issues?"

"Oh, that's all fixed," Division promised. "This place is shipshape now."

That's when we heard thunderous foot stomping, followed by, "You son of a bitch!"

I rushed upstairs. "Division is doing batt. chief interviews downstairs," I warned. Mule and the new Bull bore smiles, bare chests, and antique war swords. They scurried their bleeding torsos into another room before the chiefs made it upstairs.

Ricky covered for them. "Guys are training for the next world games. They get lively."

Division looked over his shoulder at his candidate, a fish on the line. "See. Shipshape."

I went to get a cup of coffee. Sitting by myself at the massive table, I sipped and looked at the transfer form still in my hand. I'd arrived at Belmont as Flipper and became Tiger. I'd met a Mule, a blue jay, Bulls, *Homo sapiens*, a quail, vultures, and probably some closeted bears—a zoo indeed. Yvonne was getting married, Hollywood divorced, and Morgan now had lines on his face. Mule was the only stagnant one, still trying to find a way to feel something—at the tip of Bull's sword. I didn't want to end up that way. I filled out the transfer request.

CHAPTER 12

FISSURES

Saint Helena Unit Headquarters, 1988

My new unit headquarters rested at the base of Mount Saint Helena, a 2.4-million-year-old volcanic rock spread into Sonoma, Lake, and Napa counties. I arrived before dusk and reported to the command center for assignment to a fire that had started the day before.

The command center battalion chief nodded hello while pouring himself coffee from a fresh pot. He turned to his captain. "Hey, Tanner, where's the unfilled orders on that fire?"

Tanner looked at the status board. "Looks like all the engines are staffed except . . ." He stopped.

"Except what?" The battalion chief asked.

"Well, there's an engine that just has a captain. No crew."

"That's where she's going, then."

"Well . . ."

The battalion chief stared at Tanner. Impatient. "Well what?"

"It's Verner."

"Oh. *Huh.*" He raised his eyebrows, took a sip from his mug, then nodded to Tanner.

Tanner keyed his mic to contact Verner. "Are you in position to pick up an engineer?"

"Kelsey-Cobb," a voice grunted.

Tanner scribbled down an address on a Post-it note, handed it to me, and said, "Meet him at Kelsey-Cobb Station. Don't arrive on an empty stomach." He shifted his glance to the battalion chief, with a this-should-be-interesting look.

I topped off my go-mug with coffee and walked out. Chill filled the air. It was December, but inland Lake County had proven it could burn anytime, and its winter fires were brutal. They raced through summer-cooked fuel, crackling and laughing at us while earned sweat turned to ice. I'd worked a late-season fire here with Norm and Scott six years earlier. When we bedded down, the outside of my sleeping bag froze to the ground and the inside froze to my Nomex. I had to peel myself out like a damn Popsicle.

I cranked my car heater on, found the route to Kelsey-Cobb in my map book, then followed the dark twisting highway, questioning whether I was lost the whole time. An hour in, a town called Lower Lake emerged. It reeked of acrid residential trash burned in backyard piles, but a fuzzy neon sign offered relief as it came into focus: Foster's Freeze. I ordered three full meals—two for me and one for Verner, in case he hadn't eaten. On the final stretch, I sucked down my crappy burgers and fries.

An iconic large redwood burl sign, the kind that stood in front of every state firehouse, told me I'd arrived. My headlights lit up the pitch dark. It looked like the power was out. I rolled down my window for an audible clue—maybe Verner running the engine for heat in the cab. I heard nothing but smelled cigar smoke and followed it until my headlights silhouetted Verner in the passenger seat of a fire engine.

I opened the driver's side door to introduce myself. Thick cigar smoke rolled out, forcing me to gag and threatening burger regurgitation. I stuck my hand out. "Captain Verner? I'm Clare." He looked at my hand and took another puff. *Not a hand-shaker. Got it.*

After loading my gear on the engine, I tossed his sack meal on the seat between us. "Picked up an extra burger in case you haven't eaten. It's a little

cold, but it's yours if you want it." Verner didn't move except to cut off the tip of a new cigar with his belt knife.

I buckled up. "Where to?" This put him in an awkward position. He had to talk to me.

"Back the way you came. Right on Bottle Rock."

Disoriented by the pitch dark and heady smoke, I made my way out the driveway, nervous I'd fuck it up. It took all my concentration to point the engine south, retracing my path toward Foster's Freeze. I hoped he'd tell me when we got to Bottle Rock. He didn't say anything, but he gave me hand signals, shooting his arm left or right when needed. We pulled up behind a group of engines putting in a hose lay along the fire's flank.

"I'll fill. You help them," Verner said. The engine we had was a water tender model. It held enough water to top off four engines. It would take Verner at least thirty minutes to transfer water from our tank to theirs. I jumped in to help with the hose lay, grabbing a hose pack and a roll in each hand. Cold bit through my fire gloves, making it hard to keep a grip on the rolls.

I hiked the steep grade, dropped off hose, then went for more. "Thanks," I heard. Shrouded by night and Nomex, nobody knew or cared who I was, other than a set of extra hands.

I tried to decipher details I couldn't see in the night air. Inland fires smell different from coastal fires. Night different than day. This fire smelled like oak woodland and chaparral with a grassy understory—peaty, not briny—and a hint of plastics, like a vehicle had been swept up in the blaze. Pockets of clean icy air felt like a drink of water.

Verner and I worked through the night. We'd fill the tender at an in-town hydrant, then return. I helped with hose lays as he replenished other engines. By the following afternoon, the fire died down enough for the incident commander to release us. The command center assigned us back to Kelsey-Cobb, keeping the water tender close in case the fire blew up.

We pulled into the station at dusk. The power was still out. Most stations had generators. Not this one. Verner and I built a fire in the dayroom's woodstove. I grabbed two wool blankets from the barracks. He planted himself on the couch with his blanket and endless cigar supply, which he

chain-smoked throughout the night. At some point the air became too dense for me to breathe, so I left the dayroom's warmth and headed into a frosty barracks. I swiped blankets off all the beds, piled them onto a single bunk, and crawled under them, hoping they'd crush me into a sleep that would give me a break from the cold and Verner's weirdness.

I knew I wasn't the problem. Tanner's reaction had clued me in. Plus, Berry had given me fair warning. Berry had cycled through Belmont as a prevention battalion chief. His humble charm and competence put him in a rare category. At Belmont, most of the brass got shit-talked. But not Berry. He came to work, did his job, took battalion coverage when needed, and paid extra into the coffee kitty. "He won't last here," Mule predicted. "He's too good of a guy." A year later, Berry promoted to division chief at Saint Helena.

Berry called me a week after I filed my transfer request. "Want out of the Zoo, eh?"

"Yeah. Trying to mix it up a little. Get different exposure."

"I can help with that. I have an opening for you in Lake County."

"That's awesome!" I said.

Berry remained silent too long.

"What?" I asked.

He cleared his throat. "There's a few cracked sidewalks up here, and by sidewalks, I mean people. Plus, you'd be the first permanent female."

"So," I said.

Berry laughed. "Okay. But don't say I didn't warn you."

Kelsey-Cobb's pile of blankets worked. I slept until sunrise, then crept into the dayroom. Verner lay motionless on the couch. I stared at his chest to see if it rose and fell. It did. *He's alive. That's a relief, I guess.* I stoked the woodstove, then went outside to chamois the engine.

Verner spent his days on the couch while I explored every nook of the station, cleaned every piece of equipment on the engine, and studied maps surrounding Middletown, the station I'd be assigned to once released from this prison. We ate pantry staples and C-rations heated on the woodstove. The fridge had been emptied and battened down six weeks earlier.

At night, I started in the warm dayroom. Reading by flashlight, I traded back and forth between *The Prophet*'s heady prose and *John Barleycorn*'s boozy tales. When my lungs couldn't take it, I headed to the barracks, swapping fresh air for cold toes. In a way, the cold helped. It numbed me physically, which cued an in-kind emotional response. I didn't feel anger, fear, or frustration. I was in battle mode—like when I hauled hose up a hill, not wondering why or how long I'd have to do it, placing one foot in front of the other until the fire went out.

On day four, the handheld radio clicked. The command center cleared us to return to our regular station assignments. Verner emerged from the dayroom, squinting at the bright sunlight, like a fucking zombie. Since we'd left the firefight, Verner hadn't said one word to me. We locked the station and nodded good-bye. I loaded my gear in my car, left Kelsey-Cobb behind, and drove to my new station.

<center>***</center>

Middletown Fire Station, 1988

Lack of sleep and cigar poisoning added to first-day jitters as I pulled my car into the parking lot. Situated midway between Kelsey-Cobb and Santa Helena headquarters, Middletown boasted a badass reputation with a rocking fire season call volume, promising twice the wildfire experience in half the time.

Five uniformed men stared at me unloading my gear. They stood outside the front door with crossed arms and dangling toothpicks, watching me struggle up an impossibly long walkway. I'd wrongly decided taking all my gear at once would make me look more competent.

One of them belted out, "What the fuck is that foreign tin can doing in our parking lot?"

I looked over my shoulder and saw the lineup I should have noticed when I drove in: Chevy pickup, Dodge pickup, Ford pickup, Ford pickup, Dodge pickup.

The oldest model sat lower than the others. I turned back to my welcomers with Jimmy in mind, the mechanic at Corralitos who'd taught me

the art of stringing together cuss words. "It beats the hell-fuck out of that pansy-ass, two-wheel, sissy-drive, shit-rusty dump-bucket," I said, adding a hint of twang to sell the redneck feel.

I heard one of them whisper, "Yup. She's got gonads—made it through a week with Verner." Another opened the door, "C'mon in. We'll make a pot and git to know each other after you set yer bunk up."

That's what it took to break new ground in this county—a little cussing and the command center pairing me with Verner in a four-day heatless purgatory. I'd hear about my legacy for years. "With Verner. By herself. No electricity." Some versions said a week, some a month, and some said he kept his knife blade open the whole time—which was very believable, but not true.

I settled into the winter routine with my five-man welcome wagon. Unless a big wildfire broke, we worked a normal Monday-through-Friday schedule and went home every night. We sacrificed immediate-response pay, but I loved the rhythm of it. Captain Fistler arrived first and started a fire in the woodstove. Franklin, the dozer operator, came next and brewed a pot of strong coffee. The other captain, Mort, got his coffee, visited for a bit, then disappeared into the office. The battalion chief, Childress, wandered in to read the paper and alert us to any priorities for the day. Sometimes, he brought his dog, Jeep. Chris, the other engineer, and I arrived last but went straight to work. We poured coffee in our cups, made a fresh pot, rubbed Jeep's ears, and dove into our adopted projects. Chris had chosen exterior paint touch-up, while I handled limb and leaf management. Rake. Saw. Pile. Drip torch. Burn. Sip coffee. Rake.

The meditative quality of Middletown winters let the frenzy of fire season roll off. We recharged ourselves, the station, and its equipment. Occasionally, someone would call for a medical assist or a pet in a well, but mostly we learned how to operate without the assistance of chaos. This was old-school forestry and something I hadn't experienced until now.

The bliss lasted a month, ending the morning Childress walked in with Jeep and a grimace. "Battalion 16 needs a body. Two months at Napa, two at Yountville."

Chris, Fistler, Franklin, and Mort all shook their heads, leaving Childress no option other than to swivel his head toward me and raise his eyebrows in apology.

"What just happened?" I asked.

Fistler explained, "Higher-ups wanna save money by not filling a vacancy. If someone leaves mid-winter, they look to us for cover. And we all said 'not-it' first."

I scrunched my eyes, realizing I'd just been screwed.

"We'll see you back here for fire season," Childress said.

<center>***</center>

Just outside the city limits, Napa Station felt like a small Belmont, with tamer animals. Urban engines responded to medical aids, traffic accidents, and occasional fires at businesses or vineyard-surrounded homes.

I dumped my duffel on an unblanketed bed.

"You don't want that one," an engineer told me.

I retrieved my bag, skipped past a blanketed bed, and set my bag on the next stripped one.

"You don't want that one either."

"Which one do I want?"

"That one in the corner is a safe bet."

I didn't ask why as a show of trust. That was always the priority: build trust.

The *why* presented itself to me that night: an engineer with a sleep disorder. He sleep-jumped. He kicked his covers off and jumped on his bed. Then he leapt to the bed on his left, back to his bed, then to the right—repeating until exhausted. Then he tucked himself back in.

In the morning, he recalled none of it. "That's bullshit. You're all messing with me."

But we weren't. For the two months I worked there, the beds on either side of him remained unblanketed, and I taught myself to sleep through ferocious bedspring squeaks.

When my rotation at Napa ended, I went to Yountville. Now, it's a showcase firehouse, but at the time it was a shithole—a tiny ramshackle set in the

V where two angled streets met. Two people staffed the quick-attack and a third person the quint. The quick-attack carried medical gear and half the water of a regular engine. The quint, short for "quintuple," combined engine functions (water, pump, and fire hose) with those of a truck (specialized ladders and equipment). It carried a giant generator to light a night scene, Jaws of Life for vehicle extrication, heavy rescue gear, a circular saw that could slice a steel wall like butter, and a variety of ladders, including a 100-foot snorkel that raised mechanically from a platform on top of the rig.

I'd worked with most of the tools, but this was my first "truck" assignment. The captain ran me though drills, showing me how to operate the snorkel and all the equipment. I did well with everything except the giant generator. I couldn't start it. It had a lawn mower–style pull cord I couldn't yank fast enough to turn the motor over. I pulled and pulled and pulled.

"You don't have the grip strength for this," my captain told me.

Sweat dripped from under my helmet, stinging my eyes. I'd been fire-fighting for eight years and a pull cord was defeating me. I felt like I was back at Pescadero with my enemy ladder. *What the fuck am I supposed to do now?* The only thing more important to me than being a firefighter, was *not being* a firefighter who couldn't do her job. I took deep breaths so tears wouldn't rise from anger or despair and wondered what Norm would tell me. This slowed my brain, and I could hear his voice. "Own it. Then fix it." It was simple, logical advice.

I looked at my captain. "You're right. I don't. But I will."

He nodded. "Alright, then. Let's get everything back on the rig."

Perennially scared of being an I-told-you-so cliché, I'd lost perspective. I didn't have to fret that my career was over. I simply had to shell out $4.99 for a grip-strength spring.

I carried the gripper with me everywhere, compressing its spring while standing in line at the grocery store, driving, watching TV, eating. It worked. More than that, it became a sort of pacifier for me. I still carry a gripper in my car for when I'm feeling weak or insecure.

Once settled in, I treasured my time on the truck. I enjoyed the self-sufficiency it inspired with its one-person operation. I liked it so much it blinded me into making a grave mistake.

"Can you trade shifts with me next week?" another engineer asked.

"Sure," I said. On days we worked together, he always let me cover the truck and he'd take the attack, so I felt indebted. And I'd paid zero attention to the chatter going on about "French Laundry night"—the night I'd just traded away without understanding its epicurean value. The French Laundry restaurant, steps from the firehouse, closed once a year to serve the on-duty firefighters. If the crew got a callout, they'd respond, then return. As long as it took, the restaurant made sure their hometown crew had a full meal of the best food they'd ever eaten.

Most mistakes crush you shortly after you make them. This one wouldn't raze me until twenty years later, which is when I finally understood that the French Laundry was the epicenter of an international culinary revolution creating the foodie movement.

When fire season started, I left Yountville and returned to Middletown. I loved being back there. We brought the seasonal firefighters on board in time for a fast, busy summer. High-speed blazes ripped through grass and dried oaks all over the county. I bonded with my firefighters as I led them through the season. They were hungry for action, wanting more from each incident. They reminded me of Scott and me at Big Creek, refusing to take our days off if they landed on the fire-certain Fourth of July weekend.

A month before the season ended, we got what we wanted: a furious flame front heading for a neighborhood above Clearlake. The incident commander pointed to a hilltop house in the fire's path, at the tip of the subdivision. If it caught fire, it would create enough heat and momentum to spread to the other tightly packed hillside homes. "You gotta save that house. Watch out for the propane tank."

The fire's head had spit hot brands that ignited grass under the tank. Its relief valve pitched at a high squeal, threatening a BLEVE.

"Full fog," I instructed the firefighter on the nozzle. He got a water curtain over the tank, cooling it enough to remove the threat. I called for a second line to advance toward the fire, now cresting the hill. As

we approached, the air color changed from iridescent bright to charcoal dark with an ominous peripheral glow. Hungry flames lapped at the back deck.

"Tanker 9-0, Engine 1375. Need immediate airdrop," I called over my handheld, then directed my two remaining firefighters, "On the ground." We belly-crawled the hose line toward the fire, blasting water at the approaching enemy while waiting for the drop to hit us from above.

Air-dropped retardant is made with a red-tinted powder containing chemicals that decrease the fire's temperature and slow its spread. The powder is mixed with water at airbases, then pumped into the aircraft's holding tanks. Pilots take off with full loads, anywhere from 800 to 19,000 gallons, depending on the size of the plane—1,200 the most common. Once over the fire, pilots have options. They can dump half the load (a split drop), parse it out in smaller consecutive drops (a trail drop), or dump the whole load in one spot (a salvo). That's what we needed from Tanker 9-0. And that's what it gave us: 1,200 gallons of viscous retardant that struck with a power and burn that seared almost as much as fire.

It worked. Slipping and sliding through the raspberry-colored retardant, I scrambled back to the engine to check the water level. My firefighters wrestled the hose line to the hill's edge at the back of the house and drenched flames the salvo had temporarily subdued.

At the end of it, we were a red, yellow, and black-tar mess, smiling from ear to ear. My firefighters had given one hundred percent, saved the house and the neighborhood, and capped their season with a blowout firefight.

Cold mornings returned Middletown to its off-season routine. I reclaimed the drip torch and went to work on burn piles, and Chris taught me how to build a fence from the postholes up. Then, once again, I lost my tranquil winter. This time, Fistler stole it.

"Captain's test is next fall," he said as I refilled my coffee cup. "You're taking it."

I answered as if his inflection had posed a question. "I guess so. I figure it'll take a couple tries to score high enough, so I might as well get the throwaway over with."

Fistler shook his head. "This is your last winter as engineer." He held his cup out, knowing what I didn't: that I would score well on my first try.

I topped him off. He continued, "You need a T and D run at a camp. It'll be your chance to test-drive before you buy. A quarter of new captains' positions are at camps now."

Training and Development details allowed employees to acquire familiarity with programs they'd had little exposure to—like me with the camp program. Jointly operated by the state Department of Corrections and Cal Fire, the program allows eligible inmates to seek training for and assignment to a minimum-security facility called a "conservation camp." During the workday, Corrections turns the crews over to Cal Fire to work on land-improvement projects like fuel reduction or creek bed restoration. But if an emergency breaks, they respond as an elite firefighting handcrew.

It's a good deal for everyone. The state gets thousands of extraordinarily fit handcrew members who taxpayers already fund. The inmates get improved incarceration conditions, time off their sentences, and a chance to serve a society they'd been found guilty of harming. It shouldn't work, but it does. One unarmed captain takes seventeen convicted felons into the back country with chainsaws and axes, and together they become a motivated, unparalleled workforce that flips *The Shawshank Redemption*'s chain-gang model on its head.

I heeded Fistler's advice and spent the rest of the winter at Delta Camp, located at the southeastern tip of the unit. My boss made me read *Games Criminals Play* before I showed up. It's about how inmates try to manipulate Corrections personnel. In one winter, I saw the camp inmates literally try every trick in that book. But they also impressed me. It's amazing how much work seventeen people can accomplish when they have purpose and are treated as interesting individuals. And, I discovered, if every now and then you pick up a shovel and sweat beside them, they'll work double time.

"You scared of fire?" a crew member named Jules asked me as we scraped dirt side by side on a trail restoration project.

"Not as scared as I should be," I said, pausing before asking, "What scares you, Jules?"

"No-brainer, Boss. Being alone. Ask any guy out here, he'll say the same thing."

Maybe that's why escapes were rare, and short-lived.

While most days didn't bring trouble, some did. Sometimes a fight between rival gang members prompted the captain to call a Corrections deputy to haul all the combatants back to the Big House—they'd just lost the privilege of working at a camp. Sometimes just one crew member would be in a mood. Then he'd be fine, but now he'd have a black eye that no one saw happen. The captain could roll up the whole crew or keep it working, since peace had been restored and maybe the captain just hadn't noticed the black eye earlier.

The trouble spots paled when compared to pinnacle moments the program created. My favorite was when the crew, dead-tired from a ferocious firefight, saw hand-painted signs lining a highway back to camp: "Thank You, Firefighters!!!!"

"That's us," a crew member yelled. "They thanking *us*. Damn." Then all seventeen whooped and hollered the rest of the way back to camp, ready to go again.

After Delta Camp, I returned to Middletown for another high-speed summer that burned through Lake County's golden hillsides. I almost missed Kelsey-Cobb's frozen barracks as we battled blazes during a scorching heat wave peaking at 114°F. I don't remember the skirmishes, but I recall a creek revealing itself to my crew and me after a firefight. Caked in sweat and char, we walked in—boots and all—and dipped our heads into the creek's pure, orgasmic coolness.

In early fall, the air crisped and I signed up for classes at the community college. Every semester I'd try to knock out a few more units. More often

than not, I had to withdraw when Santa Ana winds lit up Southern California. But it was always worth a shot, and it gave me access to the college pool for lap swimming.

At the time, I lived with my sister Tera, and we'd go to the pool together. Midway through October, it was almost too cold for the outdoor pool. We decided to go one last time.

The swim team must be early today, I thought, as I felt the pool water slosh around me. I didn't let it distract my pace. When I reached the pool's edge for a turn, Tera slapped my hand. I stopped and looked up. She frantically said, "Out of the pool!" I was the last one still in. There was no swim team. An earthquake 120 miles away had caused the slosh.

We drove home, listening to the news on the car radio. The 6.9 earthquake disrupted the World Series and broke the Bay Bridge. The epicenter was in Santa Cruz.

Our sister Bernadette was safe in Arizona. But Mom, Dad, Annie, Mark, and Cathy lived in Santa Cruz. Tera and I tried to call them as soon as we got home, but the Santa Cruz phone lines were down.

I called my command center. "Hey, Tanner. It's Bisbee. Where should I report?"

"Childress is taking a strike team down. Engines are covered, but he wants you riding with him. You know those mountains. He'll pick you up at Saint Helena."

"Copy. Hey, can you check with Felton HQ to see if my brother is on duty, and okay?"

"You got it," Tanner said.

Childress led his five engines south. By the time we hit the Santa Cruz Mountains, we'd heard the reports. Fifty-seven dead. Thousands injured. Two freeways collapsed. Still no phones.

I didn't talk. My chest felt tight, and I wasn't in the mood. When I needed Childress to turn, I pointed with my arms, like Verner. This was fine with Childress, who wasn't a big yakker.

Dispatch radioed us: "Your brother's fine. On duty at Belmont. Out on calls."

I sucked in a deep breath. Relief and oxygen filled my lungs. One okay, four more to go.

Childress tilted his head, keeping one eye on the road, and one on me.

When we arrived at Felton headquarters, the place I'd first signed my firefighter papers, Childress handed me his keys. "Engines are refueling. I'll confirm assignments. Go check your parents."

I grabbed the keys. To avoid a jammed freeway, I took surface streets. It gave me a front-row view of the carnage—homes and businesses reduced to rubble. Dubbed the Loma Prieta Earthquake, its rolling action—a phenomenon called liquefaction, when solids act like liquids—left patchwork damage: unscathed next to scathed. It felt like driving through a Dalí painting.

I passed St. Patrick's Church, the one my parents went to. The quake had crumbled the west half of this 1903 Gothic sanctuary, reducing its stately steeple to a debris pile. When I pulled onto my parents' street a few blocks away, I saw their house intact. I rushed inside. It was a mess, with broken dishes and glassware, toppled bookcases, and papers soaked in an earthquake soup from a leaking pipe and liquids spat from the fridge and cupboards. But Mom, Dad, and Annie were fine, and they'd heard from Cathy. Everyone accounted for, I hurried back to Felton.

I tossed Childress his keys. "Thanks, Boss."

He tossed them back. "Your stomping grounds. Your show."

For two weeks, I navigated our strike team through neighborhoods where we extinguished smoldering structures and filled out pages and pages of damage reports. We handed out bottled water and kind words to wrecked residents. If their house had been spared, they felt survivor's guilt. If not, they cried themselves dry while combing through dust, hoping to salvage a photo album or a treasured heirloom teapot. The few with burnt homes and dry eyes made us wonder if they'd pulled their treasures out before torching their own houses for the insurance.

I'd seen post-fire damage before—residents digging through ashes—but not in a 100-mile swath, displacing tens of thousands of people at once. The collective suffering was palpable and kept us from reverting to tasteless firefighter humor. Usually on long assignments someone would bust out

with an irritating *"Cha-ching!"*—shorthand for letting others know it was the start of days off, and therefore overtime pay. Even youngsters who'd never heard a mechanical cash register had adopted it. But among these ruins, it felt wrong. Instead, a bunch of us pledged our overtime to recovery efforts. I wrote my check to St. Patrick's Church.

IV.
GROWTH

Dad decided to move us from Ventura to Ashland, Oregon, shortly after I turned ten. If Ventura was free burn, Ashland was growth—the bad kind. A fire enters the growth stage when it spreads beyond the initial area. Fuels preheated by free-burning flames catch more quickly. The fire accelerates. Spreads. Destroys.

I don't remember the reason Dad gave, only that he promised this would be our final move. He bought us a trampoline, and I started fifth grade. I liked my new teacher—and a boy named Levi. He had curly brown hair and bright eyes and was nice to me on the first day, even though he had friends. We played basketball at recess and shared brown bag lunches. And eventually, the backs of our hands accidentally-on-purpose touched. He smiled, showing off cheekbones that had recently become more prominent. Then he missed school for two weeks.

After Levi's funeral—leukemia, they said—I cried inconsolably. Dad tried to comfort me. "It's okay. Your pal is at God's side now." A jealous tone seeped through. Dad had a quick wit, prone to clever puns and practical jokes, but not lately. These days, he spent family time lambasting the government and researching communes.

Dad's mood had a cascading effect. Annie's progress stalled—she became less verbal. Bernadette ran away for a few weeks. Tera began locking herself in the bathroom for long stints. Cathy earned a scholarship and left to study abroad in Thailand. Mark wasn't as available since, for the first time, we weren't in the same school. And I lost two pound puppies in a row. It was a lot of compounded loss for me. If I trace it back, this may have been when I first learned to compartmentalize, to shut down emotions that wouldn't do anything to bring back Levi, my siblings, my puppies, my dad. I'd be okay with leaving Ashland—until we did, and Dad made me drop off my new dog at the pound on the way out of town.

CHAPTER 13

FUGITIVES

State Fire Headquarters, 11 Months Left

Governor Brown declared a drought state of emergency, which played out by mid-May. We'd already had over 1,400 wildfires—twice that of "normal" for this time of year. One four-day stretch brought 120 wildfires. It was a May that felt like a July.

When I stepped outside with Brody for his morning walk, I told him, "Feels like a fire day, little B-Man." It reminded me of my days at Corralitos, when I'd retrieve the morning paper. If the air felt dry on my forearms and a northeast breeze carried the scent of the garlic fields from Gilroy, I'd come back in and say, "Garlic is in the air," and they'd all know what that meant.

But the fire activity wasn't why our Cheez-It crew congregated around Ken's conference table earlier than usual. Nursing morning coffees in front of the muted television, we were there because a banner on the bottom of the screen said BATTALION CHIEF STILL MISSING.

"No way he did it," Red said.

Ken unmuted when a picture of our battalion chief appeared on a split screen alongside the news anchor, reporting what we already knew. Moe Fleming had abandoned his bloodied response vehicle on Apricot Woods

Way, two miles from where he lived with his girlfriend, who had been murdered inside the house. And nobody knew where Moe was.

I suppose we were waiting for the news to report a twist in the tragic caper, that Moe sustained injuries while defending his girlfriend, then chased the real killer, first in his fire pickup truck, then on foot. But my gut knew better. I'd met Moe two years earlier at the academy, where he worked as a captain in my line of command. The academy chiefs wanted me to approve his promotion to battalion chief, so they asked me to join them for lunch. As soon as I sat down, I felt a creepy vibe. Moe wore a gold chain and fondled his moustache, and I remember thinking, *He seems very in love with himself.* Still, I signed the papers. I didn't want to micromanage.

Ken re-muted the television, and a collective sigh filled the air. We moved on to the business of it, stuffing our feelings down. They could seep out later, away from work. We handled press inquiries, assigned stress counselors to academy staff and cadets, set up legislative and gubernatorial briefings, arranged for security at the academy, and issued a department-wide admonishment acknowledging the gravity, but reminding everyone we had work to do in this already fire-laden year.

<p style="text-align:center">***</p>

Heading home for the weekend, I grabbed my backpack, a sandwich bag of chicken from the loft fridge, and Brody's leash. Brody plodded down the hallway while I locked the door. He stopped and waited for me at the top of the stairs. I scooted ahead of him and laid a bite of chicken on every fourth stair. At the bottom, I put several bites on the floor—booty for braving the journey. I saved enough chicken to get him up the ramp and into the back of my Jeep. This was a hard-bargained settlement. At one point it had taken me a whole chicken.

By the time we got to San Jose, Bud had gone to bed. He'd left out a bowl of popcorn and a short pour of scotch. I kicked off my boots and tapped the couch. Brody jumped up and nestled his jowls between the back cushion and my thighs. "How come you won't do stairs, but you can jump up here?" He didn't answer. He was already asleep.

With the television on low volume, I surveyed our living room, now scattered with moving boxes. Bud and I had been playing at looking for a place to retire for the last five years. I thought it would be here, but crowds and crime were on the rise. And on a trip to see Bud's sister in Reno, we stumbled on a rural hamlet backed into the Sierra Nevada foothills near Lake Tahoe, two hours northeast of Sacramento. We found a house sooner than expected, and Bud had just retired, so we sold our home and bought the new one. We'd move the next weekend. After that, Brody and I would head to the Sierra instead of to San Jose on our weekend drives home.

At daybreak, Bud and I stumbled downstairs for caffeination. Bud usually didn't speak until his second or sometimes third cup. But this morning he started right in.

"What the fuck is up with that missing battallion chief?"

"Falls squarely in the category of, 'You can't make this shit up,'" I said.

After coffee, we wrapped plates and packed boxes. I kept my phone close and the news on. Nothing new had surfaced, but the banner now called Moe a FUGITIVE ON THE RUN.

By Sunday night, we'd completed most of the packing. Bud would finish up during the week. At dawn, I grabbed chicken from the fridge and headed back to Sacramento with Brody.

All week, we circled up in Ken's office at the end of the day. He dumped Cheez-Its on the morning newspaper, obscuring salacious details squeezed from neighbors and relatives since Moe was still missing. The stories revealed that 55-year-old Moe met his 26-year-old girlfriend Sarah through an escort service. She quit when Moe opted for exclusive rights at $2,000 a month. Moe wanted Sarah to marry him, but a divorce from his previous wife was still in process, and Sarah figured out she wanted to dump Moe. On the night of the murder, Sarah went to a casino with her sister and mother, then returned home. Around midnight, the sister phoned Sarah, heard arguing, then Sarah's "bloodcurdling scream," then a dead phone. The sister went to check on things in the morning.

We crunched on Cheez-Its, trying to make sense of it.

"In the morning? That's so fucked up," I said.

"The sister must have been toasted. They'd been partying at a casino," Ken said.

"Too ripped to bloody call 9-1-1?" Griffin chimed in.

"Two grand a month?" Red focused on the fiscal aspect.

"Son of a biscuit," Turbo said, looking up from her phone and pointing at the muted television with a BREAKING NEWS ribbon claiming Moe's estranged wife had seen a videotape of Moe and other firefighters having sex with prostitutes on fire engines at the academy.

"We've landed in the middle of a goddamn Lifetime movie," Turbo said.

We scraped stray Cheez-Its into the trash, our appetites gone. If the allegation was true, it had happened on our watch: a heaping mess on top of a mad murder. If it wasn't, we were about to overreact to an unverified rumor and further disrupt an already unsettled academy—the place we indoctrinated our force with single-word posters hung on the classroom walls: HONOR, COURAGE, LEADERSHIP, INTEGRITY.

We'd have to go big and outsource the sex-tape investigation to our law enforcement counterpart, the California Highway Patrol, CHP. If we conducted it in-house and found nothing, headlines would scream COVER-UP and FRATERNAL PROTECTION. We launched the department's most extensive investigation in its known history, because it was the only way to clear our firefighters. But sometimes when you dig, you'll find dirt you weren't looking for.

The week rolled on with fires breaking in Southern California in record numbers and Moe still requiring attention. Red's shop completed paperwork terminating Moe for being AWOL—absent without leave. We couldn't fire him for alleged murder, but we could for not showing up to work. So whether or not Moe killed Sarah, he was done at Cal Fire.

Next, we had to deal with the sheriff's disturbing WANTED FOR MURDER poster.

"This has to be posted in every firehouse, camp, airbase, and command center," Ken said.

He was right. All battalion chiefs possessed a key that gave them access to every state firehouse, and Moe hadn't left his keys in his abandoned

truck. My stomach roiled as I wrestled with how this would impact the troops. Moe would be the only person besides the US president and Cal Fire's director to ever have his face posted in all 912 facilities.

At the end of the week, we sat in Ken's office again. Our chief counsel, Steph, joined us. "Where do you think he is?" she asked the group.

"I think he offed himself. They just haven't found the body yet," Ken said.

Griffin reached for a handful of crackers. "Hopped a train. He'll end up hiding in plain sight in New York City. That's what I'd do."

"I think someone is harboring him," Turbo said.

I leaned back in my chair and put my boots on the table. This was a smart group, but I had sat next to Moe at that lunch table. He was too narcissistic and cocky for suicide, flight, or an assist. "I think he's playing Survivor-Man in the backcountry."

The press kept all our bids alive. *Good Morning America, NY Daily News, Huffington Post, America's Most Wanted*, all the broadcast networks, and a barrage of local channels and papers fed off Moe's absence and the promise of a sex tape.

"Is it remotely possible Moe is innocent?" Red asked. She must have had her mom hat on. The rest of us shook our heads.

"Christ on a pony," Turbo said, while scrolling her phone screen. "New text messages released from the wife. Moe asked her to come pick him up two days before the murder, then sent a message two hours after the murder saying, 'You should have come and picked me up.' Then there's a frowny-face emoji."

"Still think he's innocent?" Ken asked Red.

"Hang 'em high," Red said. The rest of us nodded, packed away the crackers, cleaned up crumbs, and tossed the newspaper into RECYCLE. I went home for the weekend with bright orange cracker dust on the side of my navy uniform pants, having tried to wipe my fingers clean.

On Saturday morning, Bud and I loaded the back of our Penske rental truck. I would drive it and meet Bud and his pickup at our new home.

"It's going to take me a while to get over the pass," I said.

Bud kissed me. "I'll turn on lights, start a fire, and have scotch waiting for you."

I climbed into the Penske. It had been over a decade since I promoted past fire engine driving and into the chief ranks. But my hands automatically moved to 9 and 3 on the wheel, and I easily steered the 35-footer toward to the freeway. Two hundred thirteen miles and an 8,500-foot Sierra pass stood between me and my glass of scotch.

I set a good pace, knowing darkness would envelop sooner than I wanted. By dusk, I'd reached the foothills on the western side and began to climb Carson Pass. A Cal Fire engine coming the opposite direction screamed past me, Code 3. I hadn't noticed any smoke or traffic collisions on my way up.

When I rounded the curve, a van pulled out of the firehouse driveway. *This is weird*, I thought. *Why would a van leave mid-shift while the crew is on a call?* I looked closer. The van didn't have any plates. A few words on the WANTED poster flashed in my head:

> It is believed Fleming has fled the area in an unknown vehicle. He is an avid outdoorsman and frequents the Sierra Mountains. . . . Fleming has keys to Cal Fire facilities throughout the state. He might have changed his appearance by shaving his head and moustache.

Ho-ly crap. He must have stolen the van, stripped its plates, and called in a fake alarm to empty the station. Then he raided it for wilderness essentials: toilet paper, C-rations, blankets, maybe a spare pillow—items the crew wouldn't miss until end-of-month inventory.

I sped up to get a better look. The van accelerated. I pushed the Penske, getting close enough for a glimpse through the driver's-side mirror. Bingo:

a middle-aged, ball-capped white guy with no moustache and sunglasses. He had a woman passenger.

Is she another escort? Is she his wife? Did he kidnap her? Fuck. I had no cell service and no radio. The curves took him out of sight. I throttled harder, bordering on too hard. My mind charged back to my flipped fire engine.

I let up on the accelerator but leaned forward. I spotted the van fleeing onto a dirt road too rutted for my Penske. Peering through the trailing dust, I locked the van and road details in my memory. I'd wait for cell service on the other side of the pass and call it in.

My heart thundered from the pursuit. But soon I had to shift my attention. A dimming sky delivered unexpected snow flurries that formed hidden ice patches on the darkening asphalt. I moved at a painful pace, certain it was too late to track Moe off my sighting. Cresting the pass, I began a dangerous, dark descent down the ice-slicked highway. Skidding and slipping, I could smell my brakes burning through frozen air.

I learned how to skid an engine at the fire academy. The instructors taught us, "It's controlled bedlam." Moe must have taught that class dozens of times. What happened to him that he couldn't control his own slide?

The bottom of the pass spit me into a straight stretch that fed me oxygen and slowed my pulse. It quieted my mind enough to make me question myself before calling the sheriff. What would I say? *I saw Moe Fleming ninety minutes ago. He stole a van, captured a hostage, burglarized a firehouse, and evaded my Penske in a high-speed mountain pursuit. You'll know it's him because he'll be clean-shaven and he may or may not have a pillow.*

I felt an internal shift—my tectonic plates settling after a rattling. Liquefaction retreating. It became clear. I had manifested Moe. He wouldn't have let me stay on his tail for over twelve miles. He had the same driver training I did, a faster ride, and a reason to run. My fury created him, to try to fix what I had broken when I signed the damn approval form.

The psychological tremor marinated me in the horror of what he'd done. Until now, I hadn't focused on the dead, mangled 26-year-old beauty.

Or on the bloodstains on the fire vehicle upholstery that could be cleaned but never exonerated. Or on the lasting damage to the department. Years from now, new firefighters won't know why their captain calls kitchen knives "Flemings," or why the daily task board misspells the same word every Thursday: "Moe the lawn. Cut it real good."

In the privacy of my Penske, I choked up, then ranted, "Goddamn Moe. Goddamn press—making everything worse. You're not helping find him. You're not helping Sarah or her family. And you're killing a little piece of every twenty-year-old firefighter who used to don the uniform with pride. Fuckers."

This was why firefighters had to retire young. Most of us revel in the job. But none of us gets to deal with an imprinting incident before we move on to the next. Like the cargo box of my Penske, every load left a scratch or two on the inside.

I blew breath out my cheeks, composing myself as I pulled into our lighted driveway.

Brody greeted me with a long hug. "How was the drive? Little icy on the pass, eh?"

"Uneventful," I said, knowing he knew better. Inside, we collapsed into lawn chairs in front of a fire he built in our new fireplace. He poured eighteen-year-old single-malt scotch into red plastic picnic cups we clicked together in a toast. The fire crackled, transporting me to a calmer place. Now, a state and weekend away from my office, I felt I'd found a safe harbor.

Bud splashed a second finger of scotch into our cups, waiting for me to replay my run over Carson Pass. I spilled every detail.

"Wow. The press would have a field day with that," he said, smiling.

I laughed. "I can see it: Three-star chief goes mad in a Penske—sex tape still missing."

Sixteen days after the murder, a deputy sheriff found Moe near his riverbed hideout not two blocks from the murder scene. He'd been there the whole time. When he ran out of food, he got sloppy and went out in daylight. The

deputy recognized him. Moe surrendered. Ken sent out a department-wide e-mail: "Now that Mr. Fleming has been arrested by the authorities, you are free to remove the Wanted posters from all Cal Fire facilities."

And for a brief few months, Moe Fleming wouldn't be at the forefront of our minds.

CHAPTER 14

GANJA

Felton Fire Station, 1990

Two months before my twenty-fifth birthday, I made captain ten yards from where Peters had told me I wouldn't last one season. As Fistler predicted, I did well on the test, and then on an interview, thanks to the chiefs back in Saint Helena.

They'd wanted their folks to make a good showing, so they gave us study time and mock interviews with individualized reviews. Some got advice on demeanor: "Stop touching your face." Some on content: "No. Sending overtime checks to the stations so your family won't know about them is not a department priority." The advice for me: "Wear a sleeveless blouse to any interviews you get, so they can see your muscles. Don't want them stereotyping."

Coming from one of the last units to bring on a permanent female made me want to follow the advice. I bought a sleeveless top and wore it underneath my suit jacket for my first interview, which happened to be at Felton Unit Headquarters. I never took my jacket off. But there was something about being sleeveless inside it that felt rogue—like I was Grace fucking Jones in *Conan the Barbarian*, and in an instant could unleash. My mentors had thought the shirt would inspire others to have

confidence in me. Instead, it expelled my own doubt. I delivered quick, sure answers, bordering on cocky. The panel liked it and offered me the job. I'd be the new Felton Station captain, reporting to Ricochet.

After the interview, I returned to Middletown to finish out the week and clear my locker. On my last day, the same five men who'd welcomed me with hard stares and crossed arms encircled me. "We're taking the afternoon off. Ditch your uniform shirt and come with us."

Franklin, the dozer operator, lived across the street from the station. He chewed on his toothpick while setting a cooler of beers on his front porch. In our T-shirts and work pants, we pulled tabs from ice-cold cans and embellished stories about our time together, never mentioning the two elephants on the porch. They hadn't been prepared to be impressed by me as a female, nor I by them as rednecks. But they taught me the ebb and flow of rural firehouses and the Zen of building fences, spackling Sheetrock, and drip-torching late autumn leaves. And I'd learned that leadership means making the first pot of coffee for your crew on a cold winter morning.

Franklin handed me a present. They all watched as I tore wrapping paper off a shirt box. I opened it and removed a large pink T-shirt that said, "Boss Lady." I laughed, knowing I'd never wear it. I hated pink and it was way too big. I was the same size I'd been when I arrived, but maybe now they saw me as bigger.

Their effort got to me. I took a quick swig of beer, hoping to swallow the lump forming in my throat. "I'm gonna miss you guys." I followed with a long pull to make the lump inaccessible. Questions flashed through my head. *Am I ready for this? Will I hate working at a headquarters station? Can I be the leader my crew needs?*

Fistler saw my internal wheels spinning. He downed half his beer in a gulp and delivered a solid punch to my shoulder. "You're gonna do great."

"Yeah, you are," Chris said. "I'll call you for tips when I get an interview." He was waiting for a captain's opening in this unit so he wouldn't have to move his family. He raised his palm for a high five. I slapped it, then we gripped in a handshake like we did when we nailed the last board of the fence we'd built, and like we'd do again twenty-three years later working together at State Fire Headquarters.

Childress raised his beer. "Give 'em hell." We tapped cans in the center of our circle—a good-bye sending me into the wind of my next chapter.

The first captain to arrive at the scene of a call makes high-stakes decisions. What's the first move when you pull up to an apartment building with several floors on fire, or to a wildfire raging toward a cul-de-sac but also threatening hundreds of horses, or to a busy freeway with an overturned tanker truck spilling chemicals that will melt firefighter boots? More than any other rank in the department, a captain must be able to issue sound orders in an instant. But at the firehouse, a captain's job is more like that of a house parent: keep the utilities on, complete the household paperwork, maintain the grounds, and assign chores.

To cover the span, a good captain must have a heavy hand and a soft touch. I started out a crappy captain. To prove I could lead, I turned into an autocrat, micromanaging the shit out of everything from morning cleanup to a simple hose lay on an early-season fire. I thought I was doing great, capping off exemplary guidance with showy humility by always helping with the dinner dishes.

My most seasoned firefighter, eight years my senior, found a way to let me know while he washed, and I dried. "My friend in another unit works for a badge-heavy captain. Any advice I should give?" he asked. He handed me a wet bowl and held eye contact long enough for me to understand he was talking about my new badge.

I took the bowl and wiped it dry. I must have dried it four times before putting it on the counter, handing him my dish towel, and giving him a thank-you nod. "I think your friend will figure out a gentle way to say, 'Hey, Cap, don't tell us how to unroll hose, and let *us* do the dishes—it's our job,'" I said.

I made immediate adjustments, swinging too far the other direction. My new hands-off approach meant I missed it when this same firefighter and an engineer told me every day after changing into their workout clothes, "Hey, Cap, we're going to run the loop. We'll take a handheld."

Later, I learned this meant, "Hey, Cap, we're going to jog out of sight, smoke a doobie, then go to the Quik Stop for Doritos. We'll take a handheld."

My captain partner, Matt, didn't know anything about it either until another firefighter brought it to his attention. Then Matt told me. Then the two of us took it to Ricochet with a recommendation of suspension pending a law enforcement investigation.

"How long has this been going on?" Ricochet chewed his gum at speed and glared at me. Matt had more time in, but other than a cigarette habit, he was a damn Boy Scout. Ricochet didn't expect Matt to catch devious behavior.

"We just found out about it," I said.

Ricochet shook his head at me. Disappointment. I'd need to find a leadership style somewhere between badge-heavy and too trusting.

The investigation landed the pot smokers in rehab, then at new stations on probationary status. Neither would make it more than a few years before slipping off the edge again. The engineer was the son of high-ranking brass in Sacramento. Because this hadn't dissuaded Matt and me, we earned a reputation as tacklers. That's why we got Arlo.

In his early thirties, Arlo presented well—fit, with a swimmer's build, chlorine-highlighted dirty-blond hair, pressed uniform. He greeted everyone with a broad smile and an "aw-shucks" Owen Wilson drawl that made him look and sound earnest. Straight out of the engineer academy in Ione, he came to us with a few seasons under his belt in the "Emerald Triangle"—a northeastern three-county area named for its burgeoning cannabis industry. Rumors arrived with Arlo. He was "a wobbler"—someone who barely passed the academy. The brass had decided their new tacklers could take on Arlo as a make-or-break project.

Matt and I sat Arlo down in the office to give him our expectations. He took notes and nodded at everything we said, adding enthusiastic comments like "Absolutely" and "You bet." When we asked him if he had any questions, he shook his head no, then told us, "I just want you to know, I'm a former addict. But I found Christ and cleaned up. I've been clean for years and I'm super-excited to be here."

I liked it that Arlo called himself a "former addict." When my sister Cathy felt compelled to describe herself during intermittent bouts with

recovery, she always used present tense. "I'm an alcoholic in recovery," she announced, like she couldn't ever see herself beating the affliction. I knew it was in vogue, that treatment programs proclaimed, "Once an addict, always an addict." But I didn't believe the motto, because my family tree had all the addictions on it: food, sex, alcohol, drugs, gambling, sadomasochism—you name it. And those who got enough treatment before it killed them could have a drink, eat food, or have sex without spiraling.

Matt and I looked at each other and shrugged. Maybe the academy unfairly held Arlo's past against him. As far as we could tell, Arlo was eager and self-aware. He'd be an easy project.

Arlo landed on my shift. On our first morning together, I started with the obvious. "Equipment check first thing, okay? The firefighters will handle station cleanup."

"What do you want me to check?" Arlo asked.

"The equipment," I said.

"Which equipment?" he asked.

"The fire engine and the tools on it." I spoke slowly, like to a child, questioning whether I'd somehow been unclear.

"Right. But how?"

"How they taught you at the academy."

It had taken him twenty seconds to flip me. I yelled at him in my head. *How many fucking brain cells did you kill as an addict?* I felt duped by his previous avowal to Matt and me.

I drew air through my nostrils and deep into my diaphragm, then exhaled slowly. "Arlo, you're responsible for making sure the engine and everything on it is operationally ready."

He stared at me.

"Do you understand 'operational readiness'?"

The word "yes" came out of his mouth, but he shook his head no.

"Follow me."

Working on creating a balance between micromanaging and empowering, I went inside to find the firefighters. The two most seasoned, Mario and Tunheim, were showing a new rookie, Heather, how to mop station

floors using the dependable infinity motion—sideways figure eights that ensured no missed spots.

"You smell nice," Arlo blurted out, staring at Heather.

My eyes narrowed. He was going to be a problem on all fronts. I broke one of my rules and corrected him in front of his subordinates. "You can't say that, Arlo."

"Why not? She smells good."

"Because how Heather smells has nothing to do with how good a firefighter she is. It's just the lotion she buys. Focus on the firefighter stuff, Arlo, not the lotion." He looked confused.

Mario and Tunheim both raised their arms and sniffed their pits, feigning offense at Arlo's favoritism.

"The floor looks sharp. Nice job," I said. "I need to borrow you, Mario."

I left Heather and Tunheim with the mops and brought Mario out with Arlo and me. "Can you please show Arlo how to do a morning equipment check?"

"Sure, Cap. No problem," Mario said.

I retreated to the captain's office, which had a window looking out to the apparatus bay, so I could observe. Once I was out of the picture, Arlo seemed to remember at least part of what he'd learned at the academy. He worked easily with Mario, laughing and back-slapping him and completing the equipment check.

This pattern repeated itself throughout the shift. I'd give Arlo an assignment. He'd lock up. I'd have him work with Mario or Tunheim, and he'd manage his way through.

At shift change, I briefed Matt. "There's definitely a problem. Some of it seems to be retention related, but there's something else going on. I don't have it figured out yet."

The next several shifts, I continued to press him. "Arlo, you have to show me you can do this job." I ran him through pumping tests he'd passed at the academy, but couldn't pass in front of me. So I gave him a poor performance report. If he got two more like it, he wouldn't pass his probationary period and he'd need to find a new profession. Arlo didn't react when I talked him through the bad report and handed him his copy.

That night, I figured it out. After dinner, Arlo called his fiancée from a station phone next to the dayroom. At low volume, you could manage a private conversation. But I heard him very clearly when he screamed into the phone, "I'm the man, that's why! You're to do exactly as I tell you! It's what God wants! That's why *He* put it in the Bible!"

There it was. Arlo locked up around me because his religion told him men were in charge and women were to follow without question. My giving him orders apparently triggered his brain's hypothalamus, which reacts to extreme stress by entering a fight, flight, or freeze mode. It seemed my collar brass combined with my ovaries threatened his salvation and froze his brain.

It didn't infuriate me. I'd spent enough time with my God to know that his God didn't exist. I felt sorry for Arlo and scared for his fiancée. Still, I wanted him to know that I'd heard his conversation with her, so I walked past the phone. Arlo changed his volume and tone. "We'll sort this out when I get home, Sweetie." I shook my head but didn't say anything to him about it before he went off shift.

When he came back on shift the following week, his forearms were covered in cuts.

"What the hell, Arlo? Are you okay?" I asked.

According to Arlo, his fiancée had "tried to scissor herself," but he "handled it."

"She's okay now," he told me. And he'd appreciate it if I didn't use the word "hell."

"Arlo. We have employee counseling and support services. You need to call." Arlo flashed his smile at me, then got up and left the room. He went straight to Ricochet's office.

An hour later, Arlo walked out, and Ricochet called me in. Ricochet unwrapped a new pack of gum and offered me a piece. I accepted. Spearmint filled the air as he caught me up.

"Arlo asked to be taken off your shift."

"Fine," I said. "But Matt works Sundays. That's Arlo's church day."

Ricochet shook his head. "He doesn't want to work with you, *and* he doesn't want to work on Sundays."

"That shift doesn't exist," I said.

"I know. That's why I denied the request. But . . ." Ricochet paused, chomping his gum.

"But what?"

"He's filing a formal charge. Religious discrimination. You're going to be investigated."

"*I'm* getting investigated?" I said. "The dude has scissor cuts all over his arms. He needs help. His fiancée needs help. And he's incapable of following orders or completing simple engineer tasks. And you're the one that just denied his request. Why am I the target?"

Ricochet laughed. "I think we both know why. Look. Stick to the facts. You'll be fine."

A few days later, I sat in front of the investigation panel in the same room I'd been interviewed in for my promotion. This time, my captain's uniform and a fresh pour of high-octane coffee provided my confidence.

Typically, discrimination complaints involve one-on-one interviews with a lead investigator. But this time there were multiple interrogators, because Arlo also claimed I'd failed to properly train him under the guidelines of the statewide apprenticeship standards. This drew a crew from the Sacramento training office and his union representative.

The interrogators wore button-up shirts and ties, and the union guy sported a polo. One of the button-ups with a crew cut and wide shoulders started the questioning.

"Is it fair to say that you haven't had exposure to a lot of religion, that you're not religious?"

"I'm not sure where you got that intel," I said, holding back.

"It's apparent from the complaint. But yes, let's go ahead and establish it. You've had little exposure to religion, right?"

I took a sip of coffee. "I suppose it's relative," I said, easing my way into a rant.

Crew Cut placed a check mark on the sheet in front of him, ready to move on.

I looked him in the eye and spewed, "My dad was a theology professor at a Jesuit university after serving as a Trappist monk and seminarian.

My mom was educated by Catholic nuns before attending a nonsectarian university. Mom and Dad raised us Catholic but encouraged ecumenical beliefs. So, I've read from the Bible—New and Old Testaments—*The Prophet*, Marcus Aurelius, Thomas Merton, *The Book of Mormon*, the *Bhagavad Gita*, Corrie ten Boom, Buddhist and Taoist teachings, and a host of others that don't immediately come to mind. I can provide a more complete list if you'd like."

I stopped for another sip of coffee and relaunched. "I've attended countless Catholic services and a few Protestant, Lutheran, Methodist, Charismatic Christian, Quaker, Unitarian, and nondenominational ones. I went to a youth Bible camp, spent time on a Mennonite farm, stayed at a Jewish kibbutz, and visited over a dozen Christian communes. I've been to Jericho, Jerusalem, the Wailing Wall, the Islamic Dome of the Rock, and all three of Christ's supposed Bethlehem birthplaces and their gift shops. I've kissed a bishop's ring. I believe in God and have maintained a faith practiced outside of church walls, but I'm open to people believing in whatever works for them—whatever makes them the best they can be. Compared to some, that might be considered 'little exposure to religion.' So yeah, it's relative."

Ricochet smiled from ear to ear while Crew Cut stared at me with wide eyes. We spent the remainder of the session talking about training and whether I was too harsh with Arlo. Religion didn't come up again. In the end, Arlo was allowed to transfer back to the Emerald Triangle's cannabis-filled forests. I never saw him again.

The Emerald Triangle wasn't the only place with cannabis in its forests. The Santa Cruz Mountains tucked away hundreds of clandestine grows. One almost killed me.

In autumn, we got dispatched to a "smoke check" in Nisene Marks State Park. I saw white wisps spiraling through the thick redwood canopy as I turned the engine onto a back road. The trees weren't on fire, but something on the ground underneath was.

I slowed. "Looks like we might be able to access on foot through this grove," I told Mario and Tunheim. "Let's go scout it."

I pulled on the engine's hissing spring brake. We took hand tools with us. Peaty duff and coast redwood needles filled the air. It also smelled like a skunk had recently passed this way. At a fork in the footpath, I said, "You two go left. I'll go right."

About one hundred yards in, I spotted a clearing that looked like the source of the smoke. I quickened my pace. Then, I heard three sounds in rapid succession. *Click. BANG! Whir.* Something grazed the front of my Nomex shirt at warp speed. Then I heard a *clunk.*

I stood, paralyzed in the moment, trying to process what had happened and what I should do next. I looked to where I'd heard the last sound and saw a bucket mounted to a tree branch below a Polaroid camera. A green-coated wire rested on top of my right boot.

"Yo, Cap! You good?" I heard Tunheim yell.

"Yeah. But there's some kind of fucked-up booby trap out here. You both okay?"

"Yeah. We're fine. Came from your direction."

"Retrace your exact steps. Watch for wires. Meet at the engine. Now!" I followed my path back out, scanning for wires as I returned to the engine to call in law enforcement—my heart rate at full throttle.

The fire skulked around, throwing up little smoke as we waited for deputy sheriffs and a Cal Fire peace officer. This was the kind of fire that could go unnoticed for days if not for the opening in the grove. A coastal fog-soaked canopy could hold smoke down until an incipient fire gained enough momentum to consume its cover.

Deputies and my former battalion chief from Corralitos, McFlay, combed the area. McFlay returned to the engine holding a spent twelve-gauge casing in front of me.

"Buckshot from a spring gun rigged with a wire trip. If you were bigger, you'd be dead."

"Fuuuck," I said, struggling to unpack everything that meant. I examined my shirt. A buckshot pellet had ripped the fabric just above my belly button.

"We didn't find any other wires strung. You can take your hoses back there now. Steer clear of the flagged-off areas and deputies hauling out pot plants."

I waved my firefighters over. "Let's go, guys. Pull an inch and a half. Then we'll get a scratch line around it."

McFlay lit a cigarette. "Chainsaw probably started it. Pot growers topped the tree canopy to let in sunlight for their crop. Left the chainsaw on some dry leaves. When they saw smoke in the air, they knew we'd respond, so they quick-harvested what they could and bolted."

"Wow," I said, grabbing a McLeod off the engine. "I guess that explains the camera. If the trip wire failed to trigger the shot, at least they'd have a picture of an intruder dumped into that treetop bucket."

"Bingo," McFlay said. He looked me up and down. "You should go to cop school."

"Not on your life," I said, my tone implying that anyone who had gone was cracked. After a beat, I tried to clean it up. "I'm just not wired that way. Shit, I didn't even know it was a grow. I totally thought there was a skunk nearby."

McFlay laughed, then stared at me with an intensity I hadn't seen in him before. Wondering what it meant, I headed over to help with the fire. I found a meditative rhythm in scraping my McLeod across dirt and ash. Lean in. Scrape. Lean in. Scrape. Like a locomotive piston shooting forward and drawing back, then shooting forward again.

My thoughts turned inward, unearthing the twelve-gauge's magnitude. *How close did I just come to dying?* Lean. Scrape. *Closer than on Mount Whitney?* Lean. Scrape. *What if I'd taken the other fork, and sent my firefighters down the wired path? It wouldn't have missed both of them. Is this how life works, every one of us skirting death on a regular basis? Is this God's way of letting us know it isn't up to us?*

I looked up through the clearing, hoping for a glimpse at answers. The sun's setting rays flickered through trees to the west. It looked like God winking at me, saying, "I'm not answering your silly questions. All you need to do is lean, scrape, and know I'm here."

A chill passed through me, pulling me out of my head. I rested on my McLeod handle, watching my firefighters shoulder-load dirty hose.

"It's all about grape jelly, my brother," Mario said.

"You put that shit on everything. It's gross," Tunheim replied.

"It's going on my steak tonight."

"You need help, dude. You should talk to Cap about counseling."

They laughed as they hiked the char-smudged hose out my near-fatal path. I felt like a parent watching her kids play in a park, narrowly missed by an asteroid they hadn't noticed.

The ganja fire deepened my awareness of mounting grow operations. They'd become prevalent enough that harvest season now had a name: *Croptober*. Grows skyrocketed and harvesters got creative, setting blazes in the last full month of fire season. As fire engines and for-hire equipment headed in and out of the backwoods, growers hauled their crops out in box trucks, camouflaged by the activity. In the years ahead, legalization would curb but not eliminate these fires—there're still a lot of illegal aspects to many of the grow operations.

The trip wire also got me to pay attention to the meth lab scene popping up in rural areas. So when we got dispatched to a reported foul smell on Last Chance Road, I knew it wasn't a skunk and made sure law enforcement units were en route. The explosion—a common meth lab side effect—occurred while we were still making our way up the off-the-grid rutted dirt road. Black billows mushroomed in layers, pointing to the exact spot of their origin. By the time we arrived, there was little to do for the leveled house, which didn't exist according to county records. We masked up, mopped up, then left McFlay and the sheriff deputies to continue their search in the woods for a couple of long-gone homegrown chemists.

As I pulled away, I caught McFlay staring at me again—that same intense look I'd noticed on the ganja fire. Maybe he felt parental about me, I thought. But my gut told me his bottomless stare stemmed from dark, not light.

CHAPTER 15

RETINAS

Felton Fire Station, 1991

My second year as captain started out easy. On a fire in Southern California, a helitorch filled with a napalm derivative called alumigel lit the wrong side of a road, trapping our strike team between the helitorch fire and the main fire. I led the engines out of what could have been an epic story. A few weeks later, on a small local fire, I tucked and let my helmet take the brunt of a boulder that broke loose on a hillside. I played the I'm-fine game before the battalion chief sent me to get checked for a concussion. I can still feel a click in my neck, around C4.

After that, things got dicey. One of my firefighters, Denise, complained about McFlay.

"Cap," Denise called when I walked outside the barracks door. I could tell from her stride she was pissed. Smart and extraordinarily capable, Denise was well-suited for firefighting, except she resented the patriarchal rank order and let everyone know it when the mood struck.

She caught up to me and launched, "Last week I'm sitting on the steps after lunch. My head's back, eyes closed. I'm soaking up some rays. When I open my eyes, I see Chief McFlay, hovering. Like right over me, and he's totally eye-fucking me. But at the same time, it's like he's looking right

through me. Super-disturbing. Plus, I thought I smelled alcohol. I let it go, but then last night I get this bullshit drunken message from him on my home answering machine."

She shoved a small tape recorder in front of my face and hit PLAY. The recording captured McFlay slurring his way through a message a smitten middle-school boy might leave a girl.

I raised my eyebrows. The slurring didn't surprise me; I'd seen him toasted at holiday parties he and his wife hosted. But the content did. McFlay was almost double Denise's age and married with two teenage daughters. "That's creepy," I said. "I have to report this."

I took the complaint and a copy of the tape to Ricochet, who elevated it to his superiors. It fell into a black hole. We got no response.

"I guess they didn't think it warranted action," I told her. At that time, department policy aligned with the legal standard for sexual harassment claims, requiring conduct be "severe and pervasive." A weird stare and drunken voicemail probably weren't enough.

Denise's shoulders sank.

"Or," I offered, "maybe they took action and didn't tell us about it. I can try to find out."

"They didn't do shit," she said. She dropped her head and shook it, then popped her chin back up. "Hey, what if we got more damning evidence?" she suggested.

"Whatcha got in mind?"

"Let's follow the bastard home. He drives his state car. I bet we catch him buying booze and transporting it in the company ride, so he doesn't have to go back out after he gets home. I've got a camera with a zoom lens."

I felt I owed Denise more than what she'd gotten from the department. Plus, I liked capers, so I went all in. Off-shift, we borrowed another firefighter's pickup truck, which was less identifiable than my new Subaru or Denise's barely street-legal motorcycle. We loaded surveillance snacks and Denise's camera into the truck, then stuffed our ponytails under ball caps and hid behind sunglasses. I pulled the truck around the corner, and we waited for McFlay.

He emerged from his office at the usual time and backed his car out of the parking lot. I delayed long enough to not be obvious, then followed.

McFlay drove perfectly, no straying over the lines or rolling stops. But he didn't take the most expedient route to his house. We knew where he lived, because of the holiday parties.

He signaled for a right turn. I followed and saw his brake lights come on. "Shit. Is he onto us?" I asked. "He is a cop."

"No way. He's clueless. We're good," Denise said.

McFlay signaled right again, this time to turn into a strip mall driveway. "Oh, fuck yeah," Denise said. "He's going to that Quik Stop. I knew it!"

I continued past the driveway. "I'll do a U-turn and park across from the entrance. That way you can get your camera on whatever he walks out with."

I maneuvered the truck into our spot. Denise snapped several pictures of his state-badged car out front and set up for her finale shot. McFlay walked out with a brown paper bag sized to hold a fifth of something.

"Got you, motherfucker," Denise said. She clicked off shots like a machine-gunner.

McFlay reached into the bag.

"Are you shitting me?" I said. "He's gonna take a swig, front and center, in uniform?"

McFlay turned to the trash can before we could identify the bag's contents. We watched his back. He wrestled with the contraband—maybe a tricky bottle cap. When he turned back around, we could see he'd extracted one pack of cigarettes from a whole carton of them.

"Damn," Denise said.

"All he got was cigarettes," I said.

We slumped back against the truck's bench seat.

"Done?" I asked.

"Done," she said.

I drove back to Felton in silence, both of us lost in thoughts about what to do next. She and I operated differently in the male-dominated world of firefighting. I took a subversive approach, hoping to change minds by

proving bullshit stereotypes wrong to both myself and others, with occasional smart-ass callouts for overt misogyny. Denise took a more combative approach—like the nineteenth-century practice where if you were looking for a fight, you placed a wood chip on your shoulder, daring anyone to knock it off so fists could fly. Her chip said, "I shouldn't have to fight to be treated equally, but I will, ass-wipes." By the time we reached Felton, neither of us had a satisfactory McFlay plan.

I might have let it ride, we both might have, if I hadn't heard rumors that McFlay had been arrested a while back. I'd assumed it was a DUI, but now I needed to know. I owed it to Denise. I owed it to my own intuition—my gut feeling about that look in McFlay's eyes.

On my next day off, I went to the county building and did a records search. I found a divorce petition filed by McFlay's wife and a criminal disposition for violation of Penal Code Section 288, to which he'd entered a plea: *nolo contendere*—no contest. He didn't fight the charges. I tried to find 288 explained somewhere in the file available for public viewing. Finally, I gave up and went to the law library on the bottom floor of the same building. There, I found it. Penal Code Section 288: lewd or lascivious acts on a child under the age of fourteen.

I sucked in a breath of shock, wondering how it was possible. Brain cells that enabled him to finish at the top of his fire and police academies intermingled with dark matter capable of causing irreparable harm to a child.

"This is what's going on," I told Denise, showing her copies of the court records. "It looks like they held him in county jail for a few days. I don't know what his sentence is."

"Fuckers let him out. Probably just some community service and probation bullshit; it's 'just child molestation.' How does he still have a job?" she asked.

I didn't have a good answer. "I assume the chiefs know. They're probably staying tight-lipped until they figure out how to best handle this."

A week later, Ricochet called me into his office. "McFlay's gone. You can tell Denise her issue is resolved."

When I told Denise, she said *she* had resolved the matter. She had the gumption to send the recording of McFlay's drunken message to his

probation officer—something his bosses should have done as soon as Ricochet gave them the tape, something I should have thought to do for her. It provided the ammunition needed. McFlay cleared out his desk, and we never saw him again.

In a few months, I'd have occasion to research the retina, which rests at the back of the eyeball. It allows light receptors to trigger impulses from the optical nerve to the brain, forming an image. I wondered if that was the intensity both Denise and I had witnessed in McFlay's stare. Were his retinas working overtime to form images neither Denise nor I would ever want to see? Were we ever in real danger of something "severe and pervasive"? Probably not; my guess was we were too old for him.

<p style="text-align:center">*★*</p>

The reason I researched retinas came from a call at Felton on the last Sunday of summer. The radio speaker squawked with a dispatch I'd underestimate: "Vehicle accident, Highway 9, south of Toll House."

Felton station sat in a town formed along a two-lane highway that wound through redwoods and served as a back road artery into and out of Santa Cruz's famed beaches and boardwalk. All summer long, weekend travelers jammed the southbound lane before noon, and the northbound one as fog and dusk chased them home. Car crashes were expected.

Accidents became routine, always unfolding in the same manner. The captain parks the engine at an angle, protecting the workspace. One firefighter grabs the medic bag while another pulls a hose line. Crashed cars never blow up like they do on TV, so it's okay for the second firefighter to leave the hose line and help with medical—holding a neck still, administering oxygen, taking vitals. The captain reports to dispatch and assigns arriving crews and the ambulance. Cops handle traffic control and walk alongside wheeled measuring tapes. We all load any injured patients into the ambulance. Everyone returns to quarters except the first engine crew, who shovel metal and glass off the road while waiting for the tow truck.

On this Sunday, I did what I always did: checked for the thumbs-up from my two firefighters, one sitting shotgun and the other on the back of

the engine; turned on the lights and siren; and blared toward the incident. I loved driving Code 3 on this highway. It made me feel like Moses.

We wound through timbered tunnels pocketed with sheer cliffs as cars in the opposing lane strained to pull to the side before my bumper hit theirs. I pushed the pace.

"We may beat highway patrol," I said. This eliminated the question of who would take command. It would be all mine.

"Cool," shotgun said. "Want me to handle patient care when we get there?"

"Probably. Let's, *um, h-huh.*"

I stuttered because no more cars were coming toward me. My flashing lights and thoughts bounced against the redwoods lining this darkened, unoccupied stretch. The siren fell into the background.

"Let's see what we have," I said in the quiet tone I used to reign calm over my firefighters. "If there're multiple vehicles, you'll need to triage."

When I rounded the oxbow curve after Toll House, I saw it. The scene rushed at me in spirals, trying to deliver all the information at once. I concentrated hard to slow time and separate the kaleidoscopic images so I could deliver clear orders and manage the chaos.

Later, I'd learn from Bud's sci-fi that whenever you manipulate time, collateral damage to the brain results. Here, mine still manifests in spotty recall. I have no memory of which firefighters I had with me, and the incident always replays in a baker's dozen of fragments that skip like spliced film reels.

1. A silver Volvo sedan sits cockeyed but upright, crunched at its front crumple zone—a safety feature that works like the perforated "tear here" instruction on a piece of paper. It insists that a crashed car fold in one spot, so it won't fold where belted passengers sit.

2. An older man and woman stand beside the Volvo, looking stunned and unsure of the world they've just collided into.

3. A hot-pink Suzuki Samurai, ragtop removed, lies on its side.

4. The Samurai's demolished rear end reveals teenagers sprawled across the vehicle and each other. Blood, glass, and beach sand camouflage where one body begins and another ends.

5. One girl's arm hangs over a dangling tailgate. Her fingers move. Her eyes don't. Her retinas had detached on impact. She'll be permanently blind, and the only Samurai survivor. A scrunchie keeps her ponytail intact.

6. Traffic clogs beyond the bend.

7. People pour toward the chaos, wanting to help. A woman screams at us to come fix this mess that she can't stand to look at but won't turn away from.

8. I assign a bystander to control the bystanders, send my shotgun firefighter to triage the teenagers, direct my second firefighter to the older couple, radio in my report, request multiple ambulances, and check on arrival time for the next-in engine and highway patrol. All this happens in twelve seconds.

9. My shotgun firefighter shakes his head at me from beside the Samurai. He holds up one finger. I run to the smell of suntan oil, beer, blood, and gasoline. It's pungent and volatile. It sears through my nostrils, onto my taste buds, and into my memory cells. I make out four bodies.

10. The next engine arrives. I must have asked the captain to handle scene safety, pull hose lines, and set traffic flares—because that's what he does.

11. I call over an incoming firefighter. "You have one task. Hold her hand." I point to the moving fingers.

12. A fifth teenager lies outside the vehicle—a few feet away from a chunk of his scalp I'll scrape off the asphalt while waiting for the tow truck. I'll use a square-headed utility shovel we keep on the engine. That shovel had seen a lot, but never head skin adorned with teenaged sandy-brown hair awash in road oils.

13. My firefighters and I check on each other after we help load dead bodies onto gurneys. "You okay? Tough one, but yeah, I'm fine. You?" we all say.

I drove us back to the firehouse, where we made sick jokes and baked biscuits to distract us from what we're supposed to be feeling. But this time, it didn't work. I'd always been able to disassociate enough. Never squeamish with blood or the smell of burnt anything, I could push any scene out of my head within a day or two. Not this one. It broke me a little.

The fragmented splices had inked a stain on my brain. For weeks, the bystander's screams pierced through my head at every bend in a road. When I shampooed my hair, I felt the weight of the boy's scalp tipping my shovel's end. When I tried to sleep, the confused older couple stared at me, asking everything and nothing. When I looked at my eyes in the mirror, it reminded me that the blinded girl couldn't see anything new—just images from her past, always ending in the crash.

I refused to reveal any of this, forcing the rupture inward. I had to. Incident stress debriefings weren't a thing yet. It was starting to become acceptable for men to show emotion in the firehouse. But I couldn't. It would feed the presumptions I'd fought off for the last eleven years. So tears I locked out at the firehouse surfaced at home, where I was free to bubble and crack. I didn't understand. I knew how to stop hemorrhaging, suppress conflagrations, run a crew, command complex incidents, evacuate towns. But I didn't know how to stop thinking about this crash. And I didn't know how to deal with not being able to deal.

At the end-of-season party, I drank beer after beer and danced with others to an endless loop of Talking Heads' "Burning Down the House." I felt like myself again. Cocky. Invincible.

Dripping with sweat, I checked my watch. It was late. Time to go. I grabbed my keys and hugged my good-byes, catching my brother Mark last.

"You good to drive?" he asked.

"Yeah," I said, figuring he wouldn't know because he'd been drinking too.

I went outside. My reflection in the Subaru's window looked at me as I unlocked the door. The kaleidoscope attacked without warning. The crash scene looped inside my head, getting stuck on the blinded girl. Like a scratched DVD that keeps playing the same ten seconds over and over, the lens zoomed in on her damn scrunchie—the same kind harnessing my dance-drenched ponytail. She is what I would look like caked in blood with

my eyes disconnected from the visual world, my youthful body mangled by beer and jagged metal.

I walked the six miles home, realizing the blind girl and her four dead friends gave their future for mine. *Thank you. Just, thank you.*

<p style="text-align:center">***</p>

"You know, lawyers popularized crumple zones," my personal injury lawyer boyfriend said after I told him about the accident. He and I had started dating a couple months earlier. He had JFK Jr. good looks and a quirky sense of humor, and he loved push-ups.

I'd always thought of injury lawyers as leeches, but he got me to see it differently when he explained, "Car crash lawsuits result in industry design standard changes—safety upgrades. That old couple is alive because of lawyers."

"That's kind of fascinating," I said.

"It is fascinating. Law is fascinating. You'd like law school," he said.

I stared at him. *There's no way I'm smart enough for law school*, I thought before saying, "Why would I need a law degree? I'm a firefighter for life."

"You'd be surprised what you can do with a JD. You're into the union stuff. Specialize in labor law and forge new changes through the union as a firefighter," he said.

I rolled my eyes at the impossibility of it. It had taken me nine years and seven different junior colleges to complete my two-year associate degree, and I was one semester into my upper-division work at San Jose State University. Always opting to drop classes instead of turning down a long-term fire assignment during the shoulder seasons, I'd traded educational expediency for work experience and rank.

He raised his eyebrows. "You have more time now. No more studying for promotions."

He was right. I didn't want to promote past captain. I could concentrate on school.

"Plus, it would fill the hole. It's a terminal degree," he said, referring to my educational gaps easily because he didn't understand how they haunted

me. Dad's ill-timed family moves and my emancipation jettisoned good portions of second, sixth, seventh, eleventh, and all of twelfth grades, resulting in lapses that reared up more often than I liked. I worked hard to hide my shame and ignorance each time it arose.

"Like the Union in the Civil War, *huh*?" someone would say, and I wouldn't know if "the Union" meant the good or the bad guys, so I'd shift the conversation. "Speaking of which, are you going to this month's union meeting? We're voting in new officers." No one ever guessed the extent of my blank spots.

"First year of law school is the toughest," my boyfriend said, still pressing.

I told him I'd consider it, so he'd let it go. He did. But then I couldn't. His suggestion settled into my mind's recesses. Like silt at a creek's bottom, the slightest movement stirred it up. I thought about it during my classes at San Jose State, all of which bored me because I'd chosen communications as my major. In that time and place, it was a default for those who couldn't hack math, science, business, history, or computer programming. If you could read people and books on rhetoric, you could glide through the courses.

One afternoon, after finishing my homework at the campus library, I hunted for and found a book on the Law School Aptitude Test. It looked fun, filled with logic problems and analysis. I bought some study guides at the campus bookstore. After finals, I took the test and ended up with a high enough score to meet the entry requirements for a handful of nearby schools with part-time programs that could accommodate my work schedule. Employing the same hubris and impatience that secured my emancipation, I applied to law school without a bachelor's degree.

The highest-tier school I applied to was Santa Clara University School of Law. My entrance essay argued that I'd accomplished equivalency of an undergrad degree through my fire service years. I added details about becoming one of the department's youngest captains on the heels of a turbulent childhood, throwing in cheat phrases like, "caring for my Down syndrome sister," and "a keen interest in labor laws to help improve firefighter safety," and "Dad was a monk before he met Mom"—after all, it was a Jesuit law school.

Intrigued, they invited me for a meet and greet at a reception. Something about the formally dressed waitstaff with trays of tiny food and prosecco-filled flutes triggered a panic attack. I'd never had a panic attack before, so it took several minutes in a locked bathroom stall to figure out what it was. Fires didn't faze me, but apparently, canapés did. I hid until it passed, then went to mingle and pretend I belonged.

The deans kept introducing me to each other. "Clare is our *special* candidate."

At first, I couldn't tell which made me more of a spectacle: that I was a firefighter interested in a juris doctorate or that I was a successful female in the fire service. They told me with their questions.

"Tell us what it's like to be a female fire captain. Do you have any issues with the men following orders?"

Regular Clare would have answered, "It's the same as being a male fire captain, except I have a gyna and breasties instead of a wiener and testes. And no, except for Arlo, who was a bit of a religious whackadoodle."

But *special* Clare said, "For the most part, firefighters treat me how I ask to be treated. I feel fortunate to have found the profession. Hopefully, I can enhance it and myself with a law degree from a school named after my patron saint."

It worked. They let me in. And my boyfriend was right. I loved law school. All through my first semester I sat at the regal tiered desks, marveling at my book stack: *Law Dictionary, The Law of Torts, Contract Law—Cases and Materials, Legal Research & Writing.* I clenched my bottom teeth against my top to keep from letting out a shit-eating grin. Me—they let *me* into law school. I felt like both an impostor and a successful con artist.

I studied like I never had, abandoning my stack of in-progress paperbacks for law textbooks I hauled everywhere, even on the fire engine. I read case law while waiting for assignments in a staging area, or under the map light on night patrol while I let my firefighters sleep. I learned about unconscionable contracts from my firehouse bunk, about legal analysis while pedaling Felton's stationary bicycle, and about eggshell plaintiffs over morning coffee in the dayroom.

I couldn't treat law school like I had the community colleges, dropping in and out. So I applied for a captain specialist position located in the administrative offices at Belmont Fire Station. Like many counties, San Mateo contracted with Cal Fire to staff its local fire marshal office. With regular hours, the job involved conducting building-plan reviews and fire code inspections—the fire prevention side of things. As a smart-ass engineer fresh out of the academy, I'd always given prevention staff a hard time: "I could never do your job. It's a conflict of interest." Now I told myself, "Just until you get your law degree. Then you can get back into the thick of it."

When I reported to the fire marshal's office at Belmont, Mule and the others gave me a rousing greeting and shit for my new glasses. Endless hours of reading casebooks had damaged my farsighted vision—refractive properties blurring the images my retinas sent to my optical nerves. The Belmont gang quipped, "Welcome back, Poindexter." I didn't like it when they said that. I never wanted to stop looking like a firefighter, but fate had a different plan for me.

CHAPTER 16

CRITTERS

County Fire Marshal's Office, 1994

I pored over a set of residential sprinkler plans in Belmont's downstairs offices. Every day, I heard the alarm set the crew in motion upstairs. Kitchen chairs scooted across linoleum, boots clunked out to the engines, apparatus bay doors opened. I liked the detail of prevention work, but it bothered me that my job wasn't to respond to calls.

Today's alarm brought the regular commotion, and a pair of boots that stopped at the top of the stairs. "Poindexter! Let's go. We need you on this one."

I threw my red pencil on the desk and bounded upstairs. They briefed me on the way. "Pregnant gal. Birth is imminent. We're two minutes out. No females on the crew today."

All the guys on the crew were dads. They knew the trajectory of blame during labor pains, and that a woman's face in the audience might provide comfort. I gloved up between the engine and the front door. The mother-to-be was in the middle of the living room floor, on a blanket, panting. A man hovered beside her, squeezing her shoulder, looking panicked and helpless. She scanned the crew, saw my face, and reached for my hand. The dads were right.

A crew member busted open the OB kit. Every engine had one, but it was a rare event to break its seal, and it wasn't something we practiced outside of our initial Emergency Medical Technician training. Somehow, we all remembered what to do—mainly because it was letting the mother and child do their thing. I laid out sterile pads and positioned myself to "catch" the baby, placing one hand low and the other high. The mother pushed, screamed in pain, panted, and pushed again. "You're doing great. Almost there, Love," I told her when I saw a tiny head crowning. After a full head emerged, I suctioned mucus from the miniature nose and mouth and checked to make sure the umbilical cord wasn't wrapped at the baby's neck. Another scream and push, and another. Then a tiny, marbled, wrinkled, slimy miracle appeared. I flicked the baby's soles, just like I'd learned. A noise followed. It sounded like an angry goose—but beautiful in a way that stole my breath.

Everyone stared at me, like I'd forgotten something. I stared back, still kind of choked up and thinking, *We can clamp and cut the cord after the mother has held her child.* They stared harder. I looked at the newborn.

"Oh! Geez. I forgot," I said. "You, my love, have birthed a goddess." Everyone cheered.

The paramedics arrived, took care of the cord, then transported mother and child to the hospital. Shamefully, I never learned the names of the mom, dad, or child. Which means now I don't know who to thank. That day, they gave me the kind of gift that can't be repaid. It didn't change my mind about motherhood, but witnessing the wonder made me appreciate the glory of childbirth in a way a doll named Julie never could. I hope life has been good to them.

I settled into a daily routine at the fire marshal's office. Monday through Thursday, I worked ten-hour days, then attended night classes at law school. Friday through Sunday brought all-day study sessions.

By summer, I was ready for a break from desk work. Itching for dirt, sweat, and smoke, I implored my boss to let me go out on the big

ones—"campaign fires," we called them. These were fires that would take a week or month to extinguish. I was qualified to work in a number of support positions needed on the bigger incidents.

My boss said yes, and what followed were two fire assignments that colluded to land me in a surgery room where a doctor would remove all my toenails and douse my fire career.

The first was the Tecate Fire, which had burned across Mexico's border into a community called Dulzura, in the eastern front of the San Ysidro Mountains. I boarded a plane with my red gear bag. The last time I'd flown instead of driven to an assignment was for a fire in Santa Barbara County three years earlier. People on that flight spoke freely to me. "You gotta risk your life for a gazillionaire's mansion? They should be flying you first class."

I wanted to say, "Fuck you. Loss is loss, no matter how rich you are. Everything's gone except memories, now tainted by trauma. Oh, and I'm making overtime pay for their pain. I'm no hero, and they aren't villains." Instead, I repeated a line I'd heard over the years, "In California, anyone's fire is everyone's fire. It doesn't grasp boundaries, economic or otherwise."

When I arrived at incident base in Dulzura, the fire maps at the entrance said otherwise. The estimated fire perimeter spiked and jagged along mountain ridges until it flatlined at the US-Mexico border, as if the fire didn't exist in Mexico. I'd never seen a fire map like it. I'd fought fires that crossed state lines, burning from northern counties into Oregon, eastern counties into Nevada, and southern counties into Arizona, but this was my first international fire. The fake perimeter made the whole incident look eerie, like a blundered covert operation.

The incident base was typical—a local community center with acres of parking. Cal Fire had contracts all over the state for spaces that thousands of firefighters could occupy on short notice: out-of-session schools, fairground complexes, parks. Once smoke was in the air, facilities managers stood ready with keys to gates if they got the call from Cal Fire. We could usually tell in the first twenty-four hours of an incident if we'd need to make that call. If yes, Cal Fire mobilized, converging on the safest closest site, building a pop-up city with its own coms, medical, food service, security, mechanics, supplies, photocopy center, gas and diesel, and so on.

I found Tecate check-in near the entrance. "Hi. Bisbee. Order O-27. Field observer."

The check-in recorder filled out his form and the Restat unit leader told me, "You'll go out tomorrow. Grab your maps over there. Show up for the 0600 briefing. You have a ride?"

"I flew in. Rental car. It's not fireworthy."

"We'll have the div. sup. take you to a drop point. You'll be on foot patrol anyways. Go to Coms and get a handy talkie programmed to this fire. Sleeping area is that way, feeding over there, and toilets just west of that."

I knew my brother was assigned here as a public information officer, so I asked, "PIOs?"

He pointed. "That way. Three trailers over."

"Thanks," I said, then made my way through fire camp by flashlight. I found porta-toilet row, then the washing station, then my brother.

"Hey, Klotchum!" He hugged me. "You just get in?"

I nodded.

"I'll show you where I'm set up. Grab your bag."

We walked to his pickup truck. He'd been assigned a day ahead of me and had driven down. He helped me set up my sleeping bag in the dirt next to his.

"So, what's the deal here?" I asked him. "Why aren't we mapping the Mexico side? It's all part of the same fire."

"Guess it's not our job. But this is a weird fire. There's an off vibe to it. Rumor is 'international travelers' started it with a warming fire after coyotes ripped off their money, then got them lost in the desert mountains. I have no idea if it's true."

"That's super-comforting," I said.

We went to grab hot chocolate from the feeding tent, forgoing sleep to visit. We'd been in the fire service together for fourteen years now, and this was only the third fire where we could enjoy each other's on-duty company.

"Hi, Bisbees." Even though it was dark, people we'd worked with could tell it was us. I'd adopted Mark's inflection and many of his mannerisms while trailing him through childhood, so a lot of people assumed we were twins. One brainiac even asked us if we were identical twins.

We drank our cocoas, talked into the stars, and returned to our sleeping bags. Sleep came easy but ended too early. We rolled up our bags, went to the sunrise briefing, and headed out to our assignments.

As a field observer, my job was to walk the ridges, update a topographical map with precise fire line demarcations, call in any spot fires, flag hazards, and conduct spot weather checks. My pack had everything I needed: water and snack bars, maps, assorted pens and markers, binoculars, a wilderness compass, a clinometer to measure slope, rulers and grid overlays, field guides, flagging tape, and a belt weather kit like the one I'd learned how to use at Sandy Point.

With my sleeves rolled up like CK, I hiked the hills next to blackline, marking my map and wondering how it was possible I was getting paid to do this. The land under my feet smelled pleasantly of char and dust. Distant helicopter rotor blades peppered the otherwise silent air. I pulled out my binoculars to watch their drops and scan for smoke columns on my division. Then I took out the sling psychrometer. Before I read the numbers, I guessed. I missed the relative humidity by one, but got the temperature and wind speed spot-on. Gulps of water, half a snack bar, and more mapping followed.

On a long, even stretch that didn't require detailed mapping, I let my mind wander as I looked south from the ridgetop to Mexico. I half expected to see a thick, straight line. But all I saw were contiguous wildlands, some burnt, some not—all God's land. I wondered if Yaqui Indian territory was within my view. Before law school, I'd finished Carlos Castaneda's *The Teachings of Don Juan: A Yaqui Way of Knowledge*. The book celebrated peyote use as a spiritual ritual. However mind-expanding, it made me cherish my non-peyote Scottish roots.

I trekked all day, miles and miles, dusty ridge to dusty ridge. My feet started to feel it. It wasn't blisters. It was a sharp burning sensation on top of my toes. I'd have to check them back at fire camp.

When it was time to return to the drop point, I saw smoke rising in a column near my division. I took out my binoculars. Fire had spotted across the line. I radioed in. "Tecate Command, Field Obs Twelve."

No one responded.

"Tecate Command, Field Obs Twelve."

Radio silence. I changed positions even though I'd heard a repeater kick back, which meant my signal had transmitted.

"Tecate Command, Field Obs Twelve," I said it with more urgency as the smoke built.

Silence. *What the fuck? Why weren't they responding?*

"Tecate Command, I've got a column building outside the primary line at the Alpha/Bravo division break."

The column climbed, and I called it in two more times with more exact coordinates. A helicopter came and dropped a bucket. Good. Someone else must have seen it. But now, with no radio contact, how was I going to get my ride off the mountain? And what if I'd been in the line of fire? None of this seemed normal. Mark was right. This fire had an off vibe.

I transmitted again, in case my ride could hear me, "Field Obs Twelve, en route back to Drop Point 4."

Ten minutes after I got there, the division supervisor rolled up. "Load in."

"Thanks for the pickup, Div," I said. "I'm having radio problems."

"Might need to get that checked," he said.

I nodded and put my feet up on his dash for the long ride back to fire camp. My toes were killing me.

Halfway out, we saw a border patrol unit parked cockeyed on the side of the fire road.

Div stopped and rolled down his window. "Everything okay?"

The border patrol dude was a talker. "Just taking a cigarette break. We're rounding 'em up like crazy right now. They're using the fire as cover."

"So, you're good, then?" Div asked.

"Yup." Border leaned one arm on Div's open window frame, keeping him from driving off. "'Cept the fire's burning them. Nine body bags been pulled so far. Don't say anything. It's unofficial intel and we still gotta figure out which country they burned in."

I must have made a face because Border looked at me.

"Yup. I'm saving lives." He took a long drag and nodded toward his paddy wagon. "Got a boxful right now. They're all safe in there—won't burn tonight. Wanna see 'em?"

Div looked at me, mouth open, unsure how I'd respond.

I looked at the small window on the back of "the box" and saw a face split into puzzle pieces by reinforced wire between the panes. I shook my head. "No thanks." If they had been horses or cows, I would have said yes, and asked to pet them.

I wasn't right or wrong. To witness this part of an existence could be depraved or enlightened, depending on your bent and intention. It's like hunters and slaughterhouse workers willing to do the dirty work, while the rest of us shop at shiny-floored supermarkets for cleaned, cut, furless, and faceless protein. I wonder now if I should have asked to see them so I could look into their eyes and tell them, "I'm sorry you were born on one side of the line, and me on the other. My feet hurt, if that helps."

Div and I ambled out of the hills, into the flatlands, and back to incident base.

"Same time tomorrow?" I asked.

He nodded.

I exchanged radios at coms and found Mark in the chow line. He told me about his day, and I told him about mine—about "the box," the body bags, and the radio silence.

"I think they heard you and sent the chopper."

"If they heard me, why not acknowledge?"

"Well, you are just a girl," he joked—but not really.

Sometimes my brother saw it before I did because he always had my back, and because I insisted on seeing myself as a firefighter, not a female firefighter. I figured if I ignored my gender, everyone else would too. Problem solved. It hadn't occurred to me that word hadn't yet spread to the border fire stations that women belonged in the department. I expected more from those working in the same profession, in the same department, fighting the same fire. I sighed. It could be worse; at least I wasn't in a body bag or being processed at a well-lit border patrol facility.

After grub, we laid our sleeping bags back out. I examined my reddened toes under a flashlight and decided a sockless sleep and moleskin in the morning would be best remedy. For four more days, I hiked and mapped, letting my toes marinate in sweat-soaked socks and moleskin in

non-breathable fire boots—creating the perfect habitat for a flesh-eating fungus to take hold under my toenails.

Div started speaking to me in longer sentences and we chatted with the same border patrol dude who popped up on our trek out every day. He continued schooling us on ugly, fucked-up truths about his part of the world.

"Unless it's their seventh time, we just send 'em back. On the seventh time, we figure they're serious, so they're gonna get the full detainment." He paused long enough to suck on his lit cigarette, then rolled out more information. "Found two more, all burnt like the others. They don't take up much space in the body bags. Easier to haul 'em out, but they don't smell too good. You're in the business. You know that. Whatcha call 'em? Critters?"

"Crispy critters," Div said.

I nodded. It is what we called bodies found burnt to a crisp. The irreverence of the term fit within our dark-humor tendencies—which were less about getting a laugh and more about avoidance or finding a way to talk through something without being dragged into the abyss of it. Saying "crispy critters" was code for, "Yes. I've seen broiled skin, melted muscle, and cooked bones, where the skin peeled back from teeth is what made me realize the blackened form used to be a human." And Border was right. They had a unique acrid odor that left a mark on your olfactory memory. Once you smelled it, you recognized it the next time you smelled it.

At the end of our last day together, Div and I said our good-byes.

"Maybe I'll see you on a fire up in your neck of the woods one of these days," he said.

"Maybe I'll answer you on the radio," I said.

He hung his head and stuck his hand out. I shook it, happy to get the dig in and make my point without making an enemy. This was my way.

"You take care," he said.

Mark got released too, so I rode home with him, wearing flip-flops instead of boots. More than anything, my feet needed air. My toes were

inflamed and sore. And my toenails had yellowed. At our first road stop for snacks, I got a can of foot powder and emptied it onto my feet. *That should fix it*, I thought.

Mark and I exchanged border stories, snacked on licorice ropes, and took turns finding radio stations. Somewhere near Buttonwillow, we shifted to our favorite game, called, "If I were Chief, I'd . . ." Along Interstate 5 we restructured the California fire service in a way we thought perfect. Later, when we both served as fire chiefs, we found those ideas abysmal.

<p style="text-align:center">***</p>

The second fire assignment that summer, the one that did my feet in for good, was in San Luis Obispo County—mid-state with cool ocean frontage and sweltering inland hills. Fires igniting in red-flag conditions exploded throughout the county, sweeping across highways close to towns. On a 50,000-acre blaze (about the size of three and a half Manhattans), I worked as a field observer again. My feet had healed from the Tecate Fire except under the toenails, where the stubborn fungus had taken hold. I'd learned moleskin wasn't the answer. To guard against it spreading, I carried several pairs of dry socks in my pack and changed them out every two hours.

My third day in, the fire encroached into an area I'd been mapping. A "dirty burn," the fire left patches of fuel available if wind shifted the flames back to where they'd come from. That's what happened on this day. After the wind shift, I waited with an engine crew to let them knock down the flames as the fire moved through an unburned oak stand. I jumped in to help hump hose so it wouldn't burn up. The ash was still so hot, we could feel it through our boots. We high-stepped to minimize contact and a rookie firefighter made the mistake of "helping" by squirting water onto our feet. Hot, dry ash was uncomfortable but wouldn't have caused much damage. The water, however, created steam that burnt feet trapped inside tightly laced boots we couldn't high-step out of.

The medical unit checked us out at incident base. Two others had sustained minor burns that earned them feet wrapped in gauze and relief from fire duty for a week. I landed in surgery because the burns and Tecate

fungus birthed a nasty infection that, in my case, couldn't be treated topically or systemically. My toenails had to come off.

The anesthesiologist sedated me, and the surgeon plucked out all ten nails. They sent me home with a wheelchair and instructions to place my feet in stinging-hot salt water three times a day. Every time I unwrapped my feet, it shocked me. It looked like I had painted my toes with bright red polish. I took pictures I still can't look at because somehow it hurts my teeth.

On the right side of my couch, I set up a soaking station. I'd count to three, shove my feet in steaming briny water, and wait for the stabbing pain. After my first soak, I retrieved a pillow from my bed, put a soft flannel pillowcase on it, and kept it next to the torture salt. I called it my screaming pillow.

<p style="text-align: center;">***</p>

Before the fires, my personal injury lawyer boyfriend and I had split. I'd liked him enough to keep stuff in a dresser drawer at his house but moved it out when I realized that was all the space he could give me. Maybe he sensed I'd never love him as much as firefighting. We parted amicably and agreed to joint custody of our Bernese Mountain Dog, Kelly.

Kelly and I found an apartment one block away from the law school, thirty minutes from Belmont, and twenty minutes from the ex-boyfriend. He dropped off Kelly on my study days and took her back during the workweek. But after my toenail harvest, I couldn't go to work for several months. So I took Kelly during the week, and he got weekends.

Still in my wheelchair when law school classes started up, I loaded my books into Kelly's panier bags. She walked alongside as I wheeled myself to class, then waited outside next to blooming star jasmine and a water bowl. A constant stream of fawning students supplied her with ear and belly rubs. Three hours later, I reloaded her packs and she walked me home.

At first, my toes seemed to heal fine as new nails grew into place. I graduated to crutches. But then the nails on my two big toes started growing in the wrong direction. The growth cells directed them into, not over, the nail bed. It was uncomfortable, but I didn't think much of it until I brushed my

<p style="text-align: center;">200</p>

toe against a chair leg in the law school computer lab, and blood spurted all over my flip-flops and the shiny white floor in a splatter pattern befitting a Jackson Pollock piece.

Two more surgeries followed, which meant I spent most of my second law school year and some of my third on crutches. In the end, I permanently lost my two big nails and had implants installed to block regrowth. That solved it. All I needed now was a conclusive doctor's visit and workers' compensation clearance.

"I'm afraid you can't wear fire boots for at least five years," the doctor told me.

"What? You-you-never, never, never told me this," I stammered.

"Your case is rare. You're a high risk for recurrence. Your feet need a break from boots."

I couldn't digest it, so I just shook my head. When I got home, I pulled Kelly close to me and called my boss. "Doc says I have to be out of boots for five years. We need a plan."

"We can't do light duty for more than eighteen months," he said. "I'm really sorry. I wish there was something—"

Unwilling to hear my lack of options, I hung up on him. I was numb. Lost. Unsure of what to do next. I called back, apologized, and insisted there had to be a way through this. But there wasn't. I knew workers' comp law well enough to know that I needed my doctor to clear me for full duty, and that wasn't going to happen.

Eventually, I drove to Belmont to clean out my desk and say good-bye. The crew wouldn't let me sulk. They made a whipped cream pie, which one of my favorite captains happily shoved in my face. I choked on Reddi-wip sucked through nostrils. They hollered, "A-2. Can do!" making me laugh and feel like they'd always be family—like years from now, I could stop in and grab a cup of coffee or have them top off the air in my tires.

The smile lasted until I turned onto the highway. A lump hit my throat. I looked at my boots, tossed onto the passenger seat. We'd driven this highway so many times and seen so much together. Fires. Hazmat spills. Cliff rescues. Vehicle pileups. Train wrecks. Pranks. Promotions. Mistakes. Smoky sunsets. Bloody pavement. Birth. Death.

I rested my right hand on my boots as we passed stations we'd worked at over the years. The last on the route—Big Creek, where I first wore these boots—was the hardest. Agricultural fields and the Pacific Ocean shimmered on our right while tall golden grass swayed in the offshore breeze on our left, waving good-bye. I choked back briny tears, until they won and cascaded down my cheeks. Slamming my hands on the steering wheel, I let out a primal scream. And then another. And another.

Punched clear through, I felt an aching hole and exit wound. I was no longer a firefighter, and I didn't know how I could live with that.

V.
FULL DEVELOPMENT

A fire is in full development when it incinerates everything in its path. It's at max heat and out of control. And it's what life felt like at twelve years old while Dad searched for his happy place. He'd ruled out communes we visited, what with the orgies and the drugs. And a month-to-month cottage at a motel in Ellensburg, Washington, only worked until cops made it clear our liberal bumper stickers weren't welcome. And the house in Eugene, Oregon, was too suburban. So Dad settled on a closed-down school in a nearby town: Curtin, population 50.

My siblings were mostly gone—Cathy and Tera in college, and Bernadette and Mark staying with a preacher and his wife in Eugene for the school year. So it was just Mom, Dad, Annie, and me living in this abandoned elementary school. Dad planned on turning it into a nondenominational center for disadvantaged kids. He called it Christopher Community School and declared Annie its first student. Since I wasn't "disadvantaged," I took a bus to the closest junior high to start seventh grade. But I got kicked out in the second week.

"*They* jumped *me*," I explained to Mom when she came to pick me up.

"The principal had a different story. You broke his daughter's arm. Unprovoked."

"Guess it doesn't matter there were three of them. That I made the b-ball team, and she didn't. That her twiggy arm snapped when I spun away. No wonder she didn't make the team."

Mom never condoned violence. "Welcome to Christopher Community School," she said.

Annie pounded untuned piano keys. Mom drew logos for T-shirts that never got printed. Dad recruited staff: an alcoholic ex-priest and a scraggly-bearded dude who taught me how to make a battery. I shot hoops in an unheated gym and read shelves of books until we moved back to Eugene six months later. We left Oregon altogether that summer.

205

CHAPTER 17

KINGS

State Fire Headquarters, Still 11 Months Left

Brody's tail whipped back and forth when Bud and I walked in the door. We'd left him at home in Sacramento with a dog sitter for the Penske moving trip over the Sierra. I hugged him hard. Then we played chase—into the living room, back to the front door, back to the living room. Pure joy. It ended abruptly on the third round when my foot landed on top of a rawhide camouflaged by bone-colored rug. The rawhide rolled under my foot like a skateboard, then pitched my ankle sideways, snapping it at volume.

Collapsed on the floor, I wailed. Brody stuffed his muzzle in my face. *Why are you making that sound? Our game wasn't over. Are you okay?* He licked me, the only comfort I'd feel for the next four hours.

Bud got me Advil and ice and took me to the ER, where we waited for a doctor to tell us what we already knew. A cast and a knee-scooter later, we returned home. Bud set me up in bed and brought me scotch. I planned on slurping it down to dull the pain and lull me to sleep. That's when my phone started buzzing.

The first call, as usual, was from Turbo. "San Diego County is breaking fires. Expect a Ken call." I had just enough time to hobble into the living

room and get the TV on before Ken's number flashed on my screen. I watched the headlines unfold. Nine major fires. One suspected arsonist. Millions in damage. One dead.

"I'll set up a bacon call," I told Ken. An after-hours remote version of the Cheez-It congregations, these calls included North and South Ops to make sure we were all in sync. I'd set up my first one on a weekend morning when everyone was still in pajamas. We heard the unmistakable sound of bacon sizzling on a griddle—Red cooking her family breakfast. I dubbed all future remote meetings at absurd times "bacon calls."

With my foot propped on the couch, I made the call and led the discussion on response needs, investigation leads, sensitive habitats, press statements, and so on. After the call, we each had work to do. I gave the go-ahead to activate incident management teams and the State Operations Center. Then I reached out to my local, state, and federal partners. If you were eavesdropping, all you would have heard for an hour was a jumbled alphabet worthy of the armed forces: IMTs, DPA, OES, FEMA, FMAG, SOC, USFS, NIFC, MACS, MAFFS, CNG, CMFA, CCs, GO, NICS, and a dozen others.

Afterward, I fell asleep on the couch. At some point, Bud drank my scotch and draped a warm blanket over me. Brody stayed at my side, apologizing for his bone obsession.

In the morning, I rolled into the office, subjecting myself to a new nickname.

"Got the maps, Scooter?" Ken asked as we gathered in the main conference room.

Griffin and Turbo pinned them on the wall for me while Red helped pass out briefing notes my staff had worked through the night on. Even with a cast on, I felt energized. The scooter handled well, and it felt good to shift away from Moe Fleming to the type of crisis we'd been trained to handle. We worked at full throttle, slowing only in the moment Turbo told us, "Hashtag prayforsandiego is trending."

The fires kept coming. In July, the Butts Fire threatened over three hundred homes, destroyed nine buildings, and killed two civilians not far from Middletown, the station I'd worked at twenty-five years earlier. This didn't set records in terms of stats, but the fire stood out for its harbinger qualities.

Chris, my engineer partner from Middletown, now worked for me at State Fire Headquarters. Chris and I received a flurry of e-mails and phone calls from current and retired chiefs we'd worked for back in the day. They all basically said the same thing: "I've never seen fire burn like this. It feels like we're in for a storm we've never seen."

The words felt like prophecy. These were the guys we called "Fire Gods" because they'd seen fire at its almightiest and never questioned whether they'd win. But now they were nervous.

With no other major fires burning, the south tipped north, and we dumped everything we had on Butts, enabling our firefighters to control it within a few days.

I wheeled my scooter to Chris's office. "Whew. That could have been a bad one."

"No shit. It's burning this hot now? What the hell is September going to look like?"

"I say we take 'em one at a time. Let's call this a victory." We high-fived, and I wheeled myself out, singing like Sir Mix-a-Lot, "I like small Butts and I cannot lie."

"That's just wrong," Chris called from his office.

<p style="text-align:center">***</p>

The next scare came a month later when the Eiler Fire consumed the town of Hat Creek, near the top of the state in Shasta County. Lightning had struck close to town, starting a fire that sprinted through homes and businesses. The local unit chief saw the rate of spread and bypassed protocols to get engines to the fire faster. He risked ripping off resources for other fires—lightning always strikes in batches—and pissing off our federal partners. In hindsight, he'd made the right call, but it created havoc. To smooth

relationships and put eyes on the damage, the Cheez-It crew carpooled to Hat Creek.

The opposite of a dirty burn, like the fire where I'd burned my feet, the Eiler burned clean, leaving little behind. Majestic groves looked like blackened twig stands. White ash covered the town. The hotter a fire burns, the whiter its ash. More complete combustion leaves less carbon particulate, less black ash.

The town's restaurant, Fireside, was in a pile. I'd eaten at Fireside twenty-two years earlier, on my way home from the Fountain Fire just west of Hat Creek.

The Fountain Fire had moonscaped 64,000 acres. I got to fly the fire in a helicopter to check mapping accuracy. I loved riding in helicopters. They made me feel powerful, weightless, and joyful. And they reminded me of a game Mark and I played with Annie after he and I became firefighters. We called it "chopper voice." First, we'd do it to ourselves, pounding our chests as we spoke. "I've got a ten-twenty on a beauty at your one o'clock."

"Copy that. She's on the radar."

Then we'd thump Annie's back and ask her to identify herself. She'd hear her warbled voice as it came out, "Aa'n'ne, Bii'ss'bee," and smile so big it squeezed a tear out, and she'd want to do it again.

The Fountain pilot lifted the bird straight up, and in no time had us over the southern tip of the fire. The aerial view delivered a gut punch. It had been a while since I'd flown a fire. I'd forgotten that instead of seeing a bit of destruction at a time, the air displayed it all at once—miles of car skeletons, chimney stacks, ruined timber, and animal carcasses peeking through ash. The fire, unapologetic, told me, "Not the best place to build homes, eh?" I kept oscillating from awe to anger. *Wow, look how white your ash is.* Then I'd see a burnt-out trailer. *Damn you. They had next to nothing, and you took it from them.*

The Eiler Fire looked like it had burned even faster than Fountain, with stark white patches of ground replacing timber stands. Every fire I laid eyes on taught me something new about life, or myself, or fire. Like Hannibal with Clarice, fire served as a mentor with each encounter. This one told me

the white ash didn't come from lightning heat; it came from lack of water. The groves were so parched from recurring low snow and rain years, the fire tore through fuel that typically stored moisture. It looked like the trees had burned as fast as dead grass.

Eiler also taught the Cheez-It crew a little something about the residents of Hat Creek. As we drove through town, we noticed cars jammed a few driveways—neighbors staying with neighbors whose homes didn't burn to the ground. We stopped in and talked to the fire victims. Their resilience and attitudes astounded me.

"'Least we ain't dead."

"Still got friends and family. Hobart sez he's bringing ice cream by later. And Checkers is okay."

Checkers wagged his tail and made a point to greet each of us with a cordial crotch sniff.

"Still got a couple good months of trout fishing too." Not one of them complained about their circumstances. Was it a tough skin cover, or were the people here that gracious? Either way, I was impressed.

After hugs, and hang-in-theres, the Cheez-It team drove south through the ruins toward Mount Shasta, where we laid over at a lodge with rustic cabins. We stayed up late, shooting the shit around a picnic table. It felt like a family camping trip where no one wanted to go to bed.

"You're going to miss this next summer," Ken said to me.

"No doubt." I elevated my ankle onto the tabletop. It had healed enough for a walking cast, but the day's activity had inflamed it.

"Any chance we can get you to change your mind? Finish out the gov's term with the rest of us?" Ken asked.

Red dumped her candy stash on the table, and we all reached for our favorites.

"Nope. I promised Bud." I peeled back the wrapper of a mini Almond Joy, shoved it in my mouth, then spoke while I chewed. "Maybe the drought won't be as bad and all y'all will be bored stiff."

Turbo snorted. "Unlikely, Scooter," she said before taking a small bite from her miniature York Pattie. An epicurean, she treated every snack and meal like a tasting menu. Eating was the only thing she didn't do fast.

"Any chance we can get Bud to change directions?" Red asked.

Ken jumped on it. "Yeah. I bet he doesn't remember what a pain in the ass you are."

"Go for it," I dared them. I knew Bud knew exactly how much of a pain in the ass I was.

The sugar kept us at it a while longer; then we caught a few hours of sleep before heading out to another hard-won firefight on the route back to Sacramento.

We stopped at various points on the fire to thank the frontline crews now mopping it up. They were dirty, grimy, and smelling of sweat and smoke. I hobbled out of the car on my walking cast and donned my uncharred Nomex shirt, a show of solidarity, not safety. I limped across the cold black ash to shake their hands, joke with them, and tell them the reason the department works is because it operates from the ground up, not the top down. We left them with smiles that Turbo shared on Facebook, capturing me in a photo with them. If you could see behind my sunglasses, you'd be able to tell how much I missed ground attack.

On the drive back to headquarters, Turbo kept us posted from feeds on her phone.

"Red-flag conditions extended. No new lightning activity. Beyonce and Jay-Z are on the rocks. And yay, fifty likes on Chief Frank pic with the crews. Oh, Jesus H. That bastard. Don't read the comments," she told me.

"What's it say?"

"They're all good, you're supporting the troops, etc."

"Buuut?"

"I guess you'll see it anyway. A dude named Colin Fyler says, 'Awfully clean clothes to be getting so much praise,' and a Mr. Roy C. Gibson says, 'No place for women.'"

Ken turned red angry. "He's a primordial sack of dicks. Tell me he isn't one of ours."

"Checking that nooowww," Turbo said. "Nope. He's a civilian."

"I could give two shits," I said, pretending to let it roll off. But nearing the autumn of my last season, it boiled me that one stranger didn't know I'd rather be in dirty Nomex, and the other hated my second X chromosome

enough to shout it to the world. Thirty-two years ago, I'd started on a path I felt born to. I'd worked up from a seasonal and volunteer firefighter to chief of Fire Protection, a rank achieved in none of the ways I was sure Roy C. thought women secured promotions. Just eight months from retirement, I feared bullshit Facebook remarks could destroy whatever progress I'd made to smooth a path for others. Roy's comment didn't bother me that much. I knew people would read it and think he was a sexist pig. But Colin got to me, making me wonder if my pristine Nomex let down all the eight-year-old girls still getting dolls when what they wanted was a football and a chance to play.

The following month, September, an arsonist started a fire off King Mountain Road about fifty miles west of Lake Tahoe's southern shore. The King Fire was interesting for three reasons. First, it garnered attention from the capital because its atomic smoke splayed very visibly into the sky one county away. Second, the fire was heading toward Lake Tahoe, where the Ironman triathlon would kick off in seven days. And third, the fire had a record-setting run, burning a swatch of 50,000 acres in a single afternoon. Back when I was on an engine, it took fires weeks to burn that many acres.

King was acting like the Butts and Eiler fires, but was bigger and had fewer resources. Lightning strikes had once again pelted Northern California, and a different arsonist started a fire near the Oregon border, which ripped into the city of Weed, taking out homes, schools, and businesses. Our ground personnel there made outstanding tactical decisions: a battalion chief let his own house burn so he could save his neighbors' homes. And a crew prioritized saving the sawmill, the town's livelihood. But they needed aircraft reinforcement, so we diverted airtankers and helicopters away from the more remote King Fire.

The King Fire took advantage and raced toward the triathlon space. And other fires in California and neighboring western states kept diluting resource availability. We were running out of everything.

"We're at drawdown on command teams," I told Ken, meaning I'd deployed our last available team for running large-scale incidents.

His face fell. "Unfuck this, Clare."

"We gotta go out of state."

Ken winced, then nodded.

Most out-of-state teams were not as hyperactive as ours. We moved fast because we knew the next fire was coming and we had to treat summer like a game of Whac-a-Mole. Teams from other parts of the country operated with less urgency.

I explained it to Bud a couple of years earlier while trying to describe the incident commander on a team that came out west to help with a massive fire near Yosemite. "Our IC gave him the briefing. And their IC turns to our IC and says in a slow southern drawl, 'Y'all out here . . . move fa-a-ast.'"

I called the folks I'd met at the meeting in Arizona where I'd picked up my sister Annie's remains. "Hi, Florida, this is California. Hi, Tennessee. . . . What's shaking, Georgia?" We'd gratefully accept any help they could give.

Bud had to take Brody to our new home in Nevada, since I was working sixteen-plus-hour days. The approaching triathlon date kept us spinning and the governor's office wanted an in-person briefing. Mostly, he wanted to see the fire maps.

The King Fire's record-setting afternoon had given the fire an undeniable phallic shape.

"Maybe we should hang it sideways—make it less obvious," my staff chief offered.

"Nope. North always goes on top."

We hung the map on the wall in its proper orientation. The fire perimeter formed a full-on erection with testicles sagging at the bottom near the origin. Worse still, two spot fires spurted just ahead of the tip.

The dignitaries arrived and no one mentioned it at first. Then, one of the governor's staff said, "Is it just me, or does that look like—"

"Just you," I said. "Nobody else here sees that. You're depraved."

It broke the ice. But still, Ken used a pointer instead of his fingers to trace a line showing the record rate of spread along the shaft.

Ken explained, "This is attributable to how dry the fuel is and how quickly it can burn, based on what we call the energy release component."

Someone started church-laughing. Then a bunch of people did. Then someone said, "Is that what it's called these days?" Then no one could hold it in, and top leaders of the sixth-largest economy in the world were lost in a spiral of penis jokes.

<p style="text-align:center">***</p>

Swimmers warmed up in the water at Kings Beach on Lake Tahoe's north shore, readying themselves for the first leg of the Ironman. But organizers made a last-minute no-go call, canceling the event for the first time in its history. The fire hadn't reached Lake Tahoe, but its prolific smoke would've choked out race participants. The winners on that day were the local bars, swarmed with pissed-off, pent-up would-be participants and spectators.

The smoke remained bad, but we stopped the fire's momentum and were on a glide path to one hundred percent containment—the measure used to describe how much of the fire had perimeter line around it. I decided to shoot over the Sierra for a weekend with Bud and Brody.

Ken called an hour into my drive. "Governor's office call in twenty minutes. I need you to cover it."

"No problem," I said.

It wasn't ideal. I'd have to stop at Bridal Veil Falls and hold my bladder during the call. I'd planned on a bathroom break at a gas station ten miles up the road. But I'd lose reliable cell coverage up there. So I pulled into the Falls' vista point. Foliage provided the illusion of privacy. But a fire camera placed to detect early smoke anywhere in the vista gave our dispatchers a frequent show from unsuspecting travelers needing relief. I was in uniform, and no one wanted to see a three-star drop trou and squat, so I stayed in my car, crossed my legs, and waited to brief the governor.

You'd think by fifty, I'd have learned to not push my bladder's limits. But part of my flawed personality always made me push edges. Back in May, during our WAW tour up and down the state, I'd made the same mistake. The Cheez-It team flew in the department's twin turbo Beechcraft King Air, outfitted to shuttle pilots and executive staff across the state when there wasn't enough time to drive. This royally named plane was stripped

down. It had a snack basket and bottles of water but no bathroom aside from emptied water bottles and a tube hooked to the pilot's flight suit. I sat, squirming in my seat, as Red shot me an I-told-you-you-should-have-gone-when-you-had-the-chance look. Then God bounced the King Air in divine pockets of turbulence that tested my pelvic floor muscles. I believe I set a PR that day.

At the Falls vista point, I rolled my window down, then back up when I realized the falls' gushing sound didn't help my current situation. The call came, and when it was my turn to talk, I rattled off the stats the governor's office always wanted to hear: aircraft numbers, the priority of our fires against the national backdrop, FEMA status, statewide acres burned, containment and control expectations, fatalities, and political issues, like which senators' homes were threatened.

Typically, someone had follow-up questions. But not this time. The calls had achieved a rhythm over the last two weeks, and it was Friday evening. It seemed like everyone yearned for a strong drink, or for time away from all this, or for a bathroom.

I made it to the gas station before a BLEVE, then home. Bud had my popcorn and scotch ready. We sat outside and gazed at the Sierra while Brody chewed his bone. I held the scotch's caramel, nut, and fire flavors at the back of my throat. These moments of pure respite rejuvenated me. I'd need it.

CHAPTER 18

TOWERS

Santa Clara University Law School, 1997

I called my brother to tell him my fifteen-year run in the fire service was over. I didn't know how to explain everything reeling inside me. It felt like the first four stages of grief attacked all at once.

"Hey," I managed when he answered the phone.

"I heard. I was just about to call you. Howya doing?"

"Thousand times worse than leaving Ventura."

That's all the information Mark needed to understand my ache. "I'm so sorry, Klotchum," Mark said. He paused, then addressed the reality of it. "You're almost done with law school. That gives you a way forward."

"Not with anything that matters," I said.

Mark rebuffed my self-pity. "Bullshit. I totally see you as an employment-law lawyer. A pit bull holding people's feet to the fire. Remember the Motel 6 strike team?"

I smiled. "Yeah, that was pretty fun."

I'd been a captain on a strike team made up of three-person crews. After an all-day drive, the strike team leader booked motel rooms, three to a room. Two other crews had female firefighters, so he lumped the three of us together and shuffled others around, splitting up crews.

"Nah. I'm sticking with my crew," I said. "This is no different from a barracks setup."

"This is required by the sexual harassment policy," he argued.

"Have you heard the joke about the guy from Harvard and a dirt firefighter who meet in the restroom?" I asked.

The strike team leader squinted at me and shook his head.

"After using the urinal, the Harvard guy goes to the sink, while the firefighter heads for the door. The Harvard guy says, 'At Haavaad, they teach us to wash our hands.' The firefighter says, 'At the firehouse, they teach us to not piss on our hands.'"

The strike team leader tried to connect the dots but couldn't, so I fed him my point. "In my firehouse, I tell my firefighters sex is on their own time. Oh, and by the way, my method doesn't assume anyone's sexual preference. Yours does." The strike team leader caved, and I stuck with my crew.

"That's why you're going to make a kick-ass attorney," Mark said. "It's your path now."

I thought about the role fate had played in our firefighting lives. When Mark was a firefighter at Corralitos, he sliced through his boot with a Pulaski on a fire. The diagonal slice crossed the bridge of the foot clear through to the sole. But his toes somehow came out unscathed. The boot remains on a plaque in the Corralitos toolroom. Who would have thought his toes would make it and mine wouldn't?

"Guess so," I said, but my voice cracked.

I knew I had to move on. I'd moved on so many times in my life, the how of it felt familiar. That night, I made a loaf of toast and rubbed my dog Kelly's ears. And in the weeks ahead, I threw myself into workouts and law school, sweating out my grief and keeping my mind distracted from the dark hole inside me.

In my last year of law school, I busied myself with clerkships. I worked a summer in an employment law firm and a winter in a district attorney's office to try on arson prosecution. My contracts professor recommended

a deputy district attorney he thought I'd work well with—Merle Frank, aka Bud. As Bud tells it, his mom assigned him this nickname at two years old, finding his personality similar to her beloved childhood pug. The only time she called him "Merle" was when he was in trouble.

Nothing about my clerkship in the DA's office appealed to me, except Bud—and even then, I fought with myself. Bud broke all my rules. I wanted an athletic, dog-loving, quasi-Christian veterinarian who loved camping, had a truck outfitted with mountain bike racks, and was no more than a decade older than me. Bud was thirteen years my senior, a nonpracticing Jew, the proud owner of a two-seat Z-car, and hated hiking, barking, and anything involving tents. But the two of us had an undeniable spark. When my clerkship ended, we tested it by going on a date. Then on another. And on another. And on another.

He was smart, easy to talk to, and had an unconventional nature. He surprised me with his complexities: a martial arts background, a woodworking gift, an infectious smile, an ocean kayak, Gershwin's complete collection, and a bratty side to match mine.

He'd poke at me, testing my tolerance for being messed with, and underestimating it. A seminal moment in our relationship occurred the day he understood my smart-ass aptitude.

It started on a grocery trip together. I should have known from his eye twinkle and curled upper lip that he was in the mode. I ignored the cues. He made me jump when he set a frozen corn package on the back of my neck.

I raised my eyebrows at him, like "Be forewarned." He laughed and put the corn in our cart. Once we had everything, I steered to an open checkout lane. Bud dawdled at the magazine racks while I handed my credit card to the checker. It was my turn to pay. As she delivered the receipt to me, Bud walked up behind me, put his arm around my waist, and said, "Hey, Babe. I see you have eggs. How 'bout we make a night of it, and I'll make you breakfast? My name's Bud, by the way."

It caught me and the checker off guard. I looked horrified. The checker froze. She needed to know what to do next: relax or call the police. I had to signal her.

"Very funny, Bud." I kissed him to show her I knew him and I wasn't a floozy. Her shoulders lowered, but I could tell she still thought something was wrong between the two of us.

"Got you pretty good in there," Bud said as we wheeled the cart to his car.

"Yup. Wasn't expecting that," I said with a smile, logging the event for some future payback opportunity.

On the way home, we stopped at his office to pick up a file. I opted to go in with him instead of waiting in the car. While I didn't like the DA's office, I loved seeing him in his work element. He was a skilled prosecutor—good with other attorneys, judges, victims, and even defendants. It fit him the way firefighting had fit me.

I watched him strut into the county building. The confident walk complimented his business suit and graying temples, making him look like an unbeatable force. In contrast, I wore torn jeans and an oversized sweatshirt that made me look like someone turning herself in to the juvenile unit on the third floor. Maybe this was why the checker looked at us funny.

"Let's take the stairs," I said.

The building's elevators were notoriously slow. With only five stories, everyone just planned accordingly. You could spot the out-of-town lawyers rushing to their hearings, repeatedly pushing a button they somehow thought was an accelerator.

"Oh, hell no. I'm still sore from the workout you forced on me yesterday," Bud replied.

I crammed into the elevator with him and several others traveling to all five floors.

The doors closed. I could feel Bud inching toward me. He swung his arm around my waist and tugged me close, the way he had in the grocery store.

I couldn't let him get away with it again, so I wriggled away and blurted in a loud whisper, "Uncle Merle, I said stop touching me that way."

Bud removed his arm, stared straight ahead, and endured the cacophony of hate stares directed at him from visiting attorneys who didn't know

us. On the longest, slowest elevator ride in history, I wondered whether I had killed or cemented our relationship.

We got married right after I finished law school.

Federal Courthouse—San Jose Branch, 2001

My first job as a lawyer was with a big labor law firm. It paid well but felt purposeless and required attendance at parties with canapés. After I earned enough to pay off my school loans, I opted for public sector lawyering with a stint at the attorney general's office before settling in as a staff attorney for the federal courthouse. I handled prisoner cases. My time in the camp program helped me understand the culture of the cases. I liked the research, the writing, and the daily cadence: walk two miles to the office, caffeinate while working on briefs, hit the health club during lunch, grab lunch to go, spill curry sauce on my research books at my desk, banter with the clerks and judges, and walk home. Then, September 11th toppled everything.

Like most, I remember that morning clearly. News stations looped apocalyptic imagery while I got dressed for work. There was nothing I could do besides put on my suit, show up at my desk, and monitor news reports. One report showed local fire departments cobbling together rescue teams to send to New York. Another showed out-of-control West Coast wildfires. The attacks resulted in an FAA order grounding all aircraft—including airtankers dropping fire retardant in California.

Instead of working on legal briefs, I made two phone calls.

I dialed my brother Mark first. "Hey. Weird fucking day, *huh*?"

"No shit," he said.

I heard road noise. "Where are you?"

"I'm heading to a fire up north. What are you doing?"

"I'm sitting at my desk. Heading nowhere."

I liked lawyering, but it didn't satisfy me the way firefighting did—especially on a day like this. While former colleagues packed their bags

220

to help at Ground Zero and my brother drove north to protect our state, I sat in my ergonomically correct chair, shoes kicked off under my desk, feeling useless—that same black hole I'd felt on my final drive home from Belmont. I wanted so badly to help. I did the only thing I could; I called my foot doctor.

"It's been five years," I said.

"Come in for a checkup," he said.

<p style="text-align:center">***</p>

My bare feet dangled off the edge of the examination table. A cold sheet of sanitary paper crackled under my shorts as I shifted on top of it, waiting for the doctor. Outside the window, a skyscraper hotel made me think about towers: first, the fallen twins taken out by plane bombs, then the firehouse drill towers I yearned to return to. A montage of times I'd spent in those towers, setting fires inside them, and practicing extinguishment and rescue techniques, raced through my mind.

I rocked back and forth in the chilly medical office. The doctor walked in. He asked questions and poked at my toes with tools I didn't recognize. After ten minutes, he said, "You're good to go."

"What does that mean?"

"It means your feet are ready for fire boots. Keep them dry when you can."

"Really? Holy fuck." I sucked in air, like I hadn't had a breath since he walked in. "I mean . . ." I tried to reword it, but "Holy fuck" came out again. "You'll sign the job duty form?"

He laughed. "I'll sign it. Send it to my assistant."

As soon as I got home, I called the division chief in charge of hiring at my old unit headquarters in Felton.

"Hi, Chief. It's Clare . . ." I hesitated. The last time I was a firefighter, my last name was Bisbee. I took Bud's name because it mattered to him, and I wouldn't have to spell it three times whenever I ordered pizza.

"Bisbee!" he said, recognizing my voice. "How the heck are you?"

"I'm good. I'm really good. My last name is 'Frank' now." After some chatter, I laid it out. "Look, my doctor just cleared me. I want to reinstate. Do you have any openings?"

He told me he had a vacant fire marshal position at Felton. "Send in your paperwork and we'll include you in the interviews."

"Will do," I said, hanging up with a huge smile on my face. The fire marshal job wouldn't get me back in the daily dirt, but it would give me access to fire assignments and maybe even a command team. And I thought I could nail the interview with my previous fire marshal experience at Belmont, and now unbeatable familiarity with codes, regulations, and statutory schemes.

I dug my fire boots from the deepest recess of my closet and wore them around the house, waiting for Bud to come home from work so I could tell him in person.

As soon as he walked through the door, I pointed to my boots and blurted, "The doctor released me. Look! Boots!"

Bud squinted and cocked his head, not caught up with me.

I took a deep breath and laid out the plan. "I know you married a lawyer with a six-figure income that's about to be cut in half. But look how happy I am."

Bud hugged me for a long time, then said, "Did we keep the for-richer-or-poorer language in our vows, or was that one of the ones we tossed?"

"Sorry, Sweetie. Kept that one. It was the whole 'obey' thing we cut."

"Damn. Well, guess I'm stuck." He laughed. "So with the pay-cut thing, we're gonna need to curtail your jewelry habit." He pointed to my wedding band.

In four years of marriage, I'd gone through three wedding rings. I wasn't good with bling. The first ring had two small rubies and a modest diamond. I loved the ring and took better care of it than any other piece of jewelry I'd owned before. One day, I took it off at the gym to do pull-ups, placing it in my shorts pocket. Once I got home, I realized all that was in the pocket was a hole. The two subsequent rings were simple gold bands, with a comfort fit, designed to be left on during workouts. Still, I managed to leave them in unknown places.

I kissed Bud and tapped my latest ring. "It's not going anywhere," I said. I would manage to keep track of that one for a record-setting two years.

The fire marshal interview went as expected, and I got the offer. Next, I had to buy new uniforms, since I'd thrown out my old ones in a purge of fury. Then I had to tell the judges I was leaving. I made a separate appointment with each and waited for one or all of them to tell me I was flushing my hard-earned law degree and bar card down the toilet for a less honorable standing in society. But each of them surprised me.

"It's a no-brainer. Go be a firefighter." I could see envy in their eyes. In these times, they too wanted to do more than they could from their ivory tower.

✱✱✱

Felton Unit Headquarters, 2002

I loved being back in uniform, free to cuss at my coworkers. The guy who ran the headquarters supply warehouse passed me every morning on his way to the mail room. We exchanged pleasantries.

"Fuck you, Fox."

"Fuck you, Frank."

It was just a thing we did, and it made us both smile.

I dug into fire marshaling and retraining that gave me currency in all my certifications. The job was easy for me. My legal expertise proved invaluable, and I'd gained efficiency at analysis and problem solving. This left time to go back to school and finish my bachelor's degree. My educational gaps still bothered me. This time I found a major that didn't bore me. One of two fire bachelor's programs in the nation was fifteen minutes from home at a college called Cogswell Polytech. It had a firefighter-friendly low-residency format, so I didn't have to drop classes every time I left for a big fire.

The brass also assigned me to cover behind battalion chiefs when needed, handling command for larger incidents and urgent personnel issues that couldn't await the return of the regular battalion chief—like

when a fight broke out between two captains. Plus, I had time to work my way through an incident command track I'd started during my first fifteen years. Within a couple of years, I landed on one of the coveted command teams as a "plans chief," traveling all over the state to help manage campaign incidents. It was the grind I'd missed as a lawyer. I smelled bad, had smoke-filled lungs from weeks and weeks at incident base, and achieved new levels of fatigue. On one fire, I got three hours of sleep over four days. And this is likely the stretch of time that bumped my cumulative smoke exposure to a level that brought on a new incurable disorder: adult-onset asthma. I was thrilled to be back in my element.

The unit chief, who everyone called "Johnny Wallet" for his frugal tendencies, took notice, and in 2004 he bumped me up to division chief in charge of administration. Two weeks in, the job reminded me of an old movie called *How to Succeed in Business Without Really Trying*, where the protagonist follows a guidebook that tells him, "Make vice-president." He accepts a VP of advertising position, then turns to the next page of the book, which says, "vice-president of anything except advertising."

I learned more than I ever wanted to know about budgets and spreadsheets. I taught myself Excel and Visio at night while watching *Boston Legal* with Bud.

"I left the law for this." I showed Bud my latest color-coordinated budget chart.

"That's some real hero shit, Sweetie. Totally worth your pay cut."

"I'll suck it up until an Ops job opens up."

"When's that going to happen?"

"CK's in the know. I'll grill him tomorrow."

CK, from my basic firefighter training, now worked at Felton in McFlay's old job. He, Fuck-you Fox, and a captain named Mike shot hoops with me at lunch.

During an around-the-world warm-up, I asked, "Hey, CK, what's your crystal ball say on when an Ops job will open?"

CK shook his head. "Nah, man. You should apply for a chief's job." Apparently CK still saw me in a light brighter than I saw myself.

"You're crazy," I said, sinking a three-pointer.

"Remember Cloverdale?" Mike asked me, referring to a fire assignment we'd been on together. The incident command post was in a high school gym. Mike found a ball somewhere. A couple guys joined him. I walked over and he passed the ball to me, creating a two-on-two game. Mike knew I could play softball, but had no idea my heart was at point guard. The other guys didn't even bother to block my shot. I launched and hit nothing but net.

Mike captured the moment: "Not bad, for a girl." He said what every guy in the gym was thinking. Then he winked to tell me he knew better. Mike is still one of my favorite peeps.

"Not kidding," CK said, answering with his own long shot.

"But Johnny Wallet is a youngster. And talented. So he's not going anywhere," I said.

"Think about another unit, or a city. Milpitas is looking for a chief."

"No way," I said, then launched an air ball. CK had gotten into my head. The part of me attracted to dares wondered if I could be a chief. Milpitas was seven miles from my house.

I mentioned it to Bud at dinner.

He jumped on it. "Duh."

"I'm not a chief," I protested. "I'm the workhorse behind the chief. That's my zone."

"Who you kidding? You've been at the helm since we met."

"That's not true," I said.

"Who takes duty chief coverage more than anyone else?"

"We're mostly on a rotation."

"Who spent Christmas Day going to each station to chat with the firefighters and thank them for being away from their families?"

"That's not fair. I learned that from Johnny. Plus, I had the duty chief coverage that day."

"Exactly my point. I'm with CK on this one."

Bud and CK left me no choice. I had to call my touchstone: my brother, Mark.

Mark had left Cal Fire a couple of years earlier for a battalion chief position in Watsonville, a city in southern Santa Cruz County. Mark missed the bigger operations of Cal Fire, but not the endless bureaucracy that came

with its behemoth size. And a month earlier he'd gotten the fire fix of his life when Watsonville's landmark Wall Street Inn caught fire. He placed an order through dispatch for a plans chief, knowing they'd call me. Mark and I got our last opportunity to work side by side in the light of a five-alarm blaze that would draw headlines for how well he managed the incident. He was a natural and I still looked up to him. I needed his opinion on whether I should shoot for a chief spot.

"Why not a chief?" Mark asked me on the phone.

"I don't see myself as a chief."

"Why not?" Mark continued, employing the why game we played as kids. Mark was always more philosophical than me—a truth seeker. He wanted me to explore the why of my hesitation at promoting to a top spot. Perhaps he expected an answer referencing Dad and his beloved beatitudes, favoring meekness and poverty over promotions, power, and pay raises. But the part of Dad I'd inherited had to do with restless quest, not fear of success or piety. Plus, I figured no matter how high I promoted, I'd never make enough money in civil service to put me in Christ's cross hairs.

"I guess I want to be the locomotive, not the adorned train car."

"Why?" Mark persisted.

"Because that's what I respect. And don't ask 'why' again. I need your advice, not a lesson on introspection. Should I stick with spreadsheets and wait for Ops or jump to a city?"

Mark let up. "I can tell you I've had zero regrets about going the municipal route. There's no identity crisis. We're not forestry *and* fire, seasonal *and* year-around. We're not trying to be dirt *and* polish. We have the same name we've always had, and I don't have to board a plane to get to a fire."

"So you agree with Bud and CK?"

"I think you'd make a great chief. You should go for it. If it's not supposed to happen, it won't, but don't take the option away from yourself."

I hung up, still unsure of what to do. Figuring a good sweat would sort it out, I put on my running shoes. My feet set the cadence as I argued with myself. *You should apply. You shouldn't. You should apply. You shouldn't.*

226

Mark was right. There was a "why" behind my quarrel, which I got to by mile three. It was the same one I'd had at Sandy Point when CK told me I'd earned a job. I feared the precipice. As one of only a few females wearing division chief collar brass, like it or not, a failure would impact women firefighters below me. A fall from the height of chief would be an "I told you so—no place for women." *If I don't climb to the top of the tower, I can't fall from it, and I can't hurt anyone*, I thought. But opting out had repercussions too. *If I don't even try for a job I'm pretty sure I can crush, the trail-clearing slows—waits for someone else while I help adhere a glass ceiling into place.*

I made my decision and sprinted the final stretch home.

CHAPTER 19

BRASS

Milpitas Fire Department, 2005

I committed all the numbers to memory for the chief's interview. This Silicon Valley high-rise city was *51 years old,* covered *14 square miles,* and had a fire department force of *80* at *four* firehouses, responding to *5,500* calls a year, protecting *70,000* residents, another *70,000* commuters during daylight, and *2,600* inmates at the county jail. My numbers worked. The city manager offered me the job. And for the second time, I waved good-bye to Cal Fire for what I thought would be forever.

The weekend before I was sworn in as MFD's chief, Bud and I drove to the uniform store to pick up my new collar brass.

A clerk I hadn't seen before greeted us with a big smile. "I can help you," she said, looking at Bud. Granted, he had a command look and I was in shorts, flip-flops, and a braid.

Bud nodded his head toward me.

"Well, good for you. What department are you with?"

"Milpitas Fire."

"You go, Girl. I'll show you where their uniforms are."

"I already have the uniforms. Just need collar brass."

"Ra-anked. Double good for you."

"Thanks. I'll take two sets, five open."

She stopped smiling. "Um, that's for . . . Did you bring your paperwork?"

"No. I'm good. Two sets, five open."

The clerk froze, not knowing what to do.

Collar "brass" comes in two colors and several configurations. Engineers get single silver bugles. Captains, double silver. Battalion chiefs, two gold, crossed. Division chiefs, three gold, crossed. Deputy chiefs, four gold, crossed. Chiefs, five gold, crossed. Some departments have buttons with the bugles embossed. These are called "closed." Others have bugles melded at their crisscrossed intersection with space in between the bugles' bells. These are called "open."

The store owner emerged from the stockroom and saw the clerk staring helplessly.

"Everything good?" he asked her. "What department?"

"Milpitas Fire."

"Perfect, we carry their stock."

"*Um*, she's asking for five bugles."

I could see what I needed through the glass countertop. "It's right there." I pointed.

The owner glanced over, vaguely recognizing me. "Aren't you with Cal Fire?" Then he cocked his head. "Milpitas just hired a new chi—" He leaned forward. "Are you the new chief?"

I nodded. He scrambled, rushing to greet me, setting up a fresh manila folder with my information, then packaging the collar brass. He knew a chief could change a department's uniforms to a stock he didn't carry.

<p style="text-align:center">***</p>

MFD's flagship headquarters showcased Navajo-white walls, burnished floors, and tasteful bronzed lights hanging from high ceilings. Milpitas had money. My new digs were posh compared to the utilitarian stations I'd spent most of my career in.

My administrative assistant, Marilyn, was in her early forties with a soft Filipino accent, shimmering bobbed black hair, a mother's kindness, and an understated efficiency.

"The command staff is ready for you," she said eyeing the clock and suggesting with her hand the conference room direction in case I'd forgotten.

"Right. Thanks. And the coffeepot?" I asked grabbing my mug.

"I'll take care of that," she said.

"It's not your job to get my coffee."

"Just this once, then," she said, lifting the mug from my hand and giving me an almost imperceptible push in the right direction.

"Black," I said, before turning into the meeting room where my command staff of seven looked expectantly my way.

"G'morning. How about we start with some roundtable introductions." I summarized my background and told them a little about Bud.

Marilyn placed my mug in front of me and took a spot at the far end of the table with her notebook and pen.

I took a sip. "Oooh. That's the good stuff. What is it, Italian roast?" The command staff nodded.

"You guys do a monthly coffee kitty, or . . . ?"

"The budget covers it," Marilyn said.

I took another delicious sip and gave them a truncated version of my expectations. "The MFD policy manual is two inches thick. Cal Fire's is nearly a hundred inches. For me, it comes down to three rules. Act like an adult when representing the department. Use common sense. Own your mistakes. That's it. Now it's your turn."

MFD had a typical organizational structure, with a Fire Marshal's Office handling building inspections and fire ordinance enforcement designed to keep fires from starting, Fire Operations handling all aspects of response to fire and rescue calls, and Disaster Preparedness handling citizen and city staff training ahead of a disaster.

The fire marshal introduced herself and her programs first. It was clear she ran an impeccable fire-prevention shop—the best I'd seen. The others went in radio-call order. Battalion chief Alpha ran A-Shift. Bravo, B-Shift. And Charlie, C-Shift. Delta covered administrative duties. Echo ran

training, safety, and special ops. Foxtrot, a non-uniformed temp, covered disaster preparedness as a postretirement gig. He finished his introduction with a hung head.

"You should probably be aware. I recently slammed my front door in the face of a campaign candidate—our newly elected vice-mayor. I don't think it hit him."

"Yeah. See, that would fall squarely under rule two. And rule one if you were wearing anything with the department's logo on it."

"But he got rule three right. He's owning it," Bravo chimed in to defend Foxtrot.

"If you get rule three right, does it offset violating the first two?" Alpha asked.

We were off and running. Foxtrot had teed it up and now they understood my priorities well enough to debate them. But I knew this wasn't the last I'd hear about the slammed door.

When we ended the meeting, Marilyn hurried to her desk, piled with work.

"Do you like being in those meetings?" I asked.

She shrugged. "It takes a lot of time. Then to type up the minutes is more."

"You type the notes into minutes? Then what?"

"I file them in case someone forgets a task or the union makes a request."

"No," I said. "We can keep track of our own tasks and the union can ask me if they . . ."

"Is it too soon to hug you?"

"No. We're gonna need each other."

Marilyn helped with my learning curve, making sure I went to the right meetings at the right times and giving me subtle clues: a soft smile and eye roll when Finance called, a headshake when asking if I was available to take a call from the local gadfly, and a head nod when Parks and Rec Bonnie stopped in. Marilyn knew that Bonnie knew the councilmembers' favorite

drinks, the mayor's church pals, and our boss's police buddies from when he headed up the force before he became city manager.

Thanks to Marilyn, Bonnie, my command staff, and my instincts, I stayed mostly out of trouble. My only real run-in with the city manager came in my second month. At a council meeting, Finance suggested budget cuts could include shuttering Fire Station #4. The local newspaper jumped on it, shoving questions and a microphone at me.

"Closing firehouses is up to the community. They have a voice in this," I said.

The morning after it printed, the city manager called me down to City Hall.

"What the fuck were you thinking? Talking to the press and making them think we don't operate as a team? A call for community action? You don't get to do that."

"All due respect, Boss, Finance ambushed me by putting a firehouse on the chopping block without coming to me first."

"She came to me. I approved that."

"Well, someone should've told me. Maybe then I wouldn't be pitched between my own firefighters and a solution the city may or may not need. I can't lead a department that doesn't trust me. If Finance wants to run it, or if you want a pawn, go get one. I'll find a different spot."

"You got some brass balls there, Chief," he said. But he backed down, knowing it's what he would have done when he was police chief. And he knew I understood that.

Before I turned to leave, he said, "We gotta talk about something else. Your good ol' boy Foxtrot nearly gave our new vice-mayor a bloody nose."

"Yeah. I heard about that. Not smart."

"Especially not in a tight year. City council might ask you to cut his position. He's already retired, so it's an easy call. Also, don't count on filling your deputy chief slot."

I didn't know if it was a tight year or a test. I held my breath a beat to let my filter kick in, then launched. "Hurricane Katrina hit less than two weeks ago. Body count is in the thousands. All that's on TV is recovery efforts. We have three of our guys there right now on a mutual aid task force. Council

232

won't look good if they eliminate our disaster prep position. If anything, it needs perming up. I can take care of Foxtrot's tantrum another way." I took a breath. "On the deputy chief, I need time to see if anyone's ready, so I'm good on that one."

He shook his head. "Sounds like you want a bloody mess, Chief."

He was right. Budget hearings felt like a cage fight. In the end, Station #4 stayed open, along with my vacant deputy chief slot. And Council agreed to consider a permanent disaster coordinator, but it wasn't going to be Foxtrot. He was done. He collected his retirement, free to slam doors while I shoved the extra workload on my Delta battalion chief.

My brother, Mark, was promoted to chief for the city of Watsonville a few months after I'd taken the MFD job. Our two cities had a couple things in common but also some big differences. They were similar in size, and both served as the on-location filming site for panned sci-fi–horror movies—*The Milpitas Monster* in my city, and *Killer Klowns from Outer Space* in Mark's. But Milpitas was affluent and sprinklered while Watsonville was poor and old—erected before Mrs. O'Leary's cow (or drunk gamblers) knocked over a lantern and burned down Chicago, causing officials across the nation to think, *Hey, maybe we should invent fire codes.*

Mark and I compared notes weekly.

"Gimmee your rundown," Mark said.

"Someone left a *Reader's Digest* in my in-box with a cover story about one of my captains who dove into the bay and cut a whale out of a net a quarter mile offshore. Problem is he's on workers' comp leave for a bum shoulder and now I have to launch a fraud investigation. Also, yesterday a prisoner broke out of the jail, went to Taco Bell across from my office, got a burrito, then reported back to jail. And this morning, a crew did 'hose training' on the city's tennis courts to clear windstorm tree litter so Parks and Rec wouldn't have to cancel the weekend youth lessons. How 'bout you?"

"Our new tiller truck didn't slow enough at a red light during a Code 3 run and a cop car going to the same call smashed into it. A migrant family

living in a garage left the space heater on and it burned down two houses. Nobody died there, but a fatal gang shooting outside the station yesterday took out a teenager."

"You win."

"Not sure about that. Seems like I get fastballs and you get changeups," Mark said.

Mark's analogy was spot-on. Throughout my first year, I kept waiting for Milpitas to deliver a righteous calamity—a hummer straight down the middle. The city's hazardous-materials corridor, high-density neighborhoods, and toxic manufacturing posed plenty of risk. But the young city, built under new codes with an unbeatable inspection program, minimized major incidents, leaving "bread-and butter-calls" that didn't need a chief: a hot hibachi placed in a cupboard, a pileup during rush hour, medical emergencies at the jail, alarms sounding at the shopping mall, and—yes— cat rescues. I stood waiting to swing at a hundred-mile-an-hour heater. Instead, week after week, floaters dropped low in the pocket.

"Whatcha got this week?" Mark asked.

"A harassment complaint by a firefighter who knows everyone looks at him because he's gorgeous but doesn't like it if he thinks the gawker is gay. A muscle-head who didn't sound the roof and fell to the ground floor but bounced because he packs a good layer of insulation around his brawn. A new-hire paramedic who's a cool dude but too rogue for uniformed services so he's failing probation. And a pujari at a temple in a strip mall who invited me for a chief's blessing to help keep the city safe. His staff made me take off my boots and served me horrible bright-colored cookies I pretended to like. Still, I felt peace and good intention. You?"

"An apartment complex fire, and budget cuts. I can only staff two rigs a day, thanks to a blown annex deal that could've increased the tax base enough to cover my third rig, plus a library branch and PD's gang task force."

"Hang in."

"You too. Talk to ya next week."

I hung up with Mark and went to work on my latest knuckleball. Every year, the Knights of Columbus hosted an awards dinner recognizing the

firefighter, police officer, and citizen of the year. My job was to shell out sixty bucks for a couple of lukewarm buffet meals, drag Bud along as arm candy, and introduce the fire honoree with a poignant, witty, short speech. A committee of former recipients selected the year's chosen hero—who would've been a great choice, except I knew what they didn't: he'd just gotten a DUI.

I did the best I could from the podium. "What you know about this year's award winner is he's an exceptional firefighter. He also dedicates countless volunteer hours to the city's Toys for Tots program and cares deeply about this community. What you don't know is this award will humble, not inflate him. He'll work harder than he ever has on himself and on community service." I looked him in the eye. He nodded and teared up. In the months and years ahead, he'd prove me right.

The rest of the awards dinner was easier and gave me a chance to engage with the troops out of uniform. I sat and had a glass of wine with Max, a rising-star captain at MFD who I'd worked with as a Soquel Sleeper over twenty years earlier.

Then I made the rounds. One firefighter, an A-Shifter named Simonson, held an audience critiquing the fare. "The chicken was a little one-note. I would have liked different layers of rubber, a little tire, maybe some Vibram boot sole. A little more complexity is what I'm saying."

Simonson had worked as a cook while waiting to get into MFD. Then it happened; he got his dream job. Nine years in, he still couldn't wipe the smile off his face. He'd written on the corner of the training-room whiteboard, "I have the best job in the world!" None of us would have guessed that in twelve days his world would turn upside down.

<center>***</center>

I got the call around midnight. It was Alpha. "Chief, one of the guys got hurt. Off-duty. Mountain bike. Spinal injury."

"Shit. Who? How bad?"

"Simonson. Not good. C6 and C7."

I rushed into a pair of jeans and a sweatshirt and drove up to Stanford Spinal.

Surrounded by A-shifters, Simonson lay on his hospital bed, motionless, but wide awake. As soon as he heard my voice, he said, "Chief, my job. My job. I can't leave MFD."

Simonson's fearlessness had caused this—coming off a hill at speed, he splashed through a puddle that hid a tree root big enough to launch him. But now I saw only terror.

"Maybe I can beat it, Chief. Get back on an engine."

A-shifters out of his line of sight but in mine shook their heads. They'd overheard phrases from the doctor. All four limbs impacted. Quadriplegic. Bedridden.

Their fear was palpable. *Can Simonson make it through this? Could I if this was me? Will his girlfriend stick around?*

I squeezed Simonson's shoulder. "We'll figure this out. I'll do whatever I can to keep you in MFD." I suppose I saw in him the potential Norm had seen in me. When Norm inherited me, I was an unpolished mess worth working on—raw material he could macramé into its best use. I was now the same age that Norm was then, and had the wisdom to see that reckless and broken Simonson had an indomitable spirit I could help mold.

I fought to get Simonson a tryout in Foxtrot's old gig, if he could get himself mobile. He'd have to trade climbing ladders for this non-uniformed admin job, but he'd still be a member of the fire department. The nice thing about local government is that it has more agility—a small boat that can turn on a dime—compared to a state government barge with a hundred inches of policy that couldn't handle my toenails.

Simonson did his part. Relentless on rehab, he upgraded his status from bedbound to wheelchair-capable. Crews chipped in too, spending their days off installing ramps and wider doorframes at his house. And the cops helped, organizing a fund raiser yielding the best badass wheelchair made. Someone printed stickers with Simonson's initials, and we all stuck them on our helmets. Then he came back to work.

In a van with hand controls, Simonson loaded himself from his wheelchair into the driver's seat, hoisted the chair in, and headed to his meetings, where he could talk firsthand about how even the most vulnerable can prepare for disaster. The city never had a better spokesperson in

that position. And Simonson would go on to make a splash at the county, state, and national levels because his way through the injury was to ask, "What's next?" not "Why me?" Instead of waiting for a fat pitch, he smashed the spitball.

<p style="text-align:center">✶✶✶</p>

As a teenager, I worked summers and weekends at the Santa Cruz Beach Boardwalk. My bosses started me as a cotton candy spinner, but I had no gift for shaping cones, so they moved me to custom T-shirts, where I flourished. My brother had worked his way up from litter sweeper to ride operator. If I hadn't found T-shirts, I would have followed, hoping to land the grand Looff Carousel, one of the last in the country with a ring dispenser. If you picked an outside horse, you could reach out and grab a lead ring from the metal chute, then sling it at a giant clown head, hoping to land it inside the mouth, which would set off lights and bells and get you a free ride. But you had to be careful. Every now and then, the dispenser would spit out a brass ring. These were keepsakes, never to be tossed away.

Simonson's "best job in the world" quote stayed on the whiteboard because we all knew it was true. Outside of squabbles and entitlement fits that come from not working in a hardscrabble department, MFD had its shit together. There were a few jerks, but I liked everyone else and formed close friendships with my direct reports. All things considered, this was the easiest my life had been. Then it got better.

Despite me pissing him off early, the city manager gave me good reviews and pay raises. And I'd become proficient enough to take on outside responsibilities, accepting a part-time teaching gig with Cogswell Polytech and rotating into position as president of the Santa Clara County Fire Chiefs Association—a group I loved.

The ten of us met monthly to align priorities and improve interagency services, but really to share a kinship. We'd grown up in a fraternal profession, but from the top of the pyramid we felt like single parents. So we kept each other's numbers on speed dial.

We also leaned into each other's charities. If one chief supported a fund raiser, we'd all write a check for it. One city sponsored an annual "Walk a Mile in Her Shoes" event benefiting sexual violence victims with a parade of men wearing high heels. We all showed up to support our comrade chief, who wore his Class-A uniform and a pair of bright red size-14 pumps. I would have had as hard a time in heels as he did, but it would have been easier for me to find a pair that fit. He had to go to a drag shop in San Francisco. "This was not in my job description," he grumbled, in good spirits along the torturous mile.

. We always ended the year with an annual dinner including cocktails and spouses. As the outgoing president for the year, I clicked the side of my glass with a knife until the room fell silent. "Welcome to our annual chief's dinner. Here's to last year's accomplishments and next year's aspirations. It's been an honor to be your president."

We cheered and sipped, until someone clicked a glass for another toast.

"Here's to those who make it happen. To the wives!"

On autopilot, we tipped our glasses but froze midway as the words registered. All eyes shifted to Bud. He didn't miss a beat. He pointed a thumb at himself, and said, "To the wives!"

This was different from macro- and microaggressions I'd faced over the years. Here, I'd become so much a part of the same fabric, we'd forgotten to pay attention to my gender, or Bud's. In a weird way, "To the wives" became a milestone in equity.

Later that night, the most senior chief in the group pulled me aside. "You know, you made a great president. You should think about going bigger. Maybe do something with Cal Chiefs or apply for the Harvard Fellowship. Someone like you could get it."

He was talking about Harvard University's Senior Executives in State and Local Government Program. In a competitive process, four fire service giants (United States Fire Administration, International Association of Fire Chiefs, International Fire Service Training Association, and National Fire Protection Association) partnered with Harvard to award eight paid fellowships for an esteemed interdisciplinary leadership program.

I talked it over with Bud. He'd been a criminal justice research fellow at Harvard years earlier and had loved the experience. "You should go for it. And get me a new sweatshirt from the bookstore. Mine's pretty raggy."

I applied and stuck my landing. And sitting in the tiered classroom at Harvard's Kennedy School of Government gave me the same grin I'd had at law school. There I was, in my flip-flops, listening to lectures by Harvard greats, alongside classmates who aspired to be governors, senators, big-city mayors—game changers.

With a case study format, we discussed civic leadership, policy, and ethics. Some days brought outings: a Red Sox game, an Outward Bound trip to Thompson Island, a JFK Library tour. In the late afternoons, I went for runs alongside the Charles River in warm summer rain. And evenings brought continued debates in Cambridge pubs. I relished every moment, and subliminally absorbed the program's ultimate message, which JFK ripped off from the New Testament: "For of those to whom much is given, much is required."

On the flight back home, in my new sweatshirt, I wondered if I was required to do more now that I'd been privileged enough to spend the heart of summer in a higher-learning glory land. For months, the question gnawed at me. I asked Bud. I asked God. They both shrugged.

Eight months later, I found my answer on a basketball court in Emmitsburg, Maryland, home to the United States Fire Administration's National Fire Academy. I'd been asked to spend a week there on a curriculum development cadre to expand the number of fire baccalaureate programs throughout the country.

I cleared security at the sprawling colonial campus on a Sunday afternoon, then found my room, changed into gym clothes, and wandered over to the indoor basketball court. No one else was there. High windows with vintage rippled glass streamed light in magical patterns onto thick brick walls and a spongy wood floor. The place smelled like hard work

and dust. It unexpectedly brought an immediate peace to my soul. It felt like a holy place.

Maybe I'd tapped into the campus's origins. The first American-born saint, Elizabeth Ann Seton, had chosen this spot to build a groundbreaking school for girls. It must have been before the sisters turned sadistic with rulers, because I felt no malice, just pure tranquility. *This is where I want to be buried,* I thought—something I'd never thought about a place.

I launched shot after shot, rejected by tight rims on either end of the court. I slowed my breathing, found a rhythm, and started hitting nothing but net. Then, with a little nudge from Saint Elizabeth Ann, I was ready to have the conversation with myself that Harvard had urged.

"Am I supposed to be doing something more? Something bigger?"

"You're a goddamn chief. What do you want from yourself?"

I released a short jumper. "Like they said at Kennedy School: more."

"More than?"

"More than fighting with the city council over blown overtime budgets caused by their backroom negotiations. More than lovely sushi lunches with Bonnie where we dish about missing the now retired city manager because the new one's a hot mess. More than a few room-and-contents fires that don't need me. More than having to get my adrenaline rush by binge-watching Jack Bauer's *24* for twenty-four hours straight to see if it tracks in real time."

"You wanna toss your brass ring? What about your command staff? And Marilyn?"

"Command staff is fine. They've got a good pay deal and they know how to handle Milpitas. Marilyn would have to train another fire chief. I'd feel bad about that. But seven more years coasting? Doesn't feel right."

"Okay. Here's the deal. Three-pointer. If you make it, you gotta go big. State HQ, federal, or major metro. No more Felton."

I nodded, set my feet, took my deep breath, then launched the shot, trusting my body more than my head with these stakes. The ball hit the back of the rim, and rolled in.

When I got home from Maryland, I made some calls, including one to my old high school classmate Andy, who worked at State Fire Headquarters.

There was an opening on the prevention side for a deputy chief in charge of a new trailblazing program called Civil Cost Recovery, CCR for short. An underutilized statute allowed fire departments to seek suppression costs from a culpable party, like a hiker who walked away from a hot campfire, or a power company that didn't take proper precautions against lines arcing in dried vegetation. CCR needed a heavy lift and someone who could work closely with field investigators and the legal shop. Fire. Law. Game-changing. It was perfect.

That night, I gave Bud a heavy pour of scotch, then busted out with, "Soooo, you cool if I trade my 7-mile commute for a 130-mile one, with loss of a bugle and a fifty percent pay cut, to take a position with temporary funding? Oh, and we'll need to get Marilyn a fat Nordstrom gift card."

CHAPTER 20

OHMS

State Fire Civil Cost Recovery, 2009

Bud still had over two years to retirement and no interest in moving 130 miles away. And we both knew I wasn't a gracious daily driver.

"It's called the fast lane—a consti-fucking-pated turtle shits quicker."

"Ever heard of a turn signal, Einstein?"

"Gee-zus! Drive on meth much, ya ballsack."

And that was on my seven-mile commute. So we went apàrtment hunting in Sacramento, for a place I could stay during the workweek.

After looking at several moldy rentals, we found a new loft project at the front end of a regentrification effort in Sacramento's midtown—twelve studios sculpted into the second floor of a 1913 brick bakery building, near rail tracks and occasional gunfire. But it was reasonably priced, walking distance to my new job, and above a very cool bar and grill called Shady Lady.

"This is it," I declared.

On the drive home, Bud and I interlaced fingers. We understood the passing miles would be between us Monday through Friday for the next six years—when I'd be eligible to sign retirement papers.

"The time will go fast," Bud said, trying to convince himself as much as me.

"I predict you'll watch sci-fi every night and eat chili straight from the can."

"You'll leave the lights on all the time and watch those I'd-rather-slit-my-wrists-than-watch-them-with-you-no-matter-how-much-I-love-you reality shows." He paused. "No midnight walks when you can't sleep, though. Okay?"

I had a history of that, and Bud and I tried to respect that we both had inclinations a spouse should worry about but not overcontrol. When he decided he wanted a motorcycle, I said, "You have to wear a bright helmet and increase your life insurance policy." He did. Promising to stay inside during my new hood's danger hours seemed a fair quid pro quo.

I nodded and squeezed his hand tight. I could always feel it—that electrical connection between us.

<center>✳✳✳</center>

We hit the uniform store again. The bubbly clerk was confused by my request for bugles a rank lower than last time. But the store owner wasn't. "Ooohhh. You miss the big fires."

I nodded, even though it wasn't that simple. "I guess you can take that down now," I said, pointing at a newspaper article pinned to the wall behind the cash register—a story entitled "Same Blood, Same Job," about Mark and me being local sibling fire chiefs.

"I'm not taking that down. It's historical," the owner said.

It made me realize this was good-bye to an unrepeatable chapter with my brother. With me in Sacramento and him in a city chief's job, odds were we'd never be in uniform together again. A sadness enveloped me, like a fast-moving cloud that blocked the sun. I took in a deep breath, let it out in a sigh, and reminded myself: moving always has its costs.

The owner handed me my bag of goods. "Can't wait to see what you do next," he said. He understood what I didn't: that this wouldn't be my last trip to his store for collar brass.

The following Sunday, Bud brewed me a go-cup of my favorite dark roast and hugged me long enough to last the whole week. I rolled down the

Jeep windows, selected a Jimmy Cliff playlist, and waved at Bud through the open roof until he disappeared from my rearview mirror.

The hillsides along the freeway were a spring green, but the grass was short from low rainfall. Power lines rose and fell between the hills, reminding me of childhood U-Haul trips when I watched the mesmerizing poles for miles on end. I thought they were crosses signifying God's intent to keep us safe on our passage. I remember thinking it clever that God tethered them together, like my kindergarten teacher had for us on field trips to make sure no one ended up alone—although I couldn't figure out why God needed so many ropes between the crosses.

Within a few months in my new job at Cal Fire, I'd learn all about those "ropes" and the amps and volts that charged them, and the ohms needed for resistance to keep them from arcing. I'd learn about lashing wire, metallurgy, line sag, and wind load. And about how too many power poles in California were erected in wetter, greener, less-populated times when profits outweighed risk by a fairer margin.

I didn't know that fires caused by power lines would take over one hundred lives in the upcoming years and forever change how I'd view them from the road—still as crosses, but in their derivation form: crucifixes beckoning death. So I waved a friendly good-bye to them from my new off-ramp, thanking them for a safe, easy Sunday-morning voyage to the loft.

I spent the day unpacking boxes and organizing things before wandering downstairs to Shady Lady. Ragtime music and a waitress in a flapper dress greeted me.

"What's the best bet on a to-go order?" I asked.

"Shrimp po'boy." She didn't hesitate. "Comes with to-die-for fries. We use duck fat."

"Sold. Can you make the fries extra crispy for me?"

"Of course. Would you like a cocktail or glass of wine while you wait?" She looked me up and down, probably trying to figure out which agency I worked for in this government city. My jeans and flip-flops told her I wasn't a lobbyist. "I'm guessing red. But maybe a light one before dinner. Pinot?"

I laughed. "It's like you do this for a living." I took a window seat and savored the wine while looking at my new neighborhood, a hodgepodge

of trendy new eateries, state buildings, and windowless old taverns with day drinkers squinting at dusk's brightness as they exited. One government building had a glass entry door with gold-embossed lettering: DEPARTMENT OF . . . The letters stopped. They must have run out of money, I thought. The state was experiencing a serious budget shortfall. That's why I was here. This was the right time to stand up CCR. If I could prove the program would bring in more than it cost, the state would jump at funding it.

I took my po'boy and fries upstairs and laid them out on the steamer trunk.

"Hi, Charlotte," I said, kicking off my flip-flops and using the remote to select a crappy reality show, just as Bud had predicted. A contentedness washed over me. Succulent shrimp with spicy slaw, crunchy fries, and new digs that had a calming simplicity. One set of dishes. A hanging rod for my uniforms. A small dresser for jeans, shorts, and sweats. Three hooks by the door: one for a jacket, one for keys, and a third for something else. I didn't know what yet.

<p style="text-align:center">***</p>

At State Fire Headquarters, a strip of duct tape patched a crack in the lower-left corner of my office window. I sipped mediocre coffee from a chipped WORLD'S GREATEST NEPHEW mug rejected from someone's home cupboard. This was no Milpitas. But page after page of the Witch Fire investigation report told me I'd made the right decision coming here.

In October 2007, the Witch Fire combined with two smaller fires to scorch nearly a quarter-million acres about an hour southeast of Disneyland. This was the first California wildfire to cause over a billion dollars in damage and the first to call for an evacuation of half a million people. Started by power lines and fanned by Santa Ana winds, the blaze killed 2 civilians, consumed over 1,800 structures, and injured 55 firefighters. And Cal Fire spent $22 million suppressing it. Now, we were working with the state attorney general to recover those costs. If we could get even half of it, it would solidify the CCR program.

In some ways, the case looked like a no-brainer. Southern California's Santa Ana winds blew like they did almost every October. Two wind-whipped lines on a power pole grazed each other. By regulation, lines are supposed to be maintained with a tautness that prevents "line slap." For good reason. When the lines hit, their electrical current acted quickly, choosing this momentarily ohm-free path of least resistance to spit out a spark that ignited dried vegetation below, which—also by regulation—should have been cleared by the lines' owners. An additional damning fact was that even though the power company had detected three shorts in three hours on their line, it waited six hours to cut the power.

But complicating details emerged in the report's pages. The two lines that slapped together were owned by different companies. San Diego Gas & Electric (SDG&E) owned the power line and Cox owned the cable line running lower on the pole. Each company pointed a finger at the other. Our investigators couldn't tell if one or both lines were too loose when the fire started, and who hadn't cleared the vegetation.

I knew from law school this wasn't enough to absolve them. In a case called *Summers v. Tice*, two hunters recklessly fired birdshot at the same time and one or both of their pellets tore into the plaintiff's face. The court held that in instances like this, the burden shifted from the plaintiff to the defendants, who had to prove it wasn't their ammo that caused the damage. In the case of the Witch Fire, this meant two powerhouse companies went at each other with a vigor and determination that made it clear this would be a drawn-out, epic battle.

Another problem was the litigation's sheer size. We were one of 2,600 plaintiffs, and perhaps the least sympathetic. It felt unlikely a judge would prioritize our cost-recovery demand over the thousands who lost something personal: houses, horses, outbuildings, valuable timber, livestock, and, in two instances, a family member. Claims totaled $5.6 billion, far exceeding available insurance money. It was a morass. And I couldn't wait to jump in.

God starts about ten percent of the wildfires in California. Arsonists start another ten percent. The rest are unintentional. Between 4,500 and 8,500 wildfires a year in California were caused by mistakes with mower blades, hot ammo, fireworks, off-road vehicles, trains, tow chains, catalytic converters, cigarettes, campfires, debris burns, power lines, and so on.

The Witch Fire case, albeit the largest, was only one of a hundred pending cases where investigators thought they could prove negligence. Cal Fire's chief counsel cross-designated me as an attorney so I could provide legal guidance to investigators and case managers without having to push everything up to her understaffed office.

Time hadn't traveled this fast for me since my early firefighter years. Every workday passed at warp speed. Suddenly, it was seven or eight o'clock in the evening. If still light out, I went for a jog around the capitol grounds. If dark, I swam laps in the pool at the athletic club across from my office. Afterward, I spread takeout on top of Charlotte and watched *American Idol* hopefuls while continuing the day's work. On weekends, I became a geyser—spewing my whole week at Bud, like a seven-year-old who hadn't seen her bestie in five days.

"The investigators don't like the civil cases as much as the arson cases. Not as sexy. So I'm getting pushback when I ask for productivity numbers. And the only thing my North and South counterparts agree on is that neither wants to do business the same way."

"But don't you all work for . . ."

"Yeah. It's ego bullshit. At the end of the day, they're getting me what I need, but I have to use my pry tools. Oh, get this. One of the experts in the Witch Fire litigation produced a scientific analysis of Santa Ana wind patterns, concluding the fire started on a day with the fiercest wind activity in thirty years. They're trying to set up an act-of-God defense. But it's weak-ass crap. How do they claim unforeseeability when those winds blow every year? And it's not like they've never blown that hard, it's just been a while. And they'd have to prove their lines failed at top speed, not below."

"Maybe Cal Fire should sue God," Bud said. "Those are some deep pockets."

"God's judgment-proof," I said.

I always ended my spew with a perfunctory "How 'bout on your end? Anything juicy?"

He always said, "Nope. Same ol', same ol'. "

I'd worn him out. He needed his silence back.

By the end of the year, Cal Fire settled with SDG&E for $14.3 million, a number that would be hard to ignore at the budget hearing seeking permanent CCR funding. I stood in front of state congressional members in my pressed Class-A uniform, certain I'd get a yes. But then, several microphones on the dais lit up, signaling questions. The first in line came at me from a pin-striped suit. He peered over his reading glasses and furrowed his brow. "I see there's vehicles in this request. Why can't your program use Department of General Services pool cars? The state of California doesn't need to own more cars."

Was this guy fucking serious? DGS operated like a state rental car company, so our investigators trying to get to a breaking incident would have to know when the fires would start and stop, make a reservation 48 hours in advance for a "Chevy Impala or similar," fill out the forms, and return the car within an hour's time frame with a full tank of gas.

I hadn't prepared for this question, which meant I said what came to mind, filtering out the cuss words and derisive tone. "DGS might tend to disfavor it if we returned vehicles with holes drilled in the roofs for lights and sirens and destroyed undercarriages from off-road operations on wildfires inconsiderate enough to travel beyond paved areas."

The room went quiet. Then suppressed smiles broke into laughter, microphone lights disappeared, and I got my *yes*.

By the following year, we standardized procedures and tripled the staffing, adding attorneys, forensic accountants, support staff, and more investigators with more Code 3–capable SUVs. The department had given me a job to do, and I'd done it. Now, time skidded to a halt.

There was still plenty of work, but nothing new or shiny. Nothing insurmountable. Sometimes in these situations, I went into panic mode. I'm sure this malady was part nature and part nurture, inherited both genetically and psychologically from Dad. We both became restless when life began to settle. Physically, I felt agitated and fidgety, like when I endured those long sermons in confining wood church pews, itching to change into sneakers and grab my basketball. Basketball always worked for me. The fast pace. The clear goal. Someone trying to deny it to me. In my school years, when basketball season ended, I had to use softball as my sports methadone. I suppose that's where I sat now, looking for firefighting methadone.

I found it in one of the worst and best career decisions I'd make. My boss, who oversaw the civil and criminal enforcement programs, kept threatening to retire. This was a problem, because he thought I was his most viable replacement. I didn't want his job. His job meant I'd have to become a fire cop, which meant I'd have to go to a rookie police academy for six months. I was deathly scared of guns, twice the age of a typical cadet, and held a deep-seated disdain of what I called "cop attitude."

"You know, Torp wants my job," my boss said, knowing Torp was all about cop attitude and that I'd hate working for Torp.

I didn't bite. "Never gonna happen, Boss. I can't handle guns."

"Maybe you wouldn't have to qualify with cop school. Your law degree might cover it."

I shook my head. There was no way I'd serve as the department's top fire cop without going through the academy or fully understanding the burden of being an armed firefighter. "Seriously. It's not my jam. You're not gonna change my mind."

I'm not sure how Torp got wind of it. But the next day, Torp found me at the coffeepot. "Heads-up. Insane rumor going around about you going to cop school. Don't know where these people get this shit. Nobody with bones over forty can make it through."

Just like that, Torp handed me a dare with a hard game, a clear goal, and someone trying to deny it to me. Volts, amps, and ohms.

Enough happened at the police academy to make it its own story—for another time—about how my stint there changed my mind and body. When I stopped in at headquarters during the academy's holiday break, people recognized me because my voice, not my physical appearance. But headquarters had changed too. The director had unexpectedly retired. That's how Ken landed in the director spot, and Andy behind him as the chief of Fire Protection.

It left a two-star-chief vacancy behind Andy. "I encourage you to apply," Andy told me.

"Holy shit," Bud said. "That's a tap. You don't say no to a tap."

"But I'm still in the academy. And the new job doesn't include law enforcement."

Bud shook his head.

I don't know why I didn't argue. Maybe I was worn down from academy rigors. Maybe I sensed Bud needed a win after watching my body melt away under the bulletproof vest. Maybe I thought I owed Andy a yes. Or maybe I had aspirations I didn't realize. Part of me believed that wanting stars on your collar meant you were a climber, not a dirt firefighter. And nobody I respected, including myself, valued climbers more than dirt. Still, I submitted my paperwork.

"Got the call from Andy," I told Bud. "I start my new job as soon as I'm done with the police academy, or its done with me."

"I'm so proud of you." Bud gave me a bear hug.

"I have mixed feelings about it. I mean, it's exciting, but it kinda feels like I'm flushing the law enforcement stuff down the toilet."

"Not true. You know an arm of the department you didn't know before. It'll help with your next promotion," Bud said, wincing in anticipation of my reaction.

"No. No, no, no. This is it. I'm done promoting. I have four years left, and two stars is more than I ever wanted."

"Sure," Bud said, with the same look the uniform store guy gave me every time—including this time, when I went back to get two-star collar brass.

My new job covered five major programs: municipal contracts, mutual aid, inmate camps, training, and safety. Consisting primarily of programs that relied on cooperative agreements with other agencies, we called it "Co-Op." It had a massive reach and provided me with the pace I needed.

I dug in deep, again working long days to learn the ropes. I liked my staff and that I got to see the department from a different perspective, working in close collaboration with the other two-star chiefs in charge of the forestry, fire marshal, wings and wheels, and north and south region shops. One of the two-stars was ladder Stan from my engineer academy. Stan, the others, and I formed a bond that would help us through budget struggles, increased fire activity, and necessary policy work.

I'd end the days with a nice run through Sacramento's midtown and around the capitol grounds, then back to the loft for a shower, dinner, and delightfully crappy television or my latest stack of paperbacks.

After a longer run one evening, I collapsed on the couch with a bottle of cold club soda. I closed my eyes and let the cool bubbles wet the back of my throat, thinking about everything that had happened since I'd left Milpitas: standing up CCR, going to cop school, getting promoted, and tackling Co-Op. Milpitas seemed like a lifetime ago, like a fling never meant to last, but necessary to let me know how much my true love meant to me. Cal Fire was giving me more than I expected. More than I'd ever thought possible. I suppose Cal Fire and I were like Bud and me—magnetic.

When I opened my eyes, they fixated on the third hook on my coat rack. I knew what belonged there.

Bud had planted the idea over a year earlier after a particularly rough day at the police academy. "When this is all over, we should get a puppy." He didn't mean it. He just knew that's what would make me smile.

Now settled into Co-Op, I had time to handle a puppy. Before I got home that weekend, I'd done the research and located a litter of bullmastiffs in the Santa Cruz Mountains.

"Let's go check out the mom and dad, so when we're ready for a pup, we'll have already met the parents." Bud grabbed his jacket, knowing there was a better chance we'd remain puppy-free if he went along.

We came home with Brody and two sets of everything from the pet store—one for San Jose, the other for Sacramento.

When I got Brody to the loft, I hung his leash on the hook. It fit perfectly. He pushed his puppy nose into the concrete floor, scouring it for stray bits of crackers or maybe a spider. He found nothing, so he squatted and left a puddle.

"No! Not inside." I scooped him up mid-pee, hauled him out the door, and ran him downstairs and out to a dirt corner in the parking lot. We shared the lot with a dumpster and burger-joint employees on smoke breaks. By the time I set his paws on the ground, he was empty, and smiling, and my T-shirt had a wet spot.

That first week, I took him down the stairs every thirty minutes during TV time to make sure he was empty before bedtime. He started to learn the routine and liked sniffing the dirt on his outdoor bathroom. He smelled himself. No one else thought it was a good idea to have a dog in their loft.

I called Bud while waiting for Brody to get through his routine.

"He's not quick about it, which is fine when it's not raining."

"Too soon to say, 'told you so'?"

"Yes."

That night, Brody woke me up with a whimper, followed by a foul smell. I turned the light on. I hadn't supervised him closely enough on out last trip. He must have found something that missed the dumpster and gave him diarrhea. I pulled on sweatpants and shoes, navigated around the mess, grabbed the leash, and took him back down, then up. I cleaned everything, then took him back down. And back down. And back down.

By 2:30 in the morning he had nothing left to offer his potty patch. I picked him up to take him back inside. He was chewing on something.

"No. Drop it!" I dug into his mouth and grabbed ahold of something slimy. I took him over to the light by the back door. I couldn't quite tell what it was. Until I could. He'd retrieved, and now I was holding, a freshly discarded used condom. It was unclear what part of the slime belonged to Brody and what part belonged to the donor. It had taken a moment to register because the last time I had contact with a condom was over ten years ago, before Bud and I decided it best for him to cauterize any chance at us becoming surprise parents.

I hauled Brody back upstairs and disinfected everything. Twice. I tucked back into bed. Brody nestled next to me, prompting instant forgiveness and a contented smile. He grounded me—gave me the ohms I'd need to ride the Co-Op job until my planned retirement date.

Four months later, Ken and Red disrupted my plan—that fated night when I called Bud from Shady Lady's bathroom. With twenty-two months to go, wine and crunchy fries would lead me back to the uniform store, asking for three-star collar brass.

VI.
DECAY

I moved with my parents for the last time at age thirteen. Mark and Bernadette rejoined Mom, Dad, Annie, and me in Santa Cruz, California—the town I would fight to stay in. The idea I could stay came to me on April 1st, a few days before my fifteenth birthday.

Bernadette had decided Mark and I should help her steal Dad's wooden leg as an April Fool's prank. In the dawn hour, she snuck upstairs to exchange a clue scrawled on a scrap of paper for Dad's leg while Mark and I hid remaining clues.

"I got it!" she whispered while scurrying down the stairs, leg secured under her arm. We hustled it out to the garage, dodging half-filled moving boxes. Mark and Bernadette had found a place to live on their own and would be gone by the end of the month. We set the leg in a corner and pulled a tarp over it. Then, the three of us went inside to wait.

We heard Dad's signature hopping sound, *thump, thump, thump*. Then silence, then, "Okay. I'm coming to get it." We smiled at the rare lilt in his voice.

Dad hopped downstairs and foraged for a clue under the TV rabbit ears. The clue sent him back upstairs. Another back down. And so on. He wore the grin of a kid. But Mom saw it as mean. She hollered at us as best she could. "You kids give your father his leg back. This isn't funny anymore." This, of course, split us open. We couldn't stop laughing.

Twenty minutes later, Dad found his leg. We bathed in a tension-free moment, sitting next to him as he strapped the leg over his stump. *Too bad there's no prosthetic for the mind*, I thought, then decided on my plan: I'd wait a year for Dad's inevitable "We're moving" announcement. I'd decline to go with them. They'd sign my freedom papers.

I loved Mom and Dad and would keep them in my life, but my emancipation played like a fire's exit—chaos giving way to calm, and victory overshadowing the sadness of a good-bye.

CHAPTER 21

SLURRY

State Fire Headquarters, 6 Months Left

After the King Fire died down, the state got quiet. An unimpressive smattering of smaller incidents kept the station folks busy, but there were no fires with quadruple-digit acreage. No red-flag conditions. Nothing for headquarters to worry about.

I gave Brody a treat and, for the first time in six months, put on a jacket for my walk to work. Cool air matched the "Pumpkin lattes are back!" window display at a coffeehouse. I inhaled deeply, filling my lungs. This is what a waning fire season smelled like. I knew it could be a head fake. Fire season often did that. But at least for today, I'd get a breather.

At my desk, I slow-sipped coffee and scrolled through e-mails, looking for sex-tape news from the CHP investigator. Nothing yet. Next, I reviewed fire stats. We'd done well this season, keeping the damage under 625,000 acres so far, a reasonable number in a drought year. In fact, it seemed low, like fire had decided to give us a warning instead of a citation: "There's more where that came from. I burned faster and more intensely this year than ever. So, if you give me another dry winter, it's not going to go well for you."

Griffin ducked her head into my office just before noon. "Fancy a lunch walk?"

"Absolutely," I said.

Turbo was out for the day, so we went without her. We looped the pristine forty-acre capitol grounds, chatting about how we'd have more time for these walks as the weather cooled. The year had tested even our tolerance for mania, and we looked forward to a few months with a slower drumbeat. We passed the grand dome, the meandering exhibition of California's native trees, the rose garden, and various monuments, including the firefighter one. It was a simple, powerful display. Two bronze statues of geared-up firefighters created a gateway path to a long limestone wall engraved with names of those lost in the line of duty since 1850. I usually visited the wall whenever I passed close to it. But today, we didn't stop. We'd burned our lunch hour walking and talking and not thinking about fires.

Late that afternoon, my cell rang, flashing my aviation staff chief's name.

"Hey, Bill," I answered.

"Chief. No easy way to say this." His voice had a warble in it. "Tanker 8-1 just went down on the Dog Rock Fire near Yosemite."

"Oh, fuck. Is the pilot—"

"They lost contact with him. Don't know yet."

His words stole my breath. I managed a "Keep me posted," before we hung up.

I pulled up Ken's number but hesitated before pressing the dial icon. He was with South Ops and Turbo at a funeral for a retired guy they'd worked with years ago. But their guy was already dead and that wouldn't change, and this situation needed our attention. So I called.

"Shit, shit, shit." Ken answered.

"Sounds like you heard."

"South Ops just got word. Unfuck this, Clare." He wasn't joking. Sometimes Ken just needed to be mad at one of us, and for his target to ignore the dig and give him clear advice.

"We have to ground the air fleet," I said.

He didn't respond. I could tell he wanted me to fill the air with a different sentence, but he knew I was right. "How many fires are they working?" he asked.

"Nothing big. And we're almost at flight cutoff for today. I'll call the feds—see if they can cover the next few days. 'Til we know the planes and pilots are okay."

Ken agreed with the plan and said that he, Turbo, and South Ops were heading back to headquarters, "stat."

By the time they made it, the rest of us had set up at the large conference table, turning the space into a war room, the same way we had with the King Fire. The three of them plugged in without ceremony, setting up their laptops and filling coffee mugs for what promised to be a long evening.

I met Ken at the coffeepot.

He filled my mug, then his. "We haven't had a tanker crash since August twenty-seventh, two thousand one," he said in his quiet voice. He was a master of facts and could pull this from his memory bank in a blink. I would have had to look it up.

"Yeah, along those lines. I'm about to piss you off, but you'll agree with me."

He looked at me, readying his blue eyes to change from curious to furious on this day where I couldn't unfuck a plane crash.

I told him, "Like you said, we don't lose airtankers often. I'm thinking we should bring my successor in to shadow me for this."

Ken's shoulders fell, defeated. "You're sticking to your date, *huh*?"

"I promised Bud." It's not like I was in the thick of it anymore, but Bud had seen how common funerals and hospital visits were in this job. He'd supported my career choice. Hell, he'd married it, finding the uniform to his liking. But it always nagged at him that he could be getting that "we regret to inform you" phone call in the middle of the night.

"Alright. Bring Teter in," Ken said with a sigh.

Teter wouldn't need the Shady Lady. He was far more agreeable than I was. I found Teter at his desk, and told him, "Grab your laptop. You're with me."

"You got it, Boss," he said, making it seamless for everyone.

Teter observed as I issued the order to ground our planes, made sure the National Transportation Safety Board (NTSB) notifications had been made, and called my counterpart LeGarza at the US Forest Service. Yes, they'd cover us. It was no small deal to cover behind twenty-three airtankers, twenty-two now. This was how fire cooperation worked in California. All the agencies squabbled until go-time.

With our fleet grounded, I sat at the conference table and took a deep breath. There was nothing left to do except wait for word about our pilot. I took off my wedding ring and got it spinning on the table. When it fell flat, I spun it again, and again. I couldn't handle the wait. I stopped the ring mid-spin, put it back on my finger, and slammed my laptop shut. I had to go to the Dog Rock Fire. I had to lead by being present.

That's when Ken stood up and said, "Turbo, you're with me. We're going down there. Clare, you and Red handle things here." He grabbed his backpack and was out the door, with Turbo in tow.

It pissed me off. Aviation was under me. It was my program. It should have been me on the road and Ken keeping the rest of the ship on course. But Ken and I were alike this way, wanting to be closer to the action than our positions allowed, and he was the boss. So I fell back and poured myself another cup of coffee.

"There's nothing left to do here 'til we learn more," I said to the others in the conference room.

Red nodded. "Go home. Be with your families."

They filed out the door, Red taking up the rear, and me staying behind. I sat in my office dimly lit by ambient night light coming through the large windows framing a view of the state capitol dome down the street. I called Brody's adventure walker to ask if Brody could spend the night, then I called Bill back. "Ken is heading to the fire. How are the pilots taking the grounding order?"

"Half the pilots like it. The other half are bent; flying is how they deal with shit. The big worry right now is the mechanics."

It took me a beat to understand why. When there's a non-military aviation accident anywhere in the nation, the NTSB investigates and makes a finding

as to cause. There're only three causes: environment, human, machine. So either God, the pilot, or a mechanic screwed up. The mechanics took enormous pride in their care for the Cal Fire fleet, winning the FAA's top Diamond Award for the last three years running. But tonight, they'd all sit at home wondering if they missed a rivet, or a gasket, or a lube joint.

"I'll come out first thing in the morning. Talk to them."

"That might help, Chief. Thanks."

"How *you* doing, Bill?"

"Just praying right now."

"Me too, Bill."

We exchanged some small talk and hang-in-theres. As soon as we hung up, I got a call from Ken and Turbo, still on the road. "We talked to the IC. Crews are hiking in. They found the outskirts of wreckage, but no word from the pilot yet."

"Damn," I said, deciding not to share an adage I'd heard at the North Ops airbase last summer: "The ground has a PK of one hundred percent." PK stood for "probability of kill."

Turbo, as usual, was ten steps ahead. "I got some bio info since the press will be asking questions about the pilot." She rattled off his life in a breath. "Geoffrey Craig Hunt married his high school sweetheart, Sally. They have two daughters: Nancy and Sarah. He served as a lieutenant commander in the Navy for nearly twenty-three years, flying P-3s. Thirteen years ago, he left the Navy to fly S-2 airtankers under our contract with DynCorp. He goes by his middle name, Craig, and loves dogs, fishing, golf, and scuba diving."

I could tell from the way she ordered the information she already knew about PK percentages. She could convert this to a past-tense obit in ten seconds.

"Bill told me they called him 'Professor,'" I said. "I guess he teaches chemistry at UC Santa Cruz during the off-season." I felt compelled to add something to show I was connected to Craig. But I wasn't. I'd never even met him.

I stayed in my office, researching NTSB procedures and our policy manuals to make sure we weren't missing anything, waiting for the next call from Ken and Turbo to confirm what I already knew.

They called sometime after 11 p.m. "He didn't make it," Ken said.

I didn't say anything. I let Ken and Turbo take turns filling the void.

"Debris field spans a hundred fifty acres."

"Pronounced him as soon as they found him."

"Jettisoned his retardant load on a rock face above the crash area. It's eerie."

"How's everyone there?" Turbo asked.

"I'm going to talk to the mechanics at McClellan in the morning."

"Good idea. We'll be there," Ken said. He and Turbo were already low on sleep and planning on driving back overnight. It was risky. But sometimes that's how firefighters cope—distracting themselves with danger.

I hung up and stared out the window, fifteen floors above the ground, imagining what Craig's fall must have felt like. *Panic? Peace? Panic, then peace?* My brain scrambled, again trying to find some connection to him. When you don't know a person who dies under your chain of command, it brings a different type of ache. Not pain, but an internal guilt-filled cloud—like fault attaches for *not* knowing the person.

I shoved the policy manuals into my backpack and headed home, breaking my promise to Bud about walking after midnight. I justified it with the circumstances and an argument that my mood made me safe. I got this way sometimes, where I wished for someone to attack me so I could lash back. Every shadowy figure I saw, even my own, I dared: *C'mon, motherfucker. Come at me.* I had my heavy backpack and a jackknife in my pocket. *Bring it.* The shadows must have felt my fury. They steered clear.

At the loft, I made tea, spread the policy manuals out, and read into the night, intent on calling Ken and Turbo every hour to make sure they were awake at the wheel. I fell asleep on the couch, still in my uniform, sometime after my 3:00 a.m. check-in.

When I woke up, I splashed water on my face, called Ken and Turbo, changed into a fresh uniform, and headed out to buy donuts for the

mechanics on my way to the airbase. Donuts make everyone feel better—at least for a few minutes.

I walked into the spotless hangar with the big pink box. The mechanics converged on the donuts like cows toward grain laid for them on a thinning pasture. Red showed up with a warm smile, then Ken and Turbo with bags under their eyes. Ken and I addressed the group. Then we all mingled, giving our attention to anyone who wanted it. We stayed the whole morning, trying to balance being supportive with not absolving what might still be found a fatal error on someone's part. I don't remember who I talked to or what I said. Later, Turbo told me the sole female mechanic had come up to me and after I talked to her for a few minutes her shoulders dropped. I suppose I must have said something acknowledging the extra weight she bore.

<p style="text-align:center">***</p>

So many times in my career, I'd expended all of me to beat back a fire, only to have it spot over the line and take off again. Each time, everyone on the crew looked at each other, took a deep breath, and reengaged. I remember being astounded that our bodies would do what our minds asked them to no matter how hard they'd already been at it.

That's how it felt on this day as the Cheez-It team reengaged in the conference room. We looked at each other, then swung into motion—working side by side, like we were cutting fire line together.

Red activated critical incident stress debriefing for pilots, mechanics, and those on the Dog Rock Fire who needed it. Turbo was on top of all press needs. Griffin briefed key legislative members and subtly dropped soft granola bars in front of whoever needed one. She called them "quiet snacks" because you could eat one without disrupting a legislative session. Ken stayed in touch with the NTSB, Yosemite National Park, the state resources secretary, and the governor's office. North and South Ops bird-dogged every fire start in their respective regions. Teter and I worked on contingencies in case the feds had to pull their air cover. And Chief Counsel Steph set up shop to address potential legal issues. We all stayed into the dinner hour.

"Cutoff time," I announced. This was the official time when airtankers had to stop operations and leave the night firefight to other resources. I locked eyes with Ken across the table and supposed we were thinking the same thing. Grounded airtankers made us incredibly nervous, especially since the weather had turned again and we were breaking fires—the latest one forty miles northeast of headquarters, which now threatened one thousand homes. If the feds busted a fire east of California, they could reassign their tankers and we'd be bare. Ken and I both wanted his phone to ring and for the NTSB to tell us they'd made a preliminary finding that would allow us to reactivate our aircraft—a finding that would most likely mean pilot error. It felt shitty to wish for this. We both lowered our eyes, shook our heads, and checked our cell phones.

We got our wish later that night. The NTSB let us know that while the full investigation and report would not be complete for months, they had enough information to conclude the crash was not caused by air turbulence or a mechanical issue. They had reviewed the wreckage, the weather records, and a video. A Yosemite Park visitor looking for scenic footage had captured Craig's last seconds.

"You sure you want to watch it?" the aviation deputy chief asked Teter and me after the press conference the next morning. "You can't unsee it."

We nodded. I told myself it was my job. I needed to know what happened to better lead through this crisis. I'm not sure what Teter told himself. I never asked.

What we knew before pressing PLAY was that hot metal fragments— suspected sparks from a tourist's loose trailer chains striking pavement— had started the fire, which then burned 130 acres in forested canyons walled in by escarpments. It was inaccessible by engines or bulldozers. Airtankers had to slow its spread. Craig had made one 1,200 gallon retardant drop, refilled, and was on final approach for his second drop.

I shouldn't have watched the video. It didn't help me lead, but it still plays in a loop the way my crashed teenagers do—vivid and often. My imagination augments the video footage. I smell burning sequoias. I hear a wing's sheet metal ripped by a giant tree. I feel the rock face jarred by Craig's jettisoned load—his last-minute attempt to gain control. I see the

violently splattered, red-tinted fire retardant as 1,200 gallons of human blood. I taste the fear on his tongue when he realizes he's overcorrected to a warning about a hazardous tree on the right. I'd made the same error, overcorrecting from right to left, when I rolled my fire engine. My mistake tore a hole in my pants and bruised my ego. His killed him.

<p style="text-align:center">***</p>

We donned our Class-As and drove to San Jose's Church on the Hill for the memorial service. Aerial trucks, like the one I'd operated in Yountville, created an archway, with the American flag hanging between the ladders. We flanked underneath in full salute, waiting for the flyover. Uniformed ushers accompanied Craig's family inside to the front row. Bagpipes played. Craig lay in a flag-wrapped casket, still guarded by a rotating sentry from the firefighter union's honor guard. They'd made sure that Craig had company from the time he was found.

This is the part they cover in movies, showing all the pomp and circumstance. And it will put a lump in your throat. But there's crap they don't show that takes the shine off. There's a rotation of certified chaplains for these events and the lop who drew this one got Craig's wife's name wrong. The lop got taken off the roster, but still, it chapped me. There are the firefighters who don't think enough of the event to iron their slacks. And there's the sick humor we use to get through it, so Turbo had to come around to remind everyone, including Ken and me, "You don't want to be caught on camera smiling during a funeral. It will land above the fold in the *Sac Bee*, guaranteed."

Then there's shit the cameras can't catch—like the endless commotion in my head. I tried to stay engaged—be in the moment, a better, more grown-up Clare than the kid who couldn't sit still in church. But my mind bounced. As a friend talked about how much Craig loved flying tankers, I thought about the day I went to our air ops training the previous summer. We'd allowed Pixar to attach gizmos to the airtanker dashboards so they could create accurate animation sequences for the movie *Planes: Fire & Rescue*, a feature-length cartoon about anthropomorphized airtankers

fighting a fire in a national park modeled on Yosemite. They aptly captured the motion, even the rise of the nose after a retardant drop. Craig's jettisoned load replayed in my head. I willed the footage to reverse itself, but gravity was on its side. I wondered if he screamed or went silently. I wondered if he talked to God the way the Arizona hotshots must have or if it was different in the air because he was already closer to God. The Pixar movie didn't cover this part.

Back at the loft, I took off my Class-A jacket and tie, unshrouded my badge, and popped open a beer. Brody nudged me for a treat. I obliged and turned on the TV to catch the first game of the World Series: Giants vs. Royals. Nothing more instantly normalizes a day than hearing Joe Buck calling the play-by-play for a baseball game. I preferred basketball but appreciated the Zen of a ball field and its accoutrements—a certainness that made it nostalgic. Bats and stitched balls, mink-oiled gloves, a diamond in the dirt. I owed my career to it.

<center>***</center>

While my brother Mark gave me tips for my initial training, my ball play is what got me into Sandy Point. Mark had told me, "They need female players for the annual co-ed softball tournament. Family can play even if they aren't firefighters. I told them I'd ask you."

I showed up and they stuck me in right field. Feigning unreadiness and uncertainty, I took in the familiarity of it. Fresh-cut grass mingled with dusty infield air and distant dugout chatter echoed my way.

"You see the hole."

"Light it up, Jacko."

"Easy-peasy, Bro."

They mistook my well-worn glove for a borrowed one.

The batter shifted his feet, lining up for a late swing—a sure base hit and an advance of the runner on second. Maybe even a double and an RBI.

I wandered backward to compensate for his stance. Near the third-base line, hands clapped out of sync. The on-deck batter swung two bats that clanked together. Someone popped open a fresh can of beer.

The ball arced in slow motion toward the batter. He took his eyes off right field to focus on the ball. That's when I got in my ready stance. From here, I could run forward, backward, sideways, or jump, or dive. He connected. A baseline drive I had to sprint toward still landed easily in my glove. I ignored the cutoff and threw to second base behind the runner. But he hadn't underestimated me as much as the batter or dugout chatters. He was safe. And so was I.

"You ever think about becoming a firefighter?" the coach, who everyone called Ricochet, asked as I jogged into the dugout. That's how I first met him. He'd been a supporter even before I went to Sandy Point.

<p style="text-align:center">***</p>

On the loft couch, I sipped my beer and took in the game, happy the Giants were winning. Brody devoured his supper and took a loud drink from his water bowl before coming over to thank me with wet jowls that deposited a viscous slobber onto my Class-A slacks.

His drool had the same consistency as fire retardant, which we sometimes called *slurry*. This is the generic term for a solid mixed with water so that it can be transported where it can't otherwise go, like concrete mix, or blood. Our blood plasma is ten percent solid nutrients mixed with water so it can get pumped where it is needed, making us all slurry, awaiting our final place of deployment.

I thought about getting up to wipe off my pants but took another swig of beer instead. Andy's voice landed in my head. "You'll start a countdown. It'll sneak up on you. Then you'll be at a conference table and think, *This is the last time I'll be with this group. This is the last time I'll teach SUP 5.* Once that starts," he said, "it happens with everything, and you can't slow the clock down."

"This is the last time I'll have to wear my Class-As," I told Brody. But I was wrong.

CHAPTER 22

SCRAPPLE

State Fire Headquarters, 5 Months Left

The Giants took the World Series and rain ended fire season. Work finally slowed to a winter pace. There was time for bullshitting at the coffeepot, sneaking into Red's candy jar for an afternoon sugar push, and sitting in Griffin's office with Turbo, talking world politics and shoes—where they patiently explained to me what d'Orsay pumps looked like and who Christian Louboutin was.

My cell rang. It was the unit chief at Felton. I stepped out to take the call. "Hey, Shrek."

"Hey, Chief," he said with a tone that let me know this wasn't a pleasure call. "I know you two were tight. I'd thought you'd want a call before I sent the e-mail. Norm died last night."

I don't think I said anything. I just remember thinking it impossible; how does a god die?

"I'm sure his family would appreciate a few words from you at the service," Shrek said.

"Of course," I managed to whisper before hanging up. My sternum ached.

When I got to the loft, I pulled my Class-A pants out and went to work cleaning the dried Brody slurry. The next night, I steam-ironed everything

and tried to formulate what I'd say at Norm's funeral. But I couldn't focus. I kept jumping through eulogies I'd heard over the years. I'd lost track of the total count—somewhere around thirty. A lot of firefighters keep the memorial announcements tucked inside their Class-A hats. Mine got full, so I ditched the papers and wore my hat empty.

Some funerals hit harder than others. One was Eva Schicke's. A 23-year-old, gritty, ponytailed, basketball-playing firefighter assigned to the Columbia helitack crew, she died in 2004 on the Tuolumne Fire, a few months before I became Milpitas fire chief. The wind shifted and chased her and another firefighter uphill toward their safety zone, the highway. The other firefighter made it, but the fire caught Eva five feet before she reached pavement—less than a body length away. She was the first female in Cal Fire to land on the limestone wall. In a full-honors ceremony, the helicopter she'd served on hovered over our saluting teary-eyed lines. Its rotor blades provided a drumbeat while a chief presented Eva's helmet to her sobbing parents and I escaped into my own thoughts. I wondered how many times I might have been five feet from death. I got a lifetime of fire she'd never get, but she got the death I'd never get. I always thought that would be the way to go—dying in a boots-on-the-ground moment in the midst of service to others. It seemed a surefire way to land on God's side of the line.

In a way, the funerals that didn't impact me were worse. That stint lasted for a handful of them. I waited for the lump in my throat to rise, for my eyes to water, for some sign of sorrow inside. But I'd easily make it through the procession, a sibling's choked-up homily, the firefighter's prayer, the last alarm bell signifying "return to quarters," and the exit bagpipes playing "Amazing Grace." Seriously, who gets through "Amazing Grace" *on bagpipes* without it crushing some part of them? Me. I'd ossified. In full salute, I willed myself to feel something. Anything. And when I didn't, I knew I was broken—numb from too many of these.

An early lesson in firefighting is how to minimize exposure to hazardous materials. There are three ways: limit the time of exposure, keep as much distance as possible, and use protective gear to shield yourself. It became a refrain. Time–distance–shielding. We applied it to turned-over tanker trucks spilling phosphorus on the freeway, chemical plant breaches, radiation incidents. But never to funerals. I'd been saturated and they'd started to corrode me. I needed to bench myself, let my emotional cells regenerate. Time–distance–shielding. It worked. After two years of coming up with polite excuses to miss a few services, I was good as new: with working tear ducts, a refurbished glottis—the part of the throat that swells with emotion—and a retenderized heart that could feel ache again.

<p style="text-align:center">✳✳✳</p>

On the three-hour drive from Sacramento to Norm's community church in Corralitos, I worked out his eulogy—spilling the lessons he'd taught me in my first years onto a note pad as I drove. I heard them in his voice, soft with a hint of small-town twang.

Ring that dinner bell loud, and on time.

Slow is smooth, and smooth is fast.

Always carry a pen and a pad for notes, a Smokey calendar for your appointments, and a clean Kleenex in case someone needs it.

Know your knots.

Treat dispatchers right. They go to all the calls. You only go to some.

Respect collar brass, but don't be enamored by it.

Only competence matters in this job, not any of that other stuff.

Listen to country music. It's deeper than you think.

Don't shit-talk others. Those you don't care for will reveal why all by themselves.

I scribbled notes between the lines, dwelling on his wisdom and earnest respect for the profession. By the time I got to the church, I felt ready.

Mark was already there when I pulled in. I was wrong when I'd thought we'd never be in uniform together again. Here we were. We made our way

inside, stopping every few feet to shake hands or hug people we'd worked with over the years. "Hey, Bisbees."

Mark could tell I was anxious to say hi to Norm. "You go ahead. I'll meet you inside."

The smell of incense, aged hymnals, and wood oil greeted me when I opened the heavy church door. Norm's red captain's helmet sat on a display table. A photo album lay next to it, opened to a faded Polaroid of me, Norm, and Scott smiling in front of the fire engine. James must have taken the picture. I looked tiny and happy, the way a teenage girl should, I supposed. I touched the photo, maybe to take me back to that moment or maybe to say good-bye to it. Or maybe both. A church usher waited, then guided me to the dignitary seating.

When the minister signaled, I walked to the podium with confidence. But within seconds, cotton lodged in my throat. The memories whirred through my head in one mashed-together blur. I looked at the enlarged picture of Norm. His eyes smiled.

I smiled back, swallowed hard, stashed my notes into my pocket, and shared a favorite Norm story with the overfilled pews:

My turn to cook for the day. I had to get dinner on the table at 1700 hours. But our afternoon project ran long, cutting my preparation time in half. I retooled with the trusty help of our new *Betty Crocker Cookbook*—the microwave edition. Thrilled I could still make my meat loaf, I took the ingredients and did exactly as Betty instructed, plating the steamy loaf with two minutes to spare. I put the three other required food groups on the table (crispy tater tots, soft white bread, and red punch) and rang the dinner bell—loud and on time.

Norm sat in his regular spot at the head of the table. We always let him serve himself first. He took a bite of the meat loaf, chewed, and swallowed, then pushed his chair back and went to the pantry. He retrieved a jar of peanut butter, sat back down, and said, "Pass the bread, please." We all scampered to get it to him. He slathered peanut butter over a piece of bread, folded it in half, and took a big bite. He

swallowed, looked at me, and very calmly said, "If you ever make that again, I'll fire you for good."

I said, "Understood, sir," while thinking, *Fuck you, Betty. Fuck you and your damned little red cookbook*. I've never made or eaten meat loaf since.

Norm's wife's tears turned to laughter. I grinned, happy Norm and I had a final chance to do something good together. Turning to his picture, I intended to tell him, "You made us better firefighters, leaders, people, even better cooks. May God go with you, and you with us, O' Captain, My Captain." But the cotton resurfaced. All I could croak out was, "Thanks, Norm."

After the service, I sat with my brother at a splintery picnic table while kids grass-stained their church clothes and old-timers lamented Norm's fatal kidneys—"The only weak part of Ol' Ironman." A crew of new firefighters settled in across from us with pie and coffees swirled with cream. I swung my legs out from the bench. It was time to drive back to headquarters. I winked at the firefighters and said, "You should take it black. It's an easy way to say, 'I'm no priss.'"

<p style="text-align:center">✳✳✳</p>

Once I cleared traffic on the drive back to Sacramento, waves of tears soaked the cotton balls. They slid down my throat, making space for squelched grunts, then a full-volume guttural howl. I hadn't cried this hard since Annie. *Why is this one so hard for me?* Norm had retired almost fifteen years earlier, and I hadn't seen him since. We communicated through others who'd see him at the hardware store:

"That rookie of yours made chief of Fire Protection."

"A big muckety-muck, *huh*. Tell her I said hi."

"Will do."

I'd hear about it and send a message back: "Tell him I still seek his advice, which means he's an advisor to the muckety-mucks."

I sucked running snot back up into my nose, supposing this loss was harder to bear because of the role Norm had played in my firefighting life. But I shook my head at the thought. It didn't feel like I'd lost Norm today. It felt like I got to see him, and team up with him. And that we'd always find a way to communicate. So why the angst and waterworks?

"What do ya think, Norm?" I flipped the conundrum to him, wiping residual salt off my face with my white-cuffed uniform shirt.

"It's not me you're saying good-bye to. You and me, kid, we're good. But you've only got a few months left. All those people in that church today, you're saying good-bye to them. You're saying good-bye to firefighting."

When I got back to the loft, I changed into sweats and put my Class-As in the dry-cleaning bin to avoid tempting another funeral. I grabbed a beer and patted the couch. Brody jumped up, snuggled tight against my thigh, and bent toward me to kiss my salty face.

Still emotional, I told him, "I couldn't have made these last years without you, little B-Man. You're such a good boy. You're so handsome. I love you very much." He looked at me with his soulful brown eyes, then dove his muzzle in between his legs to lick his absent testicles for the next five minutes.

Norm laughed at me. I raised my beer to him, and we all watched *Chopped* reruns. One episode had scrapple in the appetizer basket. I learned that scrapple, an old-world dish made from precious meat scraps, was the original meat loaf. Peasants who couldn't afford to let any nutrient go to waste gathered offal and other bits and compressed them into a log that would keep pangs at bay.

"Nice touch," I told Norm. "I get it."

I suppose Norm was right. The funeral made me realize how much the people in that church and the profession had nourished me for nearly thirty years. Now that I was leaving, how would I feed the part of my soul that needed fire, and firefighting, and firefighters?

It's not like I hadn't thought about the impact of retirement before watching *Chopped*. I had a solid plan: sprint as hard as I could to the finish

line, collapse in Nevada to sleep for as long as I wanted, then write books having nothing to do with fire. I'd decided other interests could feed me— the ones my all-consuming firefighting life had bulldozed to the sidelines. I would give fire everything to my last day, then release it.

I hugged Brody as my mind flipped though random memories. Boxed KFC dinners helicopter-dropped on a remote smoky mountaintop at dusk. Epic water fights while washing the fire engine. Learning how to steer a bulldozer, a helicopter, and a Bronco air tactical aircraft. Cheez-It team dares to slip random words into budget and legislative meetings: salamander, avocado, robust, polyphagous.

"We'll get through this, little B-Man," I told him in a confident voice I wished I believed.

I took a long swig of beer and decided to check my phone for missed e-mails during the day. There it was, from CHP: "The investigation is complete and available for pickup."

CHP dropped off over one hundred 3-inch binders filled with documents and interview transcripts. It was their job to conduct the investigation, but our job to review their findings and come up with any necessary corrective action.

I commandeered the main conference room so Teter, Steph, and I could spread out.

"Holy mama," Teter said when he walked in. "That's a jackload of binders."

Steph scrunched her mouth to one side. "Yeah, this might take a minute."

"You guys didn't have Christmas plans, right? Or New Year's? Or Valentine's Day?"

We started with the investigation summary, which reminded me of a Gordon Graham speech. A retired highway patrol sergeant, Graham rose to fame on the public-safety speaker circuit with quirky no-nonsense messages about personnel issues. In conference rooms packed with cops and

firefighters, he told us we were good people, but not too smart. We hadn't figured out more than ten ways to get in trouble. He counted them off a finger at a time. "Sex. Alcohol. Drugs. Lying. Cheating. Reckless driving. Sex. Alcohol. Sex. Alcohol."

It proved true. The investigation revealed that sixteen firefighters were on the block for one or more of the following indiscretions: cheating on a promotional exam, lying on a time sheet, misusing a state vehicle, lying to the investigators, using a state phone to hook up with a prostitute, displaying nude pictures on a state phone, violating sexual harassment policies, off-duty groping and indecent exposure at a bar near the academy, and drinking on standby time, which is still on the clock. CHP did not, however, find any evidence of a sex tape.

This didn't stop the press from ramping back up, making sure "murder," "prostitution," "sex," or "probe" landed next to "Cal Fire" in their headlines. Thank God Turbo was handling them instead of me. The first time I'd talked to a reporter was as a seasonal on a wildfire. While I pulled hose through tangled manzanita, the reporter jammed a microphone in my face and yelled, "What's it feel like to be a female on the line?"

I yelled back, "The same as it feels for the guys, except I have chee-chees." My press skills hadn't improved much over the years.

In the HQ conference room, we plowed through binder after binder, week after week. I'd take breaks for meetings I had to attend, dragging Teter along so he'd learn the landscape.

Bean counters wanted to know why we couldn't replace our Vietnam-era helicopter fleet with the less-expensive bird CHP used. "*Um*, it's the same reason we can't use their patrol cars to put fires out," I explained.

Legislators wanted to know why we didn't embrace a new law that would keep more criminal offenders in county rather than state facilities. "*Um*, it strips opportunity away from thousands of inmates and will reduce our firefighting force by thousands before next summer."

And, on the heels of another round of mass shootings, our labor union wanted to know why the top brass wasn't pushing to get our fire cops assault rifles. "*Um*, optics. We ask now, we'll lock in a forever *no*." Then Teter and I returned to Steph and the binders.

On Friday mornings I'd make a special stop at a fortune cookie factory on my walk to work. Tucked between a noodle shop and a used vinyl records store, loud machines folded warm cookie patties into crescents. They clattered too loud to talk, which didn't matter because nobody there spoke English and I didn't speak Chinese. I held up my index finger, which meant one half-pound bag of fresh, hot, fucked-up, flat cookies the machine hadn't folded properly. It cost $2.

I dumped the cookies onto a paper plate as we unpacked the binders for the day, starting where we'd left off.

"Misfortune cookies!" Teter said.

"These are surprisingly good with coffee. They taste kinda like waffle cones," Steph said. She had an excellent palate.

I sipped coffee, crunched on misfortunes, and read interview after interview, with my boots up on the conference table. About an hour in, I grabbed the next binder. The first page made me swallow before I'd finished chewing, lodging a dry misfortune bit in my throat. I sputtered like an engine that wouldn't start. Teter rushed to get my reddened face a cup of water.

I guzzled it, got my voice back, and explained, "It's Moe's interview. Caught me off guard. Why would he even talk to them? He's not an employee. He could've said 'pound sand.'"

"*Um*, he's lonely in lockup," Teter said. "And a narcissist."

"Ohhh. That should be a good read," Steph said. To her, salacious details were plot, not personal. It's what made her a great lawyer.

Steph and Teter were both right. It was a page-turner. And Moe was a piece of work. His interview revealed that he'd viewed himself as a powerhouse who had built an academy inner circle that included four of the sixteen in trouble—a tight brotherhood that would have his back.

Red ducked her head in. "How goes it, kids?"

We grunted at her in unison.

"That bad?"

"If you put a microscope to anything, you'll find microbes," Steph said.

"Good news is, out of ten thousand employees, only found sixteen microbes," I said.

"Wouldn't you say the dude who pulled his drunk one-eyed monster out at a bar is more than a microbe?" Teter asked.

"*Allegedly* pulled it out." Steph said. "There's conflicting testimony as to whether it actually got airtime."

I nodded. "I stand corrected. So far it looks like we have about eleven microbes, the dick dude, and four guys who might think of Fleming as their cult leader."

Red raised her eyebrows. "Wow." She looked at the plate of cookies. "Misfortunes?"

"Help yourself. You guys know Moe's prelim is next week," I said.

Red and Steph nodded. Teter shook his head and asked, "Pre-limb, like a feet-first breech birth, or . . . ?" His quick, sick mind often went to body parts first, a by-product of his medic days.

"Kinda." Steph laughed. "It's the proceeding before trial. A judge has to determine if there's enough preliminary evidence to hold the defendant for a trial."

"Yeah. I don't think that's gonna go his way," Red said while crunching on a cookie.

As predicted, the prelim didn't and shouldn't have gone well for Moe. The judge set a trial date and Moe's attorney shifted to a defense strategy designed to get a more lenient verdict than first-degree murder. It worked. Moe eventually received a sentence of sixteen years to life for second-degree murder committed with bedsheets and a nine-inch knife, the tip of which the coroner had found in Sarah's scalp.

How had Moe kept this side of himself hidden from so many people? And how could his small band of brothers still not see him for what he was? These guys held the same ranks as Boran, Ebert, and Stan back when I went through the academy—so imperial to me at the time. From where I sat now, I viewed Moe's disciples as senseless pawns. Moe was right; they did have his back. During CHP's investigation, three of them snuck onto the academy grounds to remove boxes from Moe's office. It was stupid.

Everything had already been documented. What the cops needed, they'd already taken. The academy staff chief, an early bird, caught them at 5 a.m. as they were leaving. They were under a no-contact order, so they swore the meetup wasn't orchestrated, that they had landed there at the same time on the same morning by happenstance.

"*Um*, maybe next time, you shouldn't all wear matching beanies. Just a thought," the staff chief said.

As rain drenched the state, we finished making our way through the binders, briefed the Cheez-It team on all sixteen cases, and served the corrective actions. Finally, we packed the binders away, bumped fists, and went home for the first weekend off in two months.

CHAPTER 23

ETCHINGS

State Fire Headquarters, 3 Months Left

A weekend with Bud and Brody at our new home in Nevada felt a universe away from HQ. This taste of my near future thrilled and scared me. I walked laps with Brody along our new fence line. "I'll be okay without fire, little B-Man," I said to both of us, swallowing the scared portion of my emotions. I knew I'd have time to sort through it later, on this side of the state line. We walked a few more laps, then went to sit on the porch with Bud to take in the might and beauty of the Sierra. By Monday, I felt restored.

When I got to work, I loaded into the crowded elevator and saw Ken. We smiled and nodded good mornings. He too looked more rested than he had in weeks under the pressure of implacable press. By the twelfth floor, we had the elevator to ourselves. I don't remember who started it, but we broke into an elevator dance. We wiggled and shimmied and grinned—chiefs with juvenile souls on this side of the fires, the budget cycle, the academy scandal, the murder, the funerals. When the doors opened, we straightened up, bumped fists, and walked into the office.

I stuck with my plan, working hard hours, getting as much done as I could in the short time I had left. I cherished the Cheez-It time, walks and

talks with Griffin and Turbo, and hallway chats with Teter and Steph. Each day, I'd push Teter out front a little further, letting him take the lead so that by the time I had to go, he'd be an old salt. I'm sure Andy had felt the same with me—like a parent running behind a child's bicycle, saying, "I got you," then letting go when it's clear the kid doesn't need help anymore.

I began preparing the office for him, taking personal effects out every night, one backpack load at a time. While zipping it up one evening, my phone rang. It was my brother.

"I got it," Mark said.

My eyes widened as it dawned on me what "it" was. "Oh, hell yeah! Congrats. When's your start date?"

"Two weeks. Can you come to my swearing-in?"

"Absolutely," I said.

Four months earlier, Mark left his Watsonville chief's job to return to Cal Fire. This time, he'd followed my lead, stepping down to get back into the fray. He returned to Cal Fire as captain but wanted a shot at his dream job: being a battalion chief where he'd started his career. At this rank, he'd be in the thick of operations, still in the smoke, but able to go home at night and tuck his kids in. His heart had wanted this job for two decades.

It felt nostalgic pulling into Felton. Shrek, the unit chief who'd called me about Norm, greeted me with a hug. "This will be more fun than the funeral. I promise. Mark's kids are going to pin his badge. You should administer the oath. He doesn't know. It'll be a surprise."

"I'd like that."

Shrek kicked off the event. When it came time for the swearing-in, I stood. It earned a full smile from Mark. He smiled more with his eyes than his mouth, a habit from childhood after his front teeth grew in crooked. He fixed them later, but never taught himself to smile differently.

Mark's smile reminded me of how I used to feel about the job. I couldn't wait for the alarm to sound. For the phone to ring in the middle of the night. For assignments that would last weeks. For sleeping in the dirt. For flames so hot they singed my eyelashes off. But now I was weary. Happy with rain and soft mattresses. Burnt, and ready to hang with Bud in our mountain house, lounging over second cups of coffee, watching Brody

chase deer along the fence, hiking mid-week on Sierra's trails, and writing books in front of a crackling winter fire.

Mark and I stood facing each other, right hands raised. Someone snapped a photo, capturing the real last time we'd be in uniform together. "... so help me God," we finished the oath. Everyone stood and clapped for him. I smiled with pride. Always and still in awe of my older brother, I could tell that he'd outlast me by miles in this enduro-life of fire we'd chosen.

Back when we were chiefs together, we'd talked about retiring at the same time and throwing a blowout party where we could visit with everyone someplace other than at a fire or funeral. But that felt like a long time ago. He wasn't anywhere near ready. I'd chased him all these years, sometimes falling behind, sometimes inching ahead, but both of us always pulling for each other. Still, it's silly for a bullmastiff to chase a deer, the same way it was silly for me to run alongside a cross-country runner and think we'd finish at the same time, at the same line. Anyone who read our charts could have predicted this. Mark's sign is Cancer, a water sign. Water runs forever. Fire burns hot but always goes out.

On my last day, I did a final sweep of my office, setting it up for Teter. I came to an 8″ by 10″ piece of paper kept folded under my computer keyboard.

On my first morning, the day after Andy departed, I'd walked into his cleared office—this office. He'd left a bottle of wine and two glasses in a holder his brother had made from a wine barrel. A handwritten note sat next to it: "You'll need this to help you forget. And this to help you remember." Under his note was the 8″ by 10″ paper—a pencil rubbing he'd made of Eva Schicke's name etched in the limestone wall.

I stood with her name in my hand, staring out the window at the capitol dome. *I know she did enough, California. I hope I did too.* I folded the paper and slid it into my pocket, took off my collar brass, and laid it next to the wine bottle I'd gotten Teter. Then I walked out of the building with my backpack, just like I had for the last six years.

Genoa, Nevada, 2015

I don't know why I expected fire to let up when I retired, but it surprised me that first summer when smoke from a flurry of California blazes poured into Nevada. I guess part of me had thought fire would respect state borders and my need to go cold turkey for a while, allowing space for something other than fire in my life.

Reveling in my newfound freedom, I walked around in shorts and flip-flops, untethered to a cell phone or a gear bag. I dove into a creative writing master's degree program. I said yes to a Fourth-of-July vacation with Bud, a first in our married life.

But it was hard being on the outside—an observer. Helpless. Fire still had ahold of me. It had held me captive for thirty years, but also fed and housed me. I felt a loyalty to it. And I missed it. And I couldn't *not* see beauty when a charcoal-filled sky only let the longest wavelengths peer though, turning the sun bloodred. So I'd get updates and intel on the big fires from Turbo, and Griffin, and my brother. And I followed Cal Fire in the news every morning as Bud and I sipped coffee.

"Didn't you work at Middletown?" Bud asked me one morning while scrolling through the news on his phone.

"You reading about the Valley Fire?"

"Yup. Looks like a beast."

"It is. It's going to bump the Witch out of third place as California's most-destructive fire," I said. Another dry winter, an ongoing bark beetle infestation, and high winds had fast-tracked this blaze through portions of Sonoma, Lake, and Napa counties. It cremated almost 2,000 structures and skirted the edge of Middletown Fire Station, covering the footprints of several fires I'd fought in my early years.

My brother Mark was on the fire, less than a mile away from a burnover of a crew that had to deploy shelters as the fire overtook their position. The crew was unscathed by the heat, but not by the event. Same with Mark's wife, Lupita, who caught news footage of the flame lengths.

"She wants me to retire," Mark told me over the phone.

"Sounds like your two loves have you in a pinch point," I said. "Trust me, I get it."

Mark held on for one more season, then Lupita got to breathe easy.

<p style="text-align:center">✳✳✳</p>

For the first two decades of my career, we used to joke, "It's gonna to be the worst fire season ever." If it had rained a lot, we said, "Tall grass out there. Lots of fuel." If it hadn't, we said, "It's a tinderbox out there." But by the new millennium, I'd stopped joking. I could see it happening. Any way Cal Fire measured it—largest, most destructive, deadliest—new fires bumped long-standing records from the "worst" charts.

After my brother left, the record-setting escalated. In 2017, fire ravaged California with contenders vying to win, place, and show on all the charts. In the north, the Tubbs Fire took third in deadliest and first in most destructive. In the south, the Thomas Fire seized the number one spot as the largest ever. It scorched over 280,000 acres and lit up Twitter by threatening homes owned by mega-celebs. A mass of smaller fires contributed to the carbon-filled skies. Thick smoke rolled into the eastern Sierra front, dumping ash in my Genoa air—mocking me and trying to pull me back under its spell.

Since it was Mark's first season out of the fray, I knew he'd be feeling it too, so I texted him. "How ya doing against this black-sky backdrop?"

He called right away. "I couldn't just sit here. I signed up to teach some command classes and I'm going part-time to help work on higher education fire training. Lupita's cool with all of it as long as I don't go into a line spot."

I felt like a sponsor checking in on my AA guy weeks after he'd fallen off the wagon.

"Maybe I should lean in too," I said.

"Whatcha thinking?" Mark asked.

"Don't know. I've blown off offers. Haven't wanted to jump back in." I paused, knowing he'd follow with "Why?" so I tried to preempt it. "Fire is

etched so deep in me that it's all or nothing. I can't do it part-time. And I'm busy with writing projects and my masters. Plus, I feel like it's reaching back in. It's the next generation's turn to figure out how they want to tackle the issues. But this siege "

Instead of getting me to dig deeper, Mark asked, "Are you writing about any of *this*?"

"I'm working on other stuff. But fire creeps into my journal."

"Maybe writing is how you lean in. Maybe do something with those journal entries."

"They're just a mess of fire thoughts—blather, really."

"Give it time," Mark said. "When I paint, I start by putting color and texture on the canvas. I don't know what it will turn into. It takes several layers, sometimes several years."

I made no decision to write about fire but became generous with the amount of time I'd spend journaling about what was on my mind. And what was on my mind was fire.

<p style="text-align:center">***</p>

"They didn't evacuate," I told Bud while we sipped coffee on our couch, reading news updates reporting a double-digit death toll from the fires.

"Geezus. It's not like the news has been keeping this shit a secret. Why didn't they . . ."

"Some people aren't capable of leaving," I said. "I've seen it. It's like hoarders. They don't know how to choose what to take and what to leave. They're paralyzed by it. So they just stay."

"Phone, laptop, go bag, gun, Brody," Bud said.

"Really, Bud? Brody last?" I slid from my chair onto the floor and rubbed Brody's belly.

"You married it." Bud shrugged and refilled our mugs.

I stayed with my point. "Others think they can help, so they 'stay and defend.' Others feel invincible—like the fire won't destroy them or their homes."

Bud nodded, paying half attention. "Damn, that's an unfortunate name," he said handing me his phone.

I took it and read an article about a seniors' trailer park overrun by the Tubbs Fire. The fire incinerated 117 coaches, rendered the remaining 44 uninhabitable, and killed two residents who didn't make it out in time. The trailer park's name: Journey's End.

Each morning brought more confirmed deaths: store owners, veterans, charity workers, "the horse lady," a fourteen-year-old, a retired football coach, a longshoreman, a flutist, a photojournalist, a husband who stayed at his stroke-damaged wife's bedside. One article told a story about an elderly couple who escaped fire by jumping in a backyard pool. They held each other in a *Titanic* moment that lasted through the night as embers rained. But before dawn, the wife went limp, perishing from heart failure.

Each day, new heart-wrenching stories wallpapered the media, leaving little room to explore our species' role in these catastrophic times. I started scribbling about the siege from a distance, viewing it like the Goodyear blimp hovering above a football game—Fire vs. Humans:

Everyone knows the rules. Everyone understands it's dangerous. You can live in California with its Mediterranean climate and beautiful vistas atop a box canyon, or in the golden hills alongside wine country, or in a coastal community with a special commission protecting flammable vegetation, or in a matchbox trailer that cannot protect you against a fire's rage. And firefighters can earn a living risking their lives to save your home and you. But fire has been at this longer, and some years, it's gonna be a blowout Super Bowl and you're going to get the shit kicked out of you like you're Denver playing San Francisco in 1990. And that's what just happened—an annihilation. Final score: 47 dead, over 1.5 million acres burned, and over 10,000 structures destroyed. See ya next year.

What I'd spewed onto the page troubled me. My younger self never would have been this cynical. This clinical. Back then, I had to believe that nothing about firefighting was preordained—that every time I donned my helmet, it would matter. But from where I sat now, I saw an inevitability to all of it.

"Is *this* actually the worst fire season ever?" Bud began to ask every year.

My answer remained the same, "Nope, 2008 still holds that title."

Then in 2018, the Carr Fire took off, gobbling drought-ridden fuel at historical rates and producing a phenomenon I'd never seen in my thirty years: a "firenado," where a fire's intensity generates a tornado. The National Weather Service issued the first-ever firenado warning in United States history. Then the Mendocino Complex broke, then the Woolsey Fire, then the Camp Fire. And the year walked away with the belt, seizing one hundred lives, nearly two million acres and 25,000 structures, and a new media catchphrase: "We've entered the age of mega fires."

"Yes, Bud, 2018 is officially the worst fire season ever," I said.

As always, the fires waned and news stories shifted to courageous, determined survivors: "We shall rebuild."

Again, I took fire's side and turned on its victims:

"Shall" rebuild. Like it's a biblical fucking mandate. What don't you understand about living where fires have burned before? They're called "high fire hazard zones" for a reason. I've been on all those grounds before, stomping out fire that will be back again. The Camp covered at least a dozen. The Carr, over forty. The Mendocino Complex is littered with too many to count. And the Woolsey—everybody knows Malibu's canyons burn big every three to ten years. You were lucky; it waited an extra year this time. I can hear fire's voice. It's louder and more indomitable than yours. "I shall reburn."

In 2020, it didn't take long for T-shirt companies to start pumping out "Worst Year Ever" prints on their crew and V-neck models. The slogan referred to the COVID-19 pandemic and the country's landmark civil unrest. But it also applied to fire season, which required unprecedented California National Guard deployments—the state had run out of firefighters.

One of the fires was in my beloved Santa Cruz Mountains, my outdoor church for so many years. The fire burned over 86,000 acres and nearly 1,500 structures—including the old Sandy Point Training Center, now a pile of ash. It was a wrenching casualty in this devastating year. Dominating Cal Fire's worst charts, the year ended with a tally of over four million acres burned—more than double the astonishing record 2018 had put up.

Oregon was on fire too. You wouldn't think West Coast fires would capture attention on the Eastern Seaboard, but the two states' smoke plumes combined and rode the jet stream, giving New York City and New Jersey a glance at a western wildfire's brilliant scarlet sun. The *New York Times* added fire stories alongside headlines covering protests across the nation.

"I stand corrected, Bud; 2020 is officially the worst fire season ever," I said, before returning to my journal:

> *Maybe fire is like civil unrest. It makes some noise, gets some attention, then quiets down. Maybe there's a little change, awareness in people who didn't previously have it for lack of exposure. But the rest slip back to status quo. So the protests start again, "No. I'm serious. There's a problem here." There's a little more movement but not enough to quell the growing rage—the mass of accumulated flammable fuel. So fire riots, refusing to back down, refusing to be unheard. "I shall reburn."*

<p style="text-align:center">***</p>

I sat at my writing desk toggling between internet news and my knotted journal entries. They both reminded me of the piles of tangled, char-covered hose we brought back in heaps after a fire. We had to hunt for a coupling as an entry point to pull out one hose length at a time, until the mass was unraveled and laid in neat rows on the wash rack. I wondered if I could do that with my fire thoughts.

I looked to Brody, sleeping on the love seat in my writing office. The love seat had been in every office I'd had since 1997. At one point, Turbo

dubbed it "the ass-chewing couch" because most of those years I'd been the boss of someone who needed course correction on black pleather.

"Hey, little B-Man, whaddaya think? Should I try to unravel this mess?"

He opened one eye, then closed it, deciding it best to let me figure out my own shit.

Maybe that was it. Maybe spitting at others was a way for me to process my own career, which I'd spent choking off fires that the land wanted. Perhaps if I could blame others, I wouldn't have to examine the role I'd played. Fire means death but also birth. The land needs it to regenerate that which is already destined to die. Without it, there's just acres of kindling. I'd spent thirty years with no doubt as to the valor of my career choice. Everyone from fire victims to Hollywood cheered me on. Yup, I was a goddamn hero.

I'd needed time away to see it. And now I could. There are no teams driving Code 3 to stop earth, wind, or water once they're in furious motion. The earth quakes, flood waters rise, and wind whips. We don't try to stop them in their tracks. We divert the hazards or remove people from their path and handle the aftermath. But with fire, we charge in, denying Mother Nature her due.

Brody lifted his head as if to say, "Good point." Then he farted—Mother Nature punching me back.

I waited until the heavy air cleared, then snuggled against him, rubbing the spot between his eyes and nose because it made both of us feel better. My brother, Mark, was right. I needed to untangle this knot by writing about it, if for no one but myself.

So Brody and I began. We walked laps around our two acres, sorting through memories, emotions, and writing approaches. He'd slowed a bit from his puppy years but recharged quickly with breaks on the ass-chewing couch while I hammered on my keyboard. Then we'd go for another lap. He started slowing down, slower each day. Then, he couldn't move from the couch. An immune disorder caught us by surprise.

Bud and I sat cross-legged on the floor in a portable building next to the veterinary offices—the place they let you say your final good-byes. Brody

and his slobbery smile infected everyone he met. The whole front office sniffled. The vet's assistant got hiccups from trying too hard to not cry. Then she cried and hiccupped. Even the vet, who'd done this more times than he could count, had red, watery eyes as he pushed the plunger on the syringe. Brody's twenty-pound head relaxed into my hands. My teeth clenched and ground against each other, some semblance of futile stoicism that couldn't keep the dam from breaking.

<p style="text-align:center">***</p>

Bud and I walked the fence line, spreading Brody's ashes. "He can still keep the deer out this way," I reasoned, as if I was an eight-year-old girl.

Brody had patrolled the fence daily, pretending to protect our newly installed landscaping from the Genoa deer. He'd developed a complex relationship with them, chasing and barking only if he saw *we* saw the deer. Otherwise, he let them be. We'd come home from errands to find Brody on the front lawn licking his paws not six feet from a couple of does who'd hopped the fence for a Photinia snack. When Brody saw us, he made a show of it, woofing with fervor, "Hey! Get the hell out of here, ya stupid deer!" I swore I saw him wink at the lead doe as he snorted and they trotted off, easily leaping over our five-foot-tall perimeter.

I'd underestimated Brody. He seemed so simple: feed me, rub my ears, take me on walks to check my pee-mail, and give me a biscuit because I'm unbelievably handsome. But he understood what Bud and I didn't—that the deer belonged here more than we did.

At first, Brody had tried to explain it with a cocked head and questioning eyebrows. Now, from his elevated plane, he could lay it out more clearly. "They were here first. The coyotes and mountain lions keep the population in check, which is their job, not yours. That's how nature works. Sure, every so often a buck will unfelt antlers against one of your precious aspens and it'll scar the bark. They'll nibble like your landscaping install is a tasting event, even though the nursery promised you, 'They won't eat this.' And when done feasting, they'll crap on the lawn. If I were still there, I'd eat it if it was fresh or roll in it if hardened enough to give me a good back scratch.

But, and here's the point: there will be mornings when you wake up and see a deer family silhouetted against a sunrise, and afternoons with fawns frolicking in wildflowers, and evenings when you'll slow your pace to align with bucks ambling toward the river."

I inhaled deeply, shook the last of Brody's ashes from the bag, then kept shaking it.

"You okay?" Bud asked, taking the empty bag from my hands.

I nodded. "I'm just not ready for good-bye. I need a few more laps with him."

Bud kissed me and walked across the field to our house, leaving Brody and me to our thought walk. I stepped over a puddle near the wellhead. Bud and I had chosen Genoa in part because it sat above a water-rich basin. All the wells in our small neighborhood were artesian, bubbling over year-round. Our house and land didn't tread on fire's territory. But just because I didn't live in a fire-prone zone didn't mean I hadn't committed my own sin of encroachment against nature. Brody was right. We'd put up a human-made fence to deter indigenous deer from destroying our contrived vista because we wanted to be surrounded by unscarred scenery. That's the thing about nature—it is beauty and beast. All its source elements—earth, air, water, and fire—are at once wickedly brutal and unfathomably kind, bending and unforgiving, destructive and regenerative. Scarred.

I walked laps with Brody until dusk. "Thirty-six," I guessed the humidity out loud to him. As deer gathered outside the fence, looking for a place to settle, Bud waved me over to the porch, where he waited with scotch. We sat outside, sipped, and told "remember when Brody . . ." stories to each other. In a final toast, we held our glasses to the sky. Before bed, I opened the gate—in case the deer wanted to sleep close to Brody on this clear, star-filled night.

Like my cyclical laps with Brody, I knew I'd seen everything with fire, but also nothing yet. In a few months, smoke would block my stars again and a puppy named Bailey would lie in Brody's spot on the ass-chewing couch.

CHAPTER 24

BEACONS

Auburn, California, 2021

At the sound of car keys, Bailey loaded herself into the back of my capped pickup truck and circled into her spot on the plush dog bed. A blue-coated Italian mastiff, she had a very different personality from Brody. She opted out of fence line patrols but loved stairs and car rides.

I slid open the window between the cab and shell, so I could talk to Bailey on the ride. Then I kissed Bud and hopped into the driver's seat.

"Why don't you follow me since you haven't been there yet," Bud said. We were caravaning together to his sister's new house in Auburn, California, about a three-hour drive west. We'd decided to drive separately—a way to save both our vehicles if the Caldor Fire blazing into the Lake Tahoe Basin continued its run toward Genoa.

Caldor had started two weeks earlier, purportedly ignited by a father and son shooting in the woods on a Saturday evening without regard for the fire triangle: heat from projectiles and ricochets, a receptive fuel bed, and an outdoor breeze. It was mid-August in a declared drought year, with 90-degree temperatures and a massive fire to the north—the Dixie Fire. For three weeks, Dixie had torn through timberland, shrub, brush, and towns in five counties abutting the Sierra Mountains. Smoke filled every

nook, canyon, and valley formed by the northern half of the range. You couldn't not think of fire if you walked outside. But somehow, this duo had managed.

A few days earlier, Bud had asked me if we should be worried about Caldor. My answer would have been "no" for most of my fire life, but now, it drew a "yes." Caldor had scorched more than 200,000 acres so far, and it still had its sights on South Lake Tahoe and beyond. I wasn't worried about ground fire. We had basin-fed land that kept our field green, good clearance, and firewood stacked far away from the house. But windstorms aimed the fire directly at Genoa. With spotting a mile ahead, embers could easily land on our roof, on our neighbors' roofs. We were in pretty good shape with boxed eaves, metal mesh–covered vents, and composite roof tiles, but I didn't trust this fire one bit. At its current rate of spread, Caldor could reach us in two days. I told Bud, "We should leave a day ahead. Clear the road for those who won't go until the order comes."

Bud agreed and we borrowed a trailer from friends across the valley, outside Caldor's trajectory. We pulled the sixteen-foot enclosed rig into our driveway, lowered its back-door ramp, and stared into its empty space.

In all my disaster-ridden years, I'd never been on the civilian side of a fire evacuation. As a chief, I'd point at the map in front of the command team and say, "The fire is here. It's heading here. We need to evacuate these three towns." And the towns would empty, leaving behind their most stubborn—those who chose to defend possessions with garden hoses and hope—or those paralyzed by the choices one has to make during an evacuation.

Towns were easy. There were no competing interests, no picking one neighborhood over another. If they were in danger, we issued the directives: *warnings* for areas that might need to evacuate, *orders* for areas requiring imminent departure.

Bud and I sighed as we compared the trailer space to what we had in the house. The nearer a fire, the easier the evacuation. When you have ten minutes to pack, it looks a lot like the list Bud had rattled off in the wrong order: pets, meds, go bags, laptops, phones, and a firearm if that's

your thing. But when you have time to fill a trailer with a small percent of what you own, it gets more difficult. Each decision results in exponential outcomes—a *yes* to one thing means *no* to ninety-eight other things.

We operated as a team, both with cool heads. Looking back, I remember it like an out-of-body experience. I see myself directing my body to pack this thing, then that thing. I watch myself driving, towing the loaded trailer back to our friends for safekeeping. Back at our house for a final walk-through, my hand writes a note to firefighters who may need to shelter in our sturdy home: *Help yourselves to snacks and drinks we left for you in the fridge. —Chief Frank.*

Because I was an expert in compartmentalization, I'd removed myself from the gravity of the evacuation—so far that if you asked me today what I'd packed in the trailer, I'd be guessing. I'd have to rely on a quick note I fired off to a friend while packing:

> *It feels different on this side of a fire—the side with no hose or tools or collar brass. I'm packing predictable treasures: photos, a few pieces of Mom's artwork, two quilts a friend made, Bud's custom motorcycle jacket, journals I can't stand to read but can't let burn, Bud's handcrafted wood trunks, the good bottle of scotch kept in the safe, wills, and passports. But I find myself grabbing random things that surprise me: watchbands that match my favorite T-shirts, the* Poets and Writers *that just came in the mail, Bailey's completely replaceable Kong, and ashes of parents and sisters—to save them from fire. Then, it will be a backpack each, our laptops, Bailey, her food, and a road trip to blue skies, where I'll write the last chapters of my fire book.*

Bud and I drove north, then turned left onto I-80. It felt counterintuitive to drive west into California. But Auburn had clear air, and Bud's sister had room for us. And I now understood something I hadn't before: there's something about evacuating from a fire's path that drives you toward family.

As we crested Donner Summit on I-80, a pesky car worked itself between Bud's truck and mine. Bud called my cell. "That little bastard," he said.

"Yeah. What do you think his problem is? Mommy issues, or Daddy issues?"

"Small-dick issues."

"*Um*, I don't think so. It's a Hyundai."

"Fair point. Hey . . . If we lose the house, let's rebuild the workshop out back instead of in front."

"Good idea. And we should get a Wolf stove with an infrared grill."

"Absolutely. Good talk."

We hung up, knowing it was in fact a good talk. In shorthand, we'd just covered a lot of ground. We didn't want a car in between us because it was stressful driving away from the home we'd made together in Genoa, knowing it could be a smoldering ash pile when we returned. If it was, we had options. We weren't in a fire-prone area, yet Mother Nature had found a way to bring fire at us. So we'd have to decide if we wanted to relocate or rebuild. Either way, Bud would need to heal in his woodshop, so we'd make or find a first-rate one, with high ceilings and big barn-style doors for easy wood storage and movement. And I would find therapy in the classic firehouse Wolf stove, losing myself in the art of sustenance.

As hard as it would be for us if Caldor took our home, we had it easy compared to most. It was part of why we didn't soak too long in the potential tragedy. This wasn't a legacy home, lived in by generations of either side of our blood family. We hadn't raised kids who'd formed all their memories in the house—no wall with growth marks on it. We had no livestock, or horses, or chickens to rehome. We weren't caring for elderly parents tethered to oxygen machines that didn't travel well. We wouldn't lose our jobs. Insurance would cover a move or a roof over our heads during a rebuild. We had a path forward.

In a way, I embraced the experience—grateful to grow myself by seeing this side of fire, this side of the human ache when a fire approaches. But I couldn't help returning to my journal thoughts—that it's all a devastation of our own making, with no "they" to blame. As a society, we are accepting an accelerating cycle of fire.

I descended into blue skies with a tightened jaw. I knew we could do better. I knew we could curtail the destruction with some measured steps, but I had only Bailey to share my thoughts with. What would I say if I had an audience?

I'd say there's a way out if we choose it. Like with most issues these days, if we could set aside red and blue views, we could find the resolve to act. We could thin fuel (both mechanically and with prescribed fire), harden homes, restructure budget priorities, and reduce ignitions. These aren't new ideas. But we can't get traction because, "Wah, it's too hard."

People don't like prescribed burns because they put smoke in the air. They don't want ground clearing because it disturbs habitats. They hate being told how to build their homes in the WUI. Politicians and budget wonks don't want their agendas stifled. And for the love of God, don't even try forcing people to have regard for the fire triangle. It's so romantic to set flying lanterns a-sail above an autumn wedding. Dude, that dirt bike will have more power if you remove the spark arrestor! We can't possibly afford to clear around all the power lines we constructed; it would cut into our profits. No time to tighten those dragging trailer chains—the road awaits. That campfire *looks* like it's out. And my personal favorite: We can't ban fireworks in the middle of summer; it helps fund scouts.

I thought back to the saying I'd heard about anyone's fire being everyone's fire in California. But it's become bigger than that. Now, anyone's fire is everyone's fire in the West and beyond. If we want our future generations to know what a forest is, if we want breathable air and fatality reduction, we need to stop pretending fire is an unpredictable disaster.

I pulled into the driveway behind Bud. We sucked in the Auburn air—the cleanest outdoors I'd had in my asthma-scarred lungs in well over a month. Commingled Dixie and Caldor smoke had filled the Tahoe Basin and Carson Valley for weeks with a choking charcoal-brown particulate registering at levels not contemplated by the air-quality index and recorded as some of the worst air *in the world.*

Bud's sister stood at the gate, waiting for a tail-wagging Bailey and hugs. We drank wine on her patio, then walked downtown, where she showed us her favorite boutique shops, restaurants, and a community garden run by veterans trying to mend themselves with cultivation in California's sun. This quintessential rural town of 15,000 lay in overgrown wooded foothills, a poster child of WUI land, and yet we were here instead of in our safe haven in the flat bed of a valley above a water-rich basin. I felt like fire had tricked me again.

In the morning, I pulled up the status reports for Caldor. The firefighters were making amazing stops, using fuel-treated areas—the kind we needed more of—where the forest had been thinned. Where there was no treatment, flame lengths were over 100 feet. But these pockets of treated areas reduced the flame lengths to 20 feet, slowing the fire and giving firefighters a place to take a stand with hoses, hand tools, and drip torches—a toehold that, when coupled with the wind laying down, allowed evacuation warnings and orders to be lifted within two days. The fire would burn for another few weeks, but its run toward my house was over.

We drove back home. The main highways through the fire were still closed, but a back route gave us a glimpse of the fire's wreckage. Miles of destruction passed in slow motion. Blackened timber stands contrasted against a smoky gray sky and a ground that had burned so hot, the ash looked like Sierra snow. Majestic pines, firs, and cedars with six-foot-wide trunks had burned more readily than the matchsticks Fat Pat and I had toyed with forty-eight years earlier.

I thought about how much fire I'd seen over the years. I'd witnessed it demolish urban and rural homes and businesses, grand redwood groves, kids' toys and playhouses, golden rolling hills, vehicles, freeways, bridges, meth labs, critters. It had even leveled the place where I'd first learned to fight it, Sandy Point.

All the fires I'd extinguished felt like wins. But as this burnt vastness unfurled at every horizon, it felt like fire played the long game. Caldor would land in the fifteenth spot on the Largest Fires Chart, and Dixie narrowly missed first place. Collectively, they incinerated 1,185,000 acres, an area equivalent to a two-lane highway stretching over 400,000 miles—a

drive around the earth's circumference more than sixteen times. How much more must burn before we look at these fires as beacons for what lies ahead?

<p align="center">✳✳✳</p>

Bailey sat two feet from the dining table, willing something to drop on the floor as Bud and I lazed over earned lunchtime sandwiches and bubbly water poured over lemon slices and ice. That morning, we'd unpacked the trailer and returned it to our friends with a thank-you note and nice bottle of wine. I chewed my last bite slowly, scrolling through news as I ate. A headline popped up: WILDFIRE SPARKS NEAR AUBURN.

AFTERWORD

When people find out I spent a career in firefighting, two questions always follow. The first is, "Why—why did you choose to run toward fire?" I've spent a whole book doing a lesser job explaining it than Yeats did with twenty-five words in his poem about an Irish military pilot:

> Nor law, nor duty bade me fight
> Nor public men, nor cheering crowds
> A lonely impulse of delight
> Drove to this tumult in the clouds.

So, I just say, "Like Yeats said, an 'impulse of delight,'" which draws either a blank stare or a knowing nod, and the next inevitable question.

"How many are there—you know—female firefighters?" like we all know each other and play pickleball together on weekends. The National Fire Protection Association's latest study shows there are roughly 15,000 women who serve as career firefighters in the United States. Still, that makes up only *four percent* of the national total. This is an improvement from when I started. It's astonishing to me when I realize I was never a permanent direct report to another female. The odds are better now but not by much—not by enough.

If you recognize that impulse of delight in any female in your life, tell her to follow it. Tell her there's still much ground to be broken. Tell her it's worth every scar it leaves.

GLOSSARY

If you are reading this, you are officially a fire nerd. Welcome. Hopefully this compilation of *Burnt*'s technical terms will prove useful as a quick reference. I opted to omit some acronyms because their definitions won't add meaning to those not already mired in the vernacular. The definitions below come from the International Fire Service Training Association (www.ifsta.org), the National Wildfire Coordinating Group (www.nwcg.com), and my years in this delightfully jargonized fire world.

Air Tactical Aircraft: Fixed-wing observational aircraft staffed with a pilot and an air tactical officer who coordinates aerial operations like retardant drops, helitack crew insertion, and aerial reconnaissance.

Airtanker: A fixed-wing aircraft certified by the Federal Aviation Administration as being capable of transport and delivery of fire-retardant solutions.

All-Risk Fire Department: A fire department responsible for responding to all manner of emergencies, such as structure fires, medical aids, technical rescues, vehicle accidents, hazardous material spills, wildland fires, etc.—also known as All-Hazard.

Alarm: (1) A signal from a person or device indicating a fire or other situation requiring the need for emergency services response. (2) Dispatch levels for structure fire response, where "first alarm" means the initial fire department response to an emergency, and subsequent second, third, fourth, or fifth alarms add needed resources.

Apparatus: A motor-driven vehicle, or group of vehicles, designed and constructed for fire and rescue work (e.g., engines, water tenders, ladder trucks).

Apparatus Bay: A firehouse garage stall.

Backfire: A fire set along the inner edge of a fire line to consume fuel in a wildfire's path or to change the direction of the fire's convection column.

Backpump: A portable water tank fitted with backpack-style straps and a hand-pump sprayer.

Bale: The handle and control valve for a fire hose nozzle. If pulled toward the nozzle operator, water flows. If pushed away, water flow stops.

Belt Weather Kit: A belt-mounted case with weather-measuring tools for taking on-site air temperature, wind speed and direction, and relative humidity.

Black: The geographical area a wildfire has burned through—also known as *burn*.

Blacklining: The preburning of fuels adjacent to a control line; used in prescribed burning.

Boiling Liquid Expanding Vapor Explosion (BLEVE): An explosion that occurs when a pressurized container holding liquid is exposed to too much heat and the boiling liquid expands beyond the container's confines.

Box Canyon: A steep-sided, dead-end canyon.

Breathing Apparatus: Portable air tanks with regulators that allow firefighters to breathe in toxic conditions—also called a Self-Contained Breathing Apparatus or SCBA.

Brush Hook: A heavy curved cutting tool designed to cut brush at its base; it's used the same way as an axe.

Burnover: An event where a fire overtakes personnel or equipment and there is no opportunity to escape the area, sometimes resulting in equipment damage, injuries, and/or fatalities.

Cal Fire: California Department of Forestry and Fire Protection. The state's forest management, fire prevention, and all-risk fire department.

Campaign Fire: A major wildfire expected to last for days or weeks and requiring firefighters to staff the fire in shifts (typically day shift or night shift, or 24 hours on, then 24 hours rest).

Centrifugal Pump: A pump that expels water by centrifugal force through the ports of a circular impeller rotating at high speed.

Civil Cost Recovery: A statutory mechanism allowing fire departments to seek fire suppression costs from culpable parties.

Class-A Uniform: A dress uniform worn to formal events.

Code 3: Operation of an emergency vehicle using visual and audible warning devices (i.e., lights and sirens).

Collar Brass: Rank insignia worn on the uniform shirt collar and Class-A uniform jacket.

Command Center: A dispatch center, but staffed 24/7 with at least one ranked officer who assumes command of an incident until a fire officer is at the scene.

Command Team: Incident command/management team deployed to run major incidents—also known as ICT or IMT. The person in charge of any incident whether or not a team is deployed is called the incident commander or IC.

Complex: Two or more individual incidents located in the same general area, merged under a single command structure; a frequent occurrence for lightning-caused fires in close proximity to one another.

Containment: A measurement used to describe how much of the fire is surrounded by control features reasonably expected to stop the fire's spread, like a bulldozer line, or a lake, or a water curtain in structural firefighting.

Control: A measurement used to describe how much of the fire is extinguished and is expected to stay out, given current and expected conditions.

C-Rations: Now called Meals-Ready-to-Eat (MREs), these are long-shelf-life packaged meals initially used by military troops.

Crowned: A fire that rose from the ground to a tree crown and advanced from treetop to treetop.

Dayroom: A firehouse living room.

Deck: (1) The floor of an apparatus bay. (2) A platform on a fire truck used to attach a high-flow water delivery system called a "deck gun."

Dirty Burn: A fire that left behind patches or swaths of unburned fuel.

Division Supervisor: A fire officer position within the incident command system (ICS) with responsibility for operations within a defined geographic area. (It's called a "group supervisor" if the responsibility is for a function rather than for a location.)

Dragspoon: The last firefighter in line on a handcrew; responsible for scraping the fire line clean with a shovel.

Drip Torch: A handheld device for igniting fires by dripping flaming liquid fuel (diesel and gasoline) on the materials to be burned; it consists of a fuel fount, burner arm, and igniter.

Duff: The layer of decomposing organic materials lying below the litter layer of freshly fallen twigs, needles, and leaves and immediately above mineral soil.

Energy Release Component: A measurement, typically BTUs per square foot, that captures the amount of energy released within the flaming front at the head of a moving fire.

Engine: A vehicle providing specified levels of pumping, water, and hose capacity, and staffed with a minimum number of personnel—also known as a *fire department pumper.*

Federal Fire Partners: The five agencies charged with federal land management and fire protection responsibilities: the United States Forest Service (USFS), Bureau of Land Management (BLM), Bureau of Indian Affairs (BIA), National Parks Service (NPS), and Fish and Wildlife Services (FWS).

Final Approach: An airtanker is "on final" when it is on line with the target and intends to make the retardant drop on that pass.

Fire Behavior: The manner in which a fire reacts to the influences of fuel, weather, and topography. Extreme fire behavior usually involves a high rate of spread, prolific crowning and/or spotting, presence of fire whirls, and/or a strong convection column.

Fire Line: (1) A general term for the area where firefighting activities are taking place—also known as "fire ground" in structural firefighting. (2) In wildland firefighting, part of a control line that is scraped or dug to mineral soil.

Fire Season: Period(s) of the year during which wildland fires are likely to occur, spread, and cause serious damage. In many areas, "fire season" is a shrinking notion as drought conditions create a year-round fire-friendly environment.

Fire Shelter: An aluminized cloth tent that offers enhanced protection in a fire entrapment situation by reflecting radiant heat and providing a volume of breathable air.

Fire Siege: Multiple, simultaneous, long-burning wildland fires that cover large geographic areas requiring extensive coordinated response and attack plans.

Fire Storm: A violent convection caused by a large continuous area of intense fire, often characterized by destructively violent surface indrafts resulting in fire whirls.

Firenado: An extreme fire whirl—a spinning vortex column of ascending hot air and gases rising from a fire and carrying aloft smoke, debris, and flame—that has the intensity of a tornado.

Flamethrower: A device for throwing a stream of flaming liquid to facilitate rapid ignition during burnout operations on a wildfire or during a prescribed fire operation—also known as a Terra Torch.

Flat Load: Arrangement of fire hose in a hose bed or compartment in which the hose lies flat, with successive layers one upon the other.

Fog Stream: A water stream diverted by the nozzle into finely divided water particles.

Frontal Attack: A fire attack directed at the head of a wildland fire.

Fuel: Any natural or human-made combustible material.

Fuel Modification: The manipulation or removal of fuels to reduce the likelihood of ignition and/or to lessen potential damage and resistance to control (e.g., lopping, chipping, crushing, piling, burning).

Green: Unburned fuels adjacent to but not yet consumed by the wildland fire.

Ground Attack: The deployment of ground-based resources to suppress a fire (e.g., engines, handcrews, bulldozers).

Handcrew: A number of individuals organized, trained, and supervised principally for handline assignments on an incident.

Handline: A fire line constructed with hand tools.

Helitack: (1) The utilization of helicopters to transport crews, equipment, and fire retardants or suppressants to the fire line during the initial stages of a fire. (2) The crew that performs helicopter management and attack activities.

Helitorch: An aerial ignition device attached to a helicopter. It works like a giant drip torch, dripping fire into remote wildlands for backfires, prescribed burning, and dirty burn cleanup.

High Fire Hazard Zones: Predesignated wildland areas where the combination of vegetation, topography, weather, and the threat of fire to life and property create difficult and dangerous problems—also known as Fire Hazardous Areas or fire-prone areas or zones.

Horseshoe Load: The arrangement of fire hose in a hose bed or compartment in which the hose lies on edge in the form of a horseshoe.

Hose Bed: The main hose-carrying area of an engine or other piece of apparatus designed for carrying hose.

Hose Coupling: The threaded metal ends of hoses that allow lengths of hoses to be attached, or the act of attaching hose lengths together.

Hose Lay: (1) Connected lengths of fire hose, beginning at the discharge port of the engine/pumper and ending at the nozzle. (2) Connected lengths of hose from the water source (typically a hydrant) to the engine/pumper intake port.

Hose Pack: A compact bundle of hose, usually bound with straps to facilitate moving it to the needed location.

Hose Roll: A 50- or 100-foot length of hose rolled up leaving a hole in the middle of the roll for easy carrying—also called a *donut roll.*

Hotshot Crew: An intensively trained handcrew used primarily in handline construction.

Incident Base: The location at or near the incident where the logistics functions are coordinated and administered. On wildfires, the incident base is sometimes called "fire camp."

Incident Command System (ICS): A system that utilizes a standardized scalable approach to managing emerging incidents. Every incident has an incident commander and a command post, which may or may not be colocated with the incident base.

Initial Attack: An aggressive action to put the fire out by the first resources to arrive.

International Association of Fire Chiefs: A leadership and training organization for chief officers in the fire service.

International Fire Service Training Association: A nonprofit educational alliance organized to develop training materials for the fire and emergency services.

Jaws of Life: A large rescue tool with powered hydraulic arms/tips that either shear or spread. The shear function uses two blades capable of cutting through thick metal. The spread function is capable of exerting in excess of 20,000 pounds of force at its tips.

Large-Diameter Hose: A supply hose of 3½ to 6 inches in diameter used to move large volumes of water quickly with a minimum number of pumpers and personnel. Typically, it runs from a hydrant to an engine/pumper.

Lashing Wire: A metal wire used by utility and communications companies to support/secure aerial cables.

Line Slap: When two energized lines on a utility pole contact each other.

Litter: The top organic layer of a forest floor, composed of dead sticks, branches, twigs, leaves, conifer needles, etc.

McLeod: A combination hoe/scraping tool and rake.

Megafire: An extraordinary wildland fire covering a large area. It is defined by the National Interagency Fire Center as a fire exceeding 100,000 acres.

Metallurgy: The study of how metallic elements scientifically behave alone or in alloys; often used by experts to help determine fire cause when utility company wires are involved.

Model-12 Engine: An early-model Cal Fire engine designed to seat crew members in the cab instead of on the back.

Mop-Up: The work left to be done by firefighters to make the scene safe after they have extinguished the fire (e.g., douse smoldering embers, remove smoke from a building).

National Fire Protection Association: A nationally recognized organization that, among other things, develops model life safety codes and standards related to fires and other hazards.

Nomex: The trade name for a fire-resistant synthetic material used in the manufacturing of flight suits and pants and shirts used by firefighters. Aramid is the generic name.

Office of Emergency Services: State and local OES staff coordinate disaster readiness, response, mitigation and recovery efforts—comparable to FEMA but on a smaller scale.

Orders and Watch-Outs: The 10 orders and 18 watchout situations for wildland firefighters.

Orders:

1. Keep informed on fire weather conditions and forecasts.

2. Know what your fire is doing at all times.

3. Base all actions on the current and expected fire behavior.

4. Identify escape routes and safety zones, and make them known.

5. Post lookouts when there is possible danger.

6. Be alert. Keep calm. Think clearly. Act decisively.

7. Maintain prompt communications with your forces, supervisor, and adjoining forces.

8. Give clear instructions and be sure they are understood.

9. Maintain control of your forces at all times.

10. Fight fire aggressively, having provided for safety first.

Watch-Outs:

1. Fire not scouted and sized up.

2. In country not seen in daylight.

3. Safety zones and escape routes not identified.

4. Unfamiliar with weather and local factors influencing fire behavior.

5. Uninformed on strategy, tactics, and hazards.

6. Instructions and assignments not clear.

7. No communication link with crew members or supervisor.

8. Constructing line without safe anchor point.

9. Building fire line downhill with fire below.

10. Attempting frontal assault on fire.

11. Unburned fuel between you and fire.

12. Cannot see main fire; not in contact with someone who can.

13. On a hillside where rolling material can ignite fuel below.

14. Weather becoming hotter and drier.

15. Wind increases and/or changes direction.

16. Getting frequent spot fires across line.

17. Terrain and fuels make escape to safety zones difficult.

18. Taking a nap near fire line.

Origin: The exact physical location where a fire started—also called the *point of origin.*

Personal Protective Equipment (PPE): The general term for equipment worn by first responders to make their tasks safer. It includes helmets, coats, trousers, boots, eye protection, hearing protection, gloves, hoods, self-contained breathing apparatus (SCBA), personal alert safety system (PASS) devices, masks, and chemical suits.

Pincer Action: A direct attack around a fire in opposite directions by two or more attack resources.

Plans Chief: The individual responsible for collecting, evaluating, and disseminating an incident's tactical information, and for the preparing action and contingency plans.

Polyphagous: An animal able to feed on various kinds of food.

Prescribed Fire: A wildland fire originating from a planned ignition in accordance with applicable laws, policies, and regulations.

Pulaski: A hand tool used in fire line construction, which combines a single-bitted axe blade with a narrow adze-like trenching blade fitted to a straight handle.

Pump Panel: The instrument and control panel located on a fire engine.

Quick Attack: A small engine specifically designed for quick response to various emergencies.

Quint: An apparatus that combines three engine functions (water, pump, and fire hose) with two truck functions (specialized ladders and equipment).

Red-Flag Warning: A term used by fire weather forecasters to alert the public to extreme fire danger based on forecasted strong winds, low humidity, dry fuels, dry lightning, or some combination of these.

Rekindle: A reignition due to latent heat, sparks, or embers.

Resiliency: The ability of a system (ecological or human) to resist damage and recover from a disturbance or return to the predisturbance state.

Restat Unit Leader: A functional ICS unit responsible for recording the status of resources committed to the incident.

Retardant: A substance or chemical agent that reduces the flammability of combustibles—also known as slurry.

Retardant Drop: Fire retardant released from an airborne airtanker or helitanker.

Run: The rapid advance of the head of a fire, characterized by a marked transition in fire line intensity and rate of spread.

Safety Zone: An area cleared of flammable materials and used for escape if the fire closes in.

Salvo: A total airtanker retardant load dropped all at once (instead of in sequence to create a longer retardant trail). This is usually done to knock down a hotspot.

Scratch Line: An unfinished preliminary control line hastily established or constructed as an emergency measure to check the spread of fire.

Seasonal: A firefighter hired for fire season only.

Shoulder Load: A method of carrying hose on a person's shoulder.

Silviculture: The art and science behind forest management.

Sling Psychrometer: A hand-operated instrument for obtaining wet and dry bulb temperature readings and, subsequently, relative humidity.

Snorkel: An articulating boom with a platform on a fire truck that allows elevated firefighting and rescue operations.

Spot Fire: A fire ignited outside the perimeter of the main fire by a firebrand.

Staging Area: Location(s) at an incident where resources await a tactical assignment on a three-minute available basis.

State Operations Center: A facility and function activated for coordination of information and resources to support incident command/management.

Straight Stream: A water stream concentrated through a small orifice in the nozzle, providing a far-reaching solid stream (as contrasted with a fog spray).

Strike Team: A specified number of like resources (engines, trucks, handcrews, bulldozers, etc.) that operate as a single unit under a strike team leader.

Structure Fire: A fire burning any part of or all of any building, shelter, or other structure.

Supervision 5 (SUP 5): The highest-level leadership class offered by Cal Fire.

Tillered Truck: A fire truck equipped with steerable rear wheels on its trailer—also known as *tractor-drawn apparatus.*

Truck: A slang term for an aerial apparatus such as a ladder truck.

Turnout Gear: The protective clothing for structure and vehicle fires that includes coats, pants, and boots—also known as *structural gear* or *bunkers. See* Personal Protective Equipment.

Unit Chief: The fire chief for a Cal Fire unit that covers a specified geographic area within the State of California. There are 21 units in the state. There were 22 when the author started her career.

United States Fire Administration: The lead federal agency responsible for fire data collection, public fire education, fire research, and fire service training in the US.

Water Tender: Any ground vehicle capable of transporting large quantities of water—also known as a *water tanker* in some areas.

Widow-Maker: A branch or tree weakened by fire that has the potential to crush an unsuspecting person in the burn area.

Wind Load: The amount of pressure wind puts on a power line; a power line is designed to handle and must be able to handle a specified wind load by governing regulations.

Wind Speed: The wind measured in miles per hour at 20 feet above open, level ground or as adjusted to compensate for topography, terrain, or building obstructions.

Wildland-Urban Interface (WUI): The line, area, or zone where structures and other human development meet or intermingle with undeveloped wildland or vegetation fuels.

ACKNOWLEDGMENTS

The best goes first: thank you, Bud—God was looking out for me when I met you. Mom, Dad, Cathy, Tera (my sister in this life and beyond), Bernadette, Mark and Lupita (and their cool crew, Kairo and Paloma), and Annie, you formed who I was and am. I love you more than can be expressed in ink. Barbara and Joe, Dan and Jasmine, Randi (and Rick for a good part of the ride), Janna, Carley, Mason, Rachael, and Connor, I'm lucky to call you family. And Charlotte—what a gem. Thank you for Bud.

To all my fire peeps, thanks for the stories and for putting yourselves on the line. Every person I worked with in a firehouse or on a fire mattered in my journey. And because they were the last to put up with my brand of smart-ass, extra gratitude goes to those I worked with at State Fire Headquarters. I am also eternally grateful to the women who came before me—if you started in the business before 1982, I am indebted to you.

Thank you to the organizations that made my fire life possible and continue their efforts to keep the public and firefighters safe: Cal Fire, Milpitas Fire Department, International Association of Fire Fighters and Locals 2881 and 1699, Cal-JAC (and by extension, the California Professional Firefighters association), Santa Clara County Fire Chiefs Association, Cal-Chiefs, iChiefs, all the local, state, and federal fire agencies I partnered with,

and the unsung volunteer fire organizations I had the opportunity to work for and with throughout my career.

That brings us into my writing realm. Thanks to the MFA writing community at Lake Tahoe, with a special shout-out to "the Hierarchy" crew, Suzanne Roberts, and one of my favorite people in the world, Benjamin Busch (who also graced this book with his extraordinary charcoal illustrations). I'm so very appreciative of the hours you spent on my work that took hours away from yours. And Laura Yorke, thanks for plucking me out of an impossibly large pile. Your enthusiasm, belief in my stories, and keen editorial eye propelled me and this book. *Burnt* would not exist if not for you. And thank you, Abrams Press, for giving firefighting and a female perspective on it a stage. I have mad respect for my incredibly talented editor, Jamison Stoltz, and the wonderful Abrams Press cast (Sarah Robbins, Annalea Manalili, Devin Grosz, Sarah Masterson Hally, Kevin Callahan, Gabby Fisher, Christian Westermann, and Andrew Gibeley) who all helped this book come to fruition. And I can't forget the relentless support from my early readers and besties Janet and Caroline. They are proof that sisterhood doesn't require the same bloodlines.

Finally, to the locals. Thanks to my neighborhood writing haunts (Pink House, 88 Cups, Comma Coffee, Louie's Mandarin, Wild Horse, and Edgewood). They always had a table for me and my laptop. And much love to my Nevada friends and neighbors who cheered me on and plied me with food and wine when needed most; you know who you are. You are my Comstock.